© Lisa Lee

ABOUT THE AUTHOR

MICHAEL LARGO has been collecting statistics and information on the American way of dying for more than a decade. He is the author of *Final Exits: The Illustrated Encyclopedia of How We Die* and three novels.

For more information, please visit www.MichaelLargo.com.

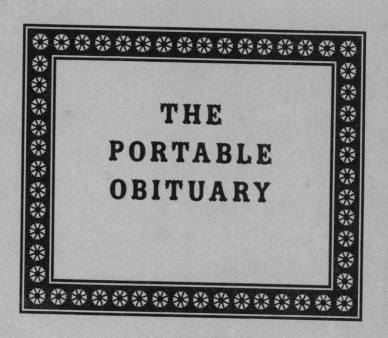

THE
PORTABLE
OBITUARY

ALSO BY MICHAEL LARGO

Nonfiction
Final Exits: The Illustrated Encyclopedia of How We Die

Fiction
Southern Comfort
Lies Within
Welcome to Miami

THE
PORTABLE
OBITUARY

*How the Famous, Rich,
and Powerful Really Died*

MICHAEL LARGO

HARPER

NEW YORK · LONDON · TORONTO · SYDNEY

HARPER

HarperCollins books may be purchased for educational, business, or sales promotional use. For information please write: Special Markets Department, HarperCollins Publishers, 10 East 53rd Street, New York, NY 10022.

FIRST EDITION

Designed by Justin Dodd

Library of Congress Cataloging-in-Publication Data has been applied for.

ISBN: 978-0-06-123166-7
ISBN-10: 0-06-123166-5

07 08 09 10 11   ID/RRD   10 9 8 7 6 5 4 3 2 1

Unfaltering in her love, no matter what I did or didn't do,

and who showed me to have another book ready to read

when one was done—for my mother, Diana

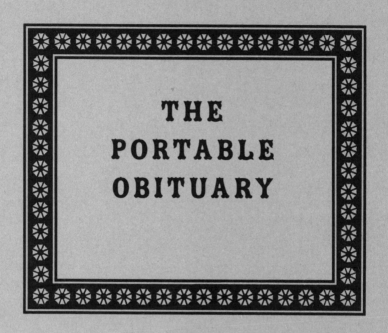

THE
PORTABLE
OBITUARY

PROLOGUE

LIFE, BACKWARD

Each week, more than fifty million people tune to TV programs that feature dead bodies. Popular forensics dramas begin when the deceased are dissected, placed on a scale, and examined under a microscope—the images can get a bit gory—but people seem compelled to watch. A typical homicide case involves unraveling how a person lived in order to discover how they died. In reality, it is no different—the manner of death is the most concise summary and perhaps the true epitaph of a person's life. In *The Portable Obituary* it is not the last words but the last days that tell of the life lived before, for as Matthew Arnold stated, "The truth sits upon the lips of dying men."

This book examines details about how a famous and celebrated person's deeds, intimate habits, and lifestyles, good or bad, ultimately influenced their mode of death and, in due course, determined their role in history and culture. The true cause of death is often the one omitted feature in popular accounts, but in fact it reveals the most poignant snapshot of an individual's life. After you read *The Portable Obituary*, I think you will agree that life, famous or not, can only be fully understood backward.

In writing this book, I choose to review the lives of the prominent, illustrious, and legendary by using their causes of death as a lens. Most traditional biographical summaries end with the date of death and rarely explain the how and why of the person's demise. By using archaeological records, published obituaries, autopsy reports, death certificates, and medical documents, I attempted to scrutinize the standard fare and instead aimed to present cultural studies and reference in a new way. This book reveals exactly how people in the news and history books who helped define our culture and our times died. By providing the ultimate days and final hours of heroes and icons, politicians and celebrities, inventors and explorers, business leaders and sports figures, as well as the unlikely endings of beauty queens, lottery winners, daredevils, and others, I hope, with considerable optimism, to make *The Portable Obituary* the definitive sourcebook on the true causes of death of public figures.

We are fascinated with celebrities who seem larger than life, but we are not often privy to how they really handled death and do not get to see how their famous deeds and accomplishments influenced their process of dying. On one level, I wanted to know if their death matched the courage, adventure, hardship, joy, or actions they portrayed in life. And on another level, it was pure curiosity: What happened to the singers and artists of our favorite songs? How did the popular stars in TV shows from the past decades die? Was the cause of death of Nobel Laureates reflected in their life pursuits? Did bestselling authors succumb to the very issues or advice they wrote about? Did saints die because they were saints, or was the quest to be saintly the thing that killed them? Did the guy who invented the wheel get killed by progress, run over, shall we say, by the very thing he created? I ultimately wanted to know how the famous, rich, and powerful, from the dawn of civilization to our modern times, really died.

The renowned have everything many would wish for: recognition, money, glamour, authority. But when it comes to death and tragedy, sometimes it makes us feel better to see that the same adversities that touch us also affect them. Perhaps, the desire to know the somber details is innate in human nature. It could be said that this form of quizzical investigation may have started when our cave-dwelling ancestors gathered information (the worse, the better) to use against potential rivals: The ones who took no interest in the details of intimate facts were ejected from the social loop. For many, though few of us like to admit it, there is a never-ending fascination when it comes to celebrity tragedy. For example, the murder of John Lennon, Kurt Cobain's suicide, Buddy Holly's plane crash, and Elvis Presley's heart attack, all struck a nerve with a generation of young people who lost an idol; the details of their fate continue to fascinate us and spur a variety of conspiracy theories that always seem to follow the untimely death of the famous. Those who were prominent and celebrated in life are oftentimes more feted in death.

Even with minor celebrities, people are captivated by the tawdry specifics of a famous person's downfall, such as Sonny Bono's skiing accident, the murder of the *Little Rascals*' Carl "Alfalfa" Switzer, or the sudden death of Anna Nicole Smith at age thirty-nine in 2007 of polypharmacy, following on the heels of her twenty-year-old son's death of methadone and antidepressant mixing. To see how many celebrities died in planes, cars, or from suicide is as illustrative as the surprising longevity of Baseball Hall of Fame inductees, multiple Oscar winners, and even circus clowns—all of whom I included in the death bios gathered in *The Portable Obituary*.

Each day, every newspaper in the country has a section for death notices and obituaries. When a person dies, the information is given to journalists in the news department, where editors decide if the person's role in the community makes the death noteworthy. An obituary is a news story that is published without charge. If a person's death doesn't merit news, it is eligible for "Death Notices," which are paid advertisements and, unlike obituaries, usually include details of funeral arrangements. For ordinary people, paying or not, there are usually three occasions when their names appear in print: birth, marriage, and death.

In contrast, for celebrities, whose every move is thoroughly Tabloided, their death is another story—for them, the true cause of death is the final detail usually omitted or concealed. There are hundreds of magazines devoted to following a famous person's smallest acts. Books and television programs document the ins and outs of their careers. But when they die, their death gets the ultimate spin; publicists, handlers, and estate trustees attempt to hold back the real truth. Though kings, politicians, and members of high society were always a source of news and gossip, the media now turns many public figures into entertainers, of a sort, whose image, even after death, needs to be "managed." Yet as Irish writer Percival Arland Ussher noted, "A man does not die of love or his liver or even of old age; he dies of being a man."

In *The Portable Obituary* we get to examine exactly what "being a man" or woman, for that matter, was to the most well-known figures in history. In fact, there is no history without death—dying has, and always will, define history. Another interesting phenomenon I've seen over and over is how the sick and supposed dead rallied and willed themselves to live longer until a time, an event, a landmark in the celebrated dying one's life was reached. That's why so many die, it seems, within weeks of their birthday, anniversary, or some other important celebration. Equally surprising are the last words or advice these famous offered before their death. Who would have thought that the prominent architect Frank Lloyd Wright, for example, would go out of his way to focus on a particular condiment when asked for the secret of his success? For many, it was the small facts about their personal lives, a lingering affliction, or lifestyle long hidden from the public that proved to be the ultimate cause of death. For others, it was a wish, not a death wish but a premonition they repeated over and over, such as the rock star who stated many times he'd never see the age of thirty, only to die in an unexplained plane crash three months shy of the timetable he had set. From baseball greats to movie stars who emulated their own heroes, they often died in a fashion similar to those they imitated, as if attracting not only the greatness but the fate as well. Once you discover these intimate details, it makes it impossible to view a notable person's life and accomplishments the same way as before.

Whether interest lies in history or in the personal particulars of movie stars or the icons of the past, I tried to offer information on topics and personalities that appeal to everyone. Who wouldn't want to know what happened to the inventor of the bar code, or the Popsicle, or the disposable camera? Everyone would like to know if the mavericks of the fast-food industry succumbed to the ravages of the diets they marketed to Americans. When we drive over a bridge or look at a river, it would be of interest to many to know about the explorers they were named after and their fates. When we hear an old song on the radio, "Under the Boardwalk," for example, it's hard to sing along quite the same way, once you've learned of the mysterious fatal doings that happened only hours before it was recorded.

From the frivolous to the sublime, browse through *The Portable Obituary* and see death as a completion, fulfillment, and culmination. Whether it's the last inning in the life and death of the "Sultan of Swat," the final shutter of those captured in the famous photograph of Iwo Jima, the unlikely death of the patron saint of fire prevention, or the final demise of the "Expert in the Workings of the

Universe," killed in a freak accident at age forty, the facts are sometimes comical, other times informative, but always fascinating.

It is my hope that we may all have long, prosperous, and peaceful lives. But I offer this advice for whatever stage of living you may be at: Write your own epitaph now. As you'll see in *The Portable Obituary*, when the day comes that someone like me sums up your life in a sentence, or writes your thumbnail bio with five hundred words or less, you might want to choose carefully the things you do and don't do. There's no telling what will make you most remembered.

INTRODUCTION

WHERE'S THE PROOF?

As early as 440 B.C. Romans counted population through the office of the cen-
sor to determine the scope of human resources available, but they kept no records of how the people scratched off the following year's census list had died.
It wasn't until the mid–1600s when formal records of death were collected in
John Graunt's *Bills of Mortality*, which listed exactly what people died from and
at what age, that the forerunner to modern death statistics began. Many of the
causes of death used in his "Table of Casualties" remained standards in necrol-
ogy (the science of the collection, classification, and interpretation of mortality statistics) for two hundred fifty years. In addition, Graunt's techniques for
gathering data were used in future models for census taking. He is also considered the first epidemiologist, studying health and illness as they relate to popu-
lations. As a man, John Graunt was self-taught, a haberdasher by trade, selling
hats and gloves from his shop in London, though noted to have "an excellent
working head . . . very rare in a trader or mechanic." His hobby of sorts seemed
morbid to some, since he had a passion to know how people died and became
a rabid collector of death statistics. The merit of his work was recognized during his lifetime, such that he was admitted into the Royal Society, even though
he was of the merchant class, not usually acknowledged by the higher echelon.
Graunt died, one week shy of his fifty-fourth birthday in 1674, of jaundice and
liver disease. Even though John was described in his obituary as "a pleasant face-
tious companion and very hospitable," he favored a good stiff drink at the end
of each day as the best remedy to take the stench out of his nostrils and the taste
of death from his mouth after having visited the morgues to see how the newly
dead met their fates.

From *Natural and Political Observations . . . upon the Bills of Mortality* in London
during a typical year in the 1650s:

Abortive, and Stillborn: 2,005
Ague, and Feaver: 6,235 (Ague meant chills, shakes, and fevers.)

Apoplex, and sodainly: 421 (Apoplex was a stroke and sodainly meant suddenly.)

Blasted: 14 (a wasted or a ravaged-looking condition to the dead body)

Bleach: 15 (This was used if the person died after turning colorless.)

Bleeding: 65 (as from mouth, ears, or orifices without visible wound)

Bloudy Flux, Scouring: 7, 858 (dysentery and cancerous tumors)

Gangrene, and Fistula: 609 (infections from wounds and fatal abscesses)

Childbed: 3,364 (during birth, or shortly thereafter, of mother)

Chrisomes, and Infants: 4, 519 (any childhood illness within the first year)

Colick, and Wind: 497 (meant excessive passing of gas in baby or adult preceding death)

Cut of the Stone: 48 (trying to pass a kidney stone)

Excessive Drinking: 2 (Only two in all of London; it's hard to imagine how much these had to drink to qualify, though this low number might be what we call denial concerning Graunt's own habits when citing this as a cause of death.)

Executed: 79

Fainted in Bath: 1

Flox, and Small Pox: 1,523

Found Dead in the Streets: 29

French Pox: 130 (syphilis)

Frighted: 9 (scared to death)

Grief: 59

Hanged, and made-away themselves: 47

Jaundice: 212 (turned yellow)

Impostume: 428 (anyone bed-bound)

Lunatique: 39 (mental disorders)

Murdered: 27

Overlayd, and starved at Nurse: 213 (possibly SIDS, or when mother died and no one was able to feed baby)

Stopping of the Stomach: 186 (constipation)

Teeth, and Worms: 3, 915 (rotted teeth and infections)

THE BUBONIC PLAGUE OF 1665 KILLED 100,000 LONDONERS, FOLLOWED BY THE 1666 GREAT FIRE THAT BURNED 80 PERCENT OF THE ENTIRE CITY. JOHN GRAUNT HAD SURVIVED BOTH EVENTS.

In America during colonial times, information on birth, marriage, and death had been kept since 1632 by ministers and trustees of different townships and churches. This method relied solely on the devotion of the individual record keepers and was usually incomplete. Between 1700 and 1910 many causes of death were the same ones found on Graunt's data. Since most diseases were not classified as they are today, reasons for death often reflected the caregiver's attempt, or those present at death, to describe the demise as best they could. "Fever," for example, a leading cause of death in the colonial period, could currently describe the end result of more than a hundred different diseases. Even stranger causes were found, such as "Commotion," listed as a reason for death in the 1700s, which was perhaps related to head injuries or concussion or used to describe how a person's head was jostled, or perhaps even "baby-shaken syndrome." "Old Age," or "Debility" was another catchall cause when anyone over fifty years passed away. Since 1951 no U.S. death certificates were accepted if "old age" was listed as a cause.

In 1989 pathologists at Johns Hopkins Hospital studied more than 45,000 death certificates, from between 1889 and 1987, and compared the cause of death written on the official certificate to autopsy reports. This study found that more than 25 percent of causes listed on death certificates were incorrect. The percentage of error is still the same today, despite efforts to use standardized codes.

COUNTING THE DEAD

The first thing the newly formed United States did do was take a head count. In May 1787, when the delegates from the thirteen original colonies met to ratify the Articles of Confederation, they decided that a census had to be taken in order to proportionally balance both the tax burden and political representation. To make it a fair system, they decided to base equity not on land wealth but on population. At the time, many believed that the biblical taboo on census taking would  make people hesitant to be counted. And families were reluctant to have their sons known to the government, in the event they should be called upon to partake in another war. Nevertheless, the patriotic spirit won out, and in 1790 the United States became the first modern nation in the world to establish a census. It has continued doing so every ten years.

The census recorded living persons, but there was still no uniform way to classify how people died, how often, or how many. The first semblance of governmental tracking of death and disease took place with the creation of Marine Hospital Service (MHS) in 1798. This government agency was designed to take care of seamen, who were a vital part of the new republic, necessary for prosperous trade and national security. Over time, the MHS, the predecessor of the

Public Health Service (PHS), was called on to do more than care for sick sailors. They took over the responsibility of supervising national quarantines, medical inspection of immigrants, and the prevention of the interstate spread of disease. They kept excellent records of seamen deaths and epidemics. Before 1850 vital statistics were not generally recorded. A person died; they buried him. Not until 1893 did the PHS start the Morbidity and Mortality Weekly Report, and it took until 1905 until a majority of the states participated. But no single national source on death was kept until World War II. As anyone searching for information on their ancestors' genealogy knows, documents are bafflingly scattered.

Today, physicians, nurses, paramedics, and even police are permitted to declare death. Filling out a death certificate is a process normally restricted to doctors, but declaring a death and executing a death certificate are two different procedures which need not be performed by the same person. A death certificate is the official declaration that a person is classified among the nonliving. But historically, even when this formal record was made, it was anything but accurate. The problem was that the precise cause of death could easily not be recognized or that whoever filled out the form had no medical knowledge of the decedent. Many times the handwriting on the certificates was illegible, and misspellings were frequent. "Natural causes"—whatever that meant—was a standard term used whenever a death certifier was in doubt. It was assumed, supposedly, that if no external trauma was evident, the death looked natural enough.

RICHMOND NEWSBOY ANNOUNCING THE REBEL SUCCESS!!!

OBITUARY vs. REALITY

Nevertheless, death certificates are usually more accurate than obituaries. Most obituaries seem reluctant to answer the most important question—how did the person die? Many do not disclose the cause, citing reasons of privacy. Death notices can be especially frustrating since it's not uncommon to still see phrases such as "died at home surrounded by friends and family" offered as the final demise, completely sidestepping the actual cause. However, certain obituaries offer clues to the habits and lifestyles that caused death. Sometimes, at the very bottom of an obituary, the family requests donations in lieu of flowers. If, for example, Leukemia Society is mentioned, chances are that a blood disorder was a contributing factor.

The art of the obituary has often changed to match the society's attitude toward death. In the early years, from 1800 to 1838, deceased persons once associated with the Revolutionary War regularly received obituaries. Nearly everyone seemed to die of an "old war wound" and had contact with George Washington or another well-known figure at one time in their life. In 1820 Daniel Boone's obituary stated he "breathed out his last breath with gun in his hands just in the act of firing," attempting to establish Boone as an icon of the much-applauded pioneer spirit, though it was a complete fabrication. Another obituary in that same year, for an ordinary woman named Christina Magill of Cumberland, Maryland, stated she died "after an illness of two weeks, leaving an infant daughter of that age." There's no doubt that complications of birth, possibly what was referred to as "Milk Leg" or "Child Bed Fever" caused this woman's death. Another woman had this obituary: "Within the short period of a year she was a bride, a beloved wife and companion, a mother, a corpse!"

As the 1800s progressed and more trained medical doctors began to practice, obituaries left behind the "long and painful illness" or the "short but distressing death" as causes and instead began to cite diseases, such as scarlet fever and "disease of the heart." During and after the Civil War when the dead were everywhere, America's attitude toward death began to change. The only way to survive the psychological magnitude of this onslaught was for people to quickly distance themselves from the dead. The funeral industry began to prosper from this point forward, and Americans from then on preferred to turn over their dealing with the dead to others. Obituaries focused on the deceased's accomplishments, usually related to the amount of wealth acquired and bequeathed, often leaving out the facts of whatever they died from as inconsequential.

Milk Leg, now known as postpartum thrombophlebitis, was an infection that caused a woman's legs to swell after giving birth; it signaled the onset of infection and death. Mothers died so frequently during birth—200 out of every 1,000 births—that it wasn't uncommon for a man to marry one woman and end up being married to the woman's sister or cousin. So great was the loss of children that many chose not to name children until they had survived at least a year.

Today, obituaries, as found in newspapers and on the Internet, are growing in popularity. According to the Readership Institute's impact study of newspapers, obituaries have the highest potential of all news items to grow readership, even if the true cause of death will require further analysis.

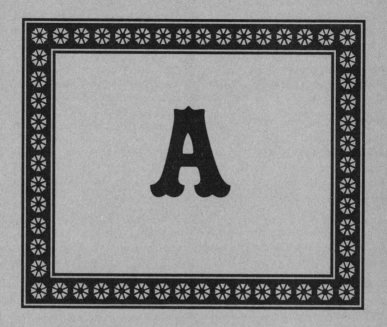

NICK ADAMS

Actor Nick Adams (Nicholas Aloysius Adamshock) had a supporting role along-side James Dean in *Rebel Without a Cause*, and he starred in the television series *The Rebel* (1959–1962), playing Johnny Yuma, an ex-Confederate soldier right-ing wrong where he saw it. In 1968 at age thirty-six Adams died of an overdose of paraldehyde. As his career options began to dwindle, and having recently returned from Japan after playing a supporting role in the sixth *Godzilla* film, Adams began to allude to his previous homosexual encounters with James Dean and Elvis Presley. A week before Elvis was scheduled to film his "Memphis Comeback" concert, Adams was found dead with enough industrial-strength paraldehyde in his veins to cause immediate unconsciousness and death. The sudden silence of this Presley bad press has made some wonder about the coin-cidence of "The Rebel's" timely death.

FELIX ADLER

Felix Adler was dubbed The White House Clown after performing for three United States presidents: Warren Harding, Calvin Coolidge, and Frank-lin D. Roosevelt. He was a happy-face clown, which made a trademark for himself by always wearing a tiny hat and carrying a miniature umbrella and a live baby pig. He was the first clown to appear on television. Adler had run away to join the circus when he was ten. They tried to make him work with the Chinese acrobats, but he was too clumsy—thus, clowning was the next best place for his talents. Although he made others smile, his smile had to be painted on—he died of ulcers in 1960 at sixty-four years old.

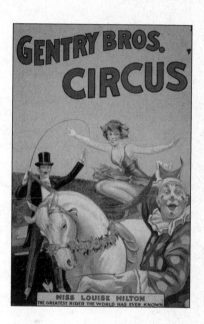

ULCERS ARE COMMONLY CAUSED BY LIFESTYLES FILLED WITH STRESS AND WORRY, AND THEY ARE AGGRAVATED BY COFFEE CONSUMPTION AND SPICY FOODS. IN 2006 THERE WERE 850,000 NEW CASES OF PEPTIC ULCER DISEASE; 4,976 DIED.

ALEXANDER

Alexander the Great had conquered most of the known world and was considered the most successful military com-mander in history. Some legends say he was poisoned by a medicine sent by Aristotle, since some believed, Alexander was angry with his teacher for not saving the life of his male lover, Hephaestion. However, descriptions of Alexander's fever are more consistent with symptoms of what we now know as West Nile Virus, a bacteria transmitted by a mosquito bite. He died in 323 B.C. at age thirty-three.

DUANE ALLMAN

Rolling Stone named Howard Duane Allman as one of the best rock guitarists of all time, second only behind Jimi Hendrix. Left fatherless at a young age when their military dad was murdered by a veteran, he and his older brother Gregg stuck together in life and in music, forming the popular Allman Brothers Band and becoming one of the most influential rock groups of the 1970s. Fame for Duane, known for "Midnight Rider," was short-lived, since his signature song turned out to be his epitaph; he was killed in a motorcycle accident at age twenty-four in 1971. Three months later the group released the album *Eat a Peach*, and fans believed the title referred to Duane's crash into the back of a peach truck in Macon, Georgia. In fact, it was a lumber truck he swerved around that caused him to fall off the bike and die. Duane looked fine, with only a few scratches, but he died of internal bleeding a few hours later, close to midnight as he had always wanted, a good-looking corpse.

MUSICIAN WRECKS

In 1955 popular accordion player of country music, **Iry LeJeune**, known for the hit "I Made a Big Mistake," did just that in choosing the wrong place to change a flat on his car; he was fatally sideswiped at age twenty-seven. In 1960 **Eddie Cochran** (Edward Ray Cochrane), known for "Summertime Blues," died from brain injuries after a car crash at age twenty-one, and the following year the singer of the hit "It Could Happen to You," **Scott LaFaro**, added new meaning to his song after he died in a car accident at age twenty-five. In 1967 "Rockin'" **Robin Roberts**, who sang "Louie Louie," a big fan of alliteration, confronted the dissonance of death when he passed away at age twenty-seven in a car crash. In 1973 **Clarence White** of the Byrds was loading instruments into a van when he was sideswiped by a drunk driver leaving one of his concerts and died of a hemorrhage at age twenty-nine. T-Rex star **Marc Bolan** "banged his gong" against the steering wheel after careening his car into a tree, killing him at age twenty-nine in 1977. Reckless driver and Steppenwolf bassist Rushton Moreve, of "Born to be Wild" fame, died in a car crash at age thirty-three in 1981. That same year, while driving his Volkswagen Beetle, **Harry Chapin** of "Cat's in the Cradle" fame, got rear-ended at a toll booth on the Long Island Expressway and died on the spot of a heart attack at age thirty-eight. And in 2002 **Lisa "Left Eye" Lopes** of TLC (nicknamed "Left Eye" because she wore a condom on the left frame of her sunglasses) died a month before her thirty-first birthday in a car crash.

ARCHIMEDES

The catapult and the business of war in Syracuse laid the ground for the great mathematician Archimedes to flourish. He devised even more outlandish weaponry, such as a claw that reached out and snatched boats sailing near the fortified walls to capsize them, all using the principles of the lever, pulley, and screw, revolutionary concepts at the time, devised and invented by his math formulas. He is also noted to have discovered the principles of buoyancy while taking a bath. He was so excited about the theory that would allow the construction of huge ships to sail and not sink, that he ran from the tub naked through the streets to share the news of his epiphany. Clutching his nuts, he shouted, "It floats!" Years later, when Roman soldiers finally did siege the city, he was not recognized and promptly impaled by a spear. He died at the age of seventy-five in 212 B.C.

LOUIS ARMSTRONG

Louis Armstrong was born on a hot, mean summer New Orleans night (August 4, 1901); a man was stabbed to death in a street brawl that raged outside his mother's bedroom as he entered the world. He was raised on the rough side of town, where at times he searched through garbage cans for a decent meal. Eventually, he turned to petty crime, including a stint as a pimp, before he was sent to reform school. It was there that he learned to blow a horn. Once Armstrong started with music, all who listened discovered that he was a natural, with perfect pitch and an innate rhythm. By the time he was twenty-three years old, he was already heralded as an innovative talent, a pioneer of jazz, and went from that point to make record after record, culminating in the release of "What A Wonderful World" (1967) and "Hello, Dolly!" in 1969.

Throughout Armstrong's life his intensity and love for music was seconded only by his propensity for gage, the jazz slang for marijuana, which he smoked nearly every day. His three cigar-size gage dubbies relaxed him, he believed, and allowed him to find the wide range of emotions that blew out of the end of his horn. This one vice may have been the thing that killed him. He was arrested for possession in 1931; his use of gage was mentioned in an FBI file the bureau kept on Armstrong. It surely affected his lungs, such that as the years progressed he was unable to play for lengths of time or with his earlier range. Prolonged use precipitated a heart problem, causing his first heart attack in 1959, which then weakened the muscles in his lips. Instead of giving up the gage, he then began to vocalize more, only hitting a few notes from the horn for effect. Satchmo, as he was called, patted at the sweat and took another toke, willing himself to live after spending three months in Beth Israel Hospital in New York when another heart attack got him in 1971. He hung in there to make it to that year's Fourth of July Newport Jazz Festival to celebrate his seventieth birthday. Two days later, on July 6, 1971, he died at age sixty-nine of a heart attack in his home in Corona, Queens. In 2001 the city of New Orleans renamed its airport: Louis Armstrong International Airport.

> "When you're dead, you're done." —LOUIS ARMSTRONG

FRED ASTAIRE

Flying Down to Rio caught the public's imagination in 1933 for an escape from reality to a venture into exotic locals, in spite of the silly lyrics: "My Rio by the sea-o." It was performed by Fred Astaire and Ginger Rogers, a dancing duo that embodied a harmony and symmetry of motion on the silver screen that was hard to find in real life. Astaire's (born Frederick Austerlitz) dance virtuosity can be seen in thirty-five additional musicals, with his last movie appearance in *Ghost Story* in 1981, before he died in 1987 at age eighty-eight of pneumonia. Ginger Rogers (Virginia Katherine McMath) made nine musicals alongside

Astaire and went on to make a total of seventy-three film appearances. When she was honored by the Kennedy Center in 1992, the heirs to the Fred Astaire estate refused to allow clips of Ginger dancing with Fred to be aired in the broadcast. She died of a myocardial infarction at the age of eighty-three in 1995.

Will Glahe started another kind of dance craze, the accordionist known for the polka: "You put your right foot in, you put your left foot out." It took some time, but Will, presumably, finally knew what it was all about when he died at age eighty-seven of heart failure in 1989.

JOHN JACOB ASTOR

John Jacob Astor came to America in 1784 from the small town of Waldorf, Germany, with seven flutes under his arm in the hope of becoming a merchant of musical instruments. Soon after settling in New York City, he discovered that fur was the "soft gold" of the New World and the commodity European markets wanted most. At first hiking alone into the then-wild regions of upstate New York to trade with Indians, trekking back with a knapsack full of pelts, he eventually established his own trading posts. With the profits from each successful venture (primarily from beaver pelts), he invested in Manhattan real estate, and by the time of his death of debility in 1848 at the age of seventy-four, he was America's first millionaire worth more than $20 million, owning nearly half of Manhattan. Before expiring, he offered final advice to his aristocratic offspring: "Serve the

classes; live with the masses. Serve the masses; live with the classes." However, **John Jacob Astor IV**, the richest person aboard the *Titanic* at the time of its demise, apparently forgot the family patriarch's counsel. His last words; "The ladies have to go first. Get in the lifeboat, to please me. Good-bye, dearie. I'll see you later." He was crushed by a fallen smokestack as the ship sank when he was forty-seven in 1912.

ATTILA

One of the most feared barbarians of all time was Attila the Hun, who ruled the largest European empire north of Rome from the steppes of central Asia, through Germany, the Netherlands, and parts of France from A.D. 433 to A.D. 453. What made Attila so feared was his desire for war for war's sake. He built palaces, though he abandoned them at a whim. He wore simple clothes, no jewelry, and preferred to drink from a wooden mug. Killing excited him, and all in his path either ran or died. He plundered villages or monasteries equally so that the rumor of his ruthlessness became larger than his actual deeds. At age forty-seven, in A.D. 453, Attila the Hun took a reprieve from pillaging to get married to his seventh wife. After a wild party Attila retired to the bridal tent with his newest bride, Ildico, a young Germanic woman known not only for her beauty but also for her powerful right jab. When he was found dead the next morning with a nosebleed, some said Attila was poisoned. Others believed that the fierce warrior liked it rough not only in battle, but in bed as well—his new wife was capable of inflicting her own measure of pain. Although Attila had long suffered from a deviated septum, making him prone to nosebleeds, it's believed that he ultimately died that night from rough sex and too much wine. His warriors, upon discovering his death, said a man of Attila's stature needs no tears. Instead, they gashed their hands and dripped drops of blood over his body. Attila left no monuments, museums, or schools; his empire was comprised of real estate. Without the fear of his sword to keep its boundaries in check, his kingdom soon collapsed.

ANONYMOUS AX

Before the invention of the ax, humans were scavengers and ranked behind hyenas on the food chain, more or less equal to buzzards. About seventy-five thousand years ago the first human found that a sharp stone attached to a stick leveled the playing field; it is considered the first tool in human history for dominating the earth. The ax inventor, as well as the anonymous inventor of other society-altering creations, like the first wheel and axle, probably died by the age of eighteen, the average lifespan of prehistoric man. From the fragments of bones that remain, murder or accident were the likely causes of death of the ax and wheel inventors.

JOHANN SEBASTIAN BACH

Johann Sebastian Bach was a prolific German composer and keyboardist with over a thousand of his pieces still surviving. He created a cerebral music and intrigued audiences of his day with simultaneous sounding of separate musical lines going on all at once and everywhere, which is now called baroque music. His compositions were not as heralded in his day as was his improvisation as a performer on the organ, and he made his living mostly by being employed by church choirs. Toward the end of his life, his eyesight was failing and he sought two doctors to perform operations to try to correct his vision. At the time, these procedures included draining his blood, dropping chemical concoctions in the eyeball, and drilling small holes near the temples to relieve pressure. These operations caused complete blindness and worsening health, and he died of a stroke at age sixty-five in 1750.

MAXIE BAER

Madcap Maxie Baer was a famous boxer during the 1930s, especially after he defeated Hitler's favorite German Max Schmeling at Yankee Stadium. Baer wore a Star of David on his trunks during that match, in honor of his Jewish grandfather, and he kept the insignia as a trademark for the rest of his career. Baer developed his strength as a boy working on cattle ranches and then as a butcher carrying carcasses. His punch was truly deadly. In 1930 he knocked fighter Frankie Campbell to the mat with only two swift blows. Campbell lay still on the canvas for nearly an hour and died of massive brain hemorrhage; Baer at 6 feet 4 inches, with his long reach, had actually knocked Campbell's brain loose from the connective tissue of the brainstem. During another fight with Ernie Schaff, Baer hit him square in the temple and sent this twenty-four-year-old, 6-foot-2-inch opponent to the mat. Schaff took three minutes to get up. After the fight he complained of memory loss and headaches. In his next bout shortly afterward, Schaff died in the ring from the first soft punch he took. Max held the world title for only a year and lost it to the underdog James L. Braddock, as portrayed in the movie *Cinderella Man*. Baer tried to make a comeback and fought Joe Louis at Yankee Stadium, but he was

knocked out in the fourth round. This was the only time Baer was TKO'd in his career, which ended in 1941 with 72 wins and 12 losses, and with more than 50 of those wins by knockout. Baer then made an acting career for himself starring in over twenty movies, opened nightclubs, and was rumored to have affairs with many Hollywood starlets. He died of a massive heart attack while shaving in the Roosevelt Hotel in Hollywood at age fifty in 1959. His son, Max Baer, Jr., starred as Jethro Bodine in the *Beverly Hillbillies*.

THE YEAR 1953 HAS THE MOST DEATHS OF PROFESSIONAL BOXERS WITH 25. BETWEEN 1979 AND 2001 THERE WERE 118 DEATHS OF BOXERS IN THE RING.

VASCO NÚÑEZ DE BALBOA

Balboa was a likable, easygoing man that had tried his hand as a pig farmer on Hispaniola with his first New World earnings. He failed at the venture only to return to conquistadoring, exploring, and taking the natives' gold as a more profitable means of advancement. He established the first Western colony on the mainland in Panama and eventually went by land to discover the Pacific Ocean during an exploration to acquire more riches. In 1513 he waded into the water and raised his sword into the air claiming dominion for Spain over all he saw. However, six years later, because of rivalry among succeeding governors and an old grudge held by another Spanish seafarer envious of Balboa's charm, he was eventually accused of being disloyal to Spain. Despite Balboa's having received title and honor for his discovery, his accusers devised a quick trial and condemned him to die. "Lies!" he said as he was led to the block, hero status among his peers being only a liability. He was beheaded at age forty-four. His head was displayed for a few days before it was discarded and fed to pigs.

LUCILLE BALL

Until 1951 every TV show was broadcast live. One of the first pre-recorded programs was *I Love Lucy*. The show ranked number one in the nation for four of its first six full seasons until it ended in 1957. It established the half-hour situation comedy, or sitcom, as a TV staple. The show featured Lucille Ball and her husband Desi Arnaz (Ricky Ricardo). The show has never been off the air and is still airing somewhere in the world every moment of the day. Lucy is considered one of the

greatest female comedians, though when the cameras were off, she was no clown but rather a serious perfectionist with a low tolerance for fools. Her love-at-first-sight marriage to Cuban bandleader Desi Arnaz was riddled with infidelity and only added to her somber outtake on reality, making her tougher to deal with and, to many, seemingly mean-spirited. Lucy finally divorced Desi in 1960, though they remained friends until he died of lung cancer in 1986 at age sixty-nine. In old age Lucy refused to retire, even though her later films were flops. She busied herself with talk show appearances and award events. She only stopped by default, when put under anesthesia for surgery. She never woke up and died during the procedure for a ruptured aorta in 1989 at age seventy-seven.

*The American with most kills in World War I, totaling twenty-six, was the unstoppable, former race car driver **Eddie Rickenbacker**. Not only did he return home safe from the war but he also went on to establish Pan American Airlines. During his civilian years he survived numerous near-death experiences, including being adrift at sea for three weeks and crashing in one of his commercial planes in 1941 near Atlanta. He died from complications of a stroke in 1973 at age eighty-two.*

RED BARON

World War I saw heroes taking to the skies, flying canvas, wood-frame planes that reached speeds of no more than 100 miles per hour. On the German side, former horse trainer Manfred von Richthofen, known as the Red Baron, dominated the skies and tallied eighty kills. When his bright red Fokker Albatros appeared, it sent terror through the clouds. He died at age twenty-five from a shot through his chest while in the air from an unknown soldier on the ground. Many had claimed to be the one who gunned down the Baron, but medical records, considering trajectory of bullet and other forensic evidence, indicate that the fatal shot could only have come during a hail of bullets fired from hillside machineguns when Richthofen swooped too low. During his final flight, he ignored all procedures he himself had initiated to ensure survival; namely, he became fixated during that flight on a target he could not hit. His apparent disregard for personal safety could be attributed to a form of heroic suicide that often happened to combatants suffering from battle fatigue.

JACK BARRY

Jack Barry was the producer and host of the most notorious game show in TV history, *Twenty-One*, which aired in 1956. The idea of the show was to put contestants in soundproof booths and ask questions, but after the first show Barry realized that the average person couldn't answer any of the questions. Instead of losing the show's deep-pocket sponsor Geritol, the show's producers decided to feed answers to the challenging contestant that the audience seemed to like best. However, when one contestant was scripted to lose and give the wrong answer, even though he knew the right one, he later blew the whistle, which precipitated a Senate investigation into game-show rigging. The stress from the debacle never left Barry, and he died of a heart attack while jogging around Central Park in 1984 two weeks before his sixty-sixth birthday.

COME ON DOWN

Game shows have been cheap to produce and have had high ratings since TV began. Over a thousand TV programs have ventured forth with the game-show format, featuring many famous actors and three U.S. presidents. "Come on down" was the line from *The Price Is Right*, but for a few listed here the phrase had a whole different meaning: Larry Blyden, host of *What's My Line?*, died in a car crash, swerving over the white line while touring in Morocco in 1975 at age forty-nine; Paul Lynde, the center square of the *Hollywood Squares* was found dead, alone in his home of a heart attack at age fifty-five; Ray Combs, host of *Family Feud*, hanged himself with bed sheets due to a feud with a business partner over finances, among other things, in 1996 at age forty; George Fenneman of *You Bet Your Life* died doing just that, from smoking and emphysema, in 1997; announcer on *Concentration*, Art James, was too serious, some say, and died in 2004 at age seventy-four of heart failure; announcer Ron Roddy (*Price Is Right*) died of cancer in 2003; *Your Number's Up* game-show regular Nipsey Russell held on a considerable time before his number was up in 2005 at age eighty of stomach cancer.

JOHN AND LIONEL BARRYMORE

Lionel Barrymore won an Oscar as best actor for the role of a pathetic, alcoholic lawyer Stephen Ashe in *A Free Soul* in 1931. Barrymore died from chronic myocarditis (impairment of heart function due to decrease in bloodflow) after suffering from acute lung edema (excess fluid) and nephritis (kidney problems) in 1954 at age seventy-six. His younger brother, actor John Barrymore, never won an Oscar or played an alcoholic on screen but instead did so in his personal life. Some say Lionel acted with authenticity in his Oscar-winning role by studying his brother. John Barrymore died of myocarditis, had nephritis like his brother, in addition to cirrhosis of the liver. He died in 1942 at age sixty. According to John's obituary, he was "considered one of the premier interpreters of Shakespeare of the twentieth century." It's no surprise his last words were "Die? I should say not, dear fellow. No Barrymore would allow such a conventional thing to happen to him."

During the first half of the twentieth century the alcoholic content of liquor was five percentage points more potent than it is today. In 1950, 80 percent of liquor sold could be categorized as whiskey. Today, 80 percent of all alcoholic beverages sold is beer. Then as now approximately 4 percent of adult drinkers became alcoholics. Each year 100,000 people achieve premature obituary status via alcohol.

WARNER BAXTER

The unfortunate distinction of being the first and last Oscar winner to receive a lobotomy belongs to Warner Baxter. He won best actor for his role as the Cisco Kid in *In Old Arizona* (1929), even though he got the part after the intended star, Raoul Walsh, had to leave the film because of a wacky accident: A jackrabbit smashed through the window of Walsh's car, which caused the actor to lose one eye. Baxter turned the win into a success for a while, and in 1936 he was named the number-one box-office draw and the highest-paid actor. Soon after, the stress to stay on top got to him and he suffered a nervous breakdown. By the 1940s he was lucky to get a few roles in B-movies. He blamed his arthritis and not his waning popularity for his demise. In 1951 he agreed to undergo a lobotomy, oddly believing this was a way to retrieve his health. He subsequently died from complications of the procedure at age sixty-two.

LUDWIG VAN BEETHOVEN

Ludwig van Beethoven is arguably the most well known classical composer of all time. His big-show, cannon, cymbal, and dramatic-ending symphonies, brimming with emotional intensity, are still performed at least once a day throughout the world. He was taught by his father, a court musician and alcoholic, who, it was said, tied young Beethoven to the piano stool with bedsheets, demanding perfection and dedication of the five-year-old would-be genius. When the father died, Beethoven took over court duties and began at the early age of twenty-two to hobnob with royalty, who eventually became his patrons. By the age of thirty he began to go deaf, a fate far worse for a musician than blindness. His works were immediately recognized as the masterpieces they were, and he was sought out by music publishers. Although by the end of his life he was wealthy, he partook in few social activities, wishing to hide his impairment, consequently never marrying, and enjoying instead, since his youth, the company of prostitutes. Stone-deaf, he went on to write his best work, hearing the music only in his head and feeling the subtle vibration of the piano keys. Officially, he died of dropsy in 1827 at age fifty-six, but the cause of death was actually cirrhosis due to worsening syphilis and lead poisoning. The day he died there was a violent thunderstorm

In those times dropsy was any disease in which a person had difficulty standing or suffered from weakness and fell or fainted. Lead was not known to cause illness and was used to sweeten wines, preserve foods, and make pewter drinking cups and dishware. It was also used in medicines to cure dropsy and many other ailments.

shaking the windowpanes, at which Beethoven supposedly shook his fists at the heavens before taking his last breath. At the time, a lock of his hair was clipped and a piece of his skull was removed before burial as a sort of relic of the great man. Theses items were tested with modern techniques and found to contain large quantities of lead, one possible reason for his deafness.

SAUL BELLOW

Saul Bellow won the Nobel Prize in 1976 after a long career that started with writing book reviews. He was heralded by many, including Philip Roth, who called him, "the backbone of twentieth-century American literature," even if now Bellow's work is considered by some conventional and old-fashioned. In

1976 he also won the Pulitzer Prize for *Humboldt's Gift*, which effectively celebrates the melancholy of the human soul. The accolades he received kept him cantankerous and sharp-witted until the end when he died in 2005 at age eighty-nine, some say, of perpetual irritability.

INGRID BERGMAN

Ingrid Bergman, the statuesque, natural Swedish beauty, known best for her role as Humphrey Bogart's love in the 1942 classic film *Casablanca*, won two best actress Oscars: *Gaslight* (1944) and *Anastasia* (1956). She died of breast cancer in 1982, but always the ambassador of class and politeness, she held on until after her sixty-seventh birthday party was over.

MILTON BERLE

Early TV advertisers were so important that they regularly put their product's name in the show's title: *The Texaco Star Theater* featuring Milton Berle made its debut a few years earlier, but by 1951 it was the highest-rated show on TV, capturing 87 percent of all viewers. At age forty, after thirty-five years in show business, Berle, known as Uncle Miltie, found himself to be the first "overnight sensation" created by television, a phenomenon the medium would produce over and over again. Berle was also referred to as Mr. Television because his popularity was credited for the astronomical boom in television set sales; more and more people bought TVs just to see what all

the fuss was about. The show burned out by 1956, although Berle kept performing into his eighties. His three marriages and a long list of partners, including Lucille Ball and Marilyn Monroe, left another legacy; it was reported that Berle had a giant penis. According to Berle's son, Bradley Lewis, his father owned a plaster statue of his member that stood over one foot tall. Uncle Miltie supposedly kept it in his attic and occasionally brought it down to stun dinner guests. Despite his lifelong cigar habit, some say the pride he took in his virility was the thing that kept him alive so long. When Berle died of colon cancer in 2002, at the age of ninety-three, no one could find the statue. The whereabouts of the Berle family heirloom remains a mystery.

IRVING BERLIN

Irving Berlin (Israel Isidore Baline) had a big hit with "The Song Is Ended" in 1927, and as if it cast a curse on his talent, he couldn't write another song for five years; he had a writer's block that put him on the doorsteps of the poorhouse. His place in music history and culture is hard to match: Berlin wrote "God Bless America" (1918), "White Christmas" (1942), "There's No Business Like Show Business" (1954), and 3,000 other songs, 17 film scores, and 21 Broadway musicals. In his later years he became a virtual recluse and died of a heart attack in 1989 at age one hundred and one.

CLARENCE BIRDSEYE

Frozen foods, TV dinners, and the microwavable entrees many Americans eat today were the inventions of Clarence Birdseye. A college dropout, he got a government job stationed at the North Pole, where he noticed that freshly caught fish stopped flopping once placed on the ice. Up there, in icy wind and frigid temperatures, the fish froze solid almost immediately. When he thawed the same fish, he discovered that it still had almost all of its fresh qualities. He marketed this concept and started the refrigerated shipping industry. He caught a cold and died of pneumonia, and ultimately a heart attack, at age sixty-nine in 1956.

ON THANKSGIVING, 13 PERCENT OF ALL HOME-COOKED TURKEYS ARE LEFT TO DEFROST IMPROPERLY AND BECOME CONTAMINATED WITH *SALMONELLA*, CAUSING 1.3 MILLION ILLNESSES AND AN ADDITIONAL 500 DEATHS A YEAR.

ELIZABETH BLACKWELL

America's first woman doctor was admitted to New York's Geneva College in 1847 as a joke, and was expected to flunk out within months. Nevertheless, Blackwell prevailed and triumphed over taunts and bias while at medical school to earn her degree two years later. While in her last year of medical training, she was cleaning the infected eye of an infant when she accidentally splattered a drop of water into her own eye. Six months later she had the eye taken out and had it replaced with a glass eye. Afterward, American hospitals refused to hire her. She then borrowed a few thousand dollars to open a clinic in New York City, which she called the New York Infirmary for Indigent Women and Children. She charged patients only four dollars a week, if they had it, for full treatment that might cost at least two thousand dollars a day at the going rate. During the Civil War she set up an organization to train nurses, Women's Central Association of Relief, which later became the United States Sanitary Commission. In 1910 at age eighty-nine she died after a fall from which she never fully recovered.

SONNY BONO

In 1998 Sonny Bono sang to Cher "I Got You Babe," and later did a rendition of it with a tree, which he crashed into, killing himself while skiing at age sixty-two. During the seventies, Bono and his then-wife Cher were one of the most recognized couples in America through their popular TV variety shows, which aired under various names from 1970 until 1977. When the audience tired of his goofball routine, and after a divorce from Cher, he turned to the restaurant business and there too made a huge success. Despite or, some say, because of his Cher affiliation, he turned to politics later in life, and there, proving the naysayers wrong again, was actually elected to Congress. Salvatore Bono, born into a poor Italian immigrant family, a high school dropout, left behind a sizable estate, with royalties from his music still bringing in over a million a year. He was last seen leaving the ski trail at a Lake Tahoe resort to ski solo among the trees at 1:30 P.M. on January 5. Six hours later his frozen body was retrieved, dead from crashing into a 40-foot pine tree. His epitaph reads: "And the Beat Goes On."

MUSICIAN ACCIDENTS

In 1954 **Danny Cedrone** (Donato Joseph Cedrone), member of Bill Haley and His Comets, plummeted down a flight of stairs and died at age thirty-four. That same year blues artist **Johnny Ace** (John Marshall Alexander, Jr.) lost at a backstage game of Russian Roulette and died at age twenty-five. In 1973 **Roger Durham,** singer of "Natural High," was looking for just that when he died after falling off a horse at age twenty-seven. In 1978 a member of Chicago, **Terry Kath,** a gun enthusiast, attempted to calm his band mates when after a gig he began to clean one of his 9-mm semiautomatic pistols: "Don't worry, it's not loaded," he said and put the barrel to his head. He was mistaken and died from a self-inflicted gunshot a week before his birthday at age thirty-one. In 1993, known for performing with abandon, **Wong Ka Kui** of the band Beyond, was filming a segment for a TV show when he fell off the stage eight feet above the floor and died at age thirty-one.

DANIEL BOONE

Daniel Boone, America's most famous pioneer hero, had set off into a hostile world without roads, toting only a flintlock musket and a knife; the region was so wild he reportedly killed over ten thousand bears while he surveyed and settled vast virgin wildernesses of Kentucky, West Virginia, and Missouri. In 1820, at the age of eighty-five, Boone went on his final hunting trip near his home in St. Charles, Missouri, caught pneumonia, and died. Although he spent his life in the woods and claimed a lot of property for himself and family, he lost it all to the slick dealings of investors using issues of unclear titles and creditors liens to strip him of all but his name. His funeral was held in his son's barn instead of the house; hundreds showed up unexpectedly to pay their respects. Many remember a TV show that portrayed Daniel Boone wearing a coonskin cap. He actually wore a felt-brim hat in the Quaker style now seen on boxes of oatmeal. The TV theme song: "Daniel Boone was a man. Yes a big man. With an eye like an eagle and as tall as a mountain was he," was also a stretch. Boone was 5 feet 8 and weighed about 175 pounds. He did have a keen and active mind and stayed physically fit, a fact that kept him alive long after what is currently considered retirement age.

> "I have never been lost, but I will admit to being confused for several weeks."
> —DANIEL BOONE

BETTY BOOP

Helen Kane (Helen Schroeder) portrayed the ditzy flapper or party girl of the Roaring Twenties when she sang the 1928 hit "I Wanna Be Loved by You, Boop-Boop-a-Doop," in a squeaky-voice, cutie-pie delivery with a distinct Bronx accent that made her an adorable sensation for a while. She made another twenty-two song recordings during the height of her fame, which was pretty much over by 1930. Although she was the obvious inspiration for the Betty Boop cartoons, she received none of those royalties and lost the lawsuit she brought against the cartoon creators. She opened a restaurant in New York, Healy's Grill, and owned it until she died at age sixty-three in 1966. At the time, few took notice that "Betty Boop" had succumbed to breast cancer.

GAIL BORDEN

Condensed milk was invented by Gail Borden in 1853. After one bad invention followed by another, he finally hit on the idea of food concentrates as an economical way to safeguard the food supply. He once said he conceived the notion by observing his wife adding sugar to her milk to keep her full-figured voluptuousness, a sign of beauty and wealth at the time (left). Before, milk was shipped in unsanitary oak barrels, and it spoiled quickly. Although he didn't invent the tin can, his marketing skills in effect launched the canned food industry. Canning food diminished the possibility of food-storage spoilage, subsequent short supplies from the whims of natural elements, and contamination by vermin. He died in Borden, Texas, of a gastrointestinal flu (possibly from drinking from a dented container) in 1874 and had his body packed in a tin can of a railroad car to be buried in Woodlawn Cemetery in New York.

TIN CANS CONQUER THE WORLD

The technique to mass produce the tin can is credited to Peter Durand who was granted a license by the King of England in 1810. Previously, iron pots with lids served as the means of storage; lead poisoning, botulism, and salmonella killed many. It was Napoleon who is the mastermind behind alternate means of food preservation. He offered a prize to anyone who could find a way to preserve and transport unspoiled food to his troops, saying "the military moves on its stomach." Du-

rand borrowed from French prizewinner Nicolas Appert, who had discovered that any means of preservation had to be airtight. (Appert used bottles sealed with a cork and wax.) Without the tin can, England wouldn't have built an empire. Preserved food allowed sailors to travel long distances and feed the armies abroad. The Civil War wouldn't have lasted as long if it wasn't for Gail Borden's milk cans keeping soldiers fed. Today, Americans use 130 billion cans each year. People who eat food from jars with loose lids, swollen or dented cans, or food left in opened cans get food poisoning from the bacteria botulism, which caused over 25,000 fatalities since 1975.

SYLVANUS BOWSER

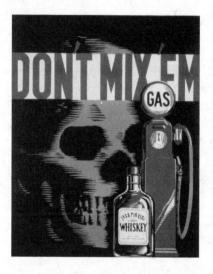

At the onset of the automobile age, gas was purchased by the bucketful at general stores and repair shops. Sylvanus Bowser came up with the idea of a water pump that used a wooden plunger that could raise a column of fluid upward to the surface. This led to the development of the first "filling station" in 1905, when he sold his devices to Standard Oil of California (now Chevron). It was said he kept a can of gasoline in his office that he sniffed when he could not get out in the field to oversee new filling pump installations. He said that he loved the smell of gas, and once wrote that to him, "It smelled like money." Once he was wealthy, he built his mansion within view of his gasoline pump factory in Fort Wayne, Indiana. Today, his obsession with inhaling gas fumes is called huffing, an addiction to the hydrocarbons in gasoline, which leads to deterioration of the central nervous system, as well as liver damage, high blood pressure, and digestive disorders. When Bowser died in 1938 at age sixty-six, his obituary praised his invention but did not mention his cause of death or his supposed penchant for gas sniffing. His death certificate cited the cause of death as "hematologic [blood] problems."

BOZO

Bob Bell played Bozo the Clown for twenty-five years. Even though there were many who played Bozo, this most famous Bozo died at age seventy-five in 1997 of heart disease. No clown was seen by more people than Bell's Bozo, with his sticky orange hair pointing out from his white face and white bald head, similar to Krusty the Clown seen on *The Simpsons*. The clown character of Bozo was not owned by Bell and belonged to Bozo's trademark holder Larry Harmon, who bought the image from Capitol Records. Nevertheless, it was Bob who won an Emmy for his antics in 1970, was a write-in candidate for the 1984 presidential election, was inducted into the Clown Hall of Fame in 1996, and remains, to loyal fans, the best Bozo among Bozos.

EVEN SAD CLOWNS LIVE LONG

Emmett Kelly, Sr., began as a trapeze performer before he found his niche as the clown- hobo Weary Willy. His sad face, sad-eyed clown persona was one of the most recognizable clown images of the twentieth century and appears on more velvet paintings and mass-produced lithographs than that of any other performer. After sixty-five years in the circus, he retired, though he kept busy doing trade show appearances and sad, small performances at local malls. In 1979, at eighty, he died in Sarasota, Florida, of heart failure.

JOHANNES BRAHMS

Johannes Brahms was the last of the great composers from the classical and romantic period, though less passionate than Beethoven, with a more logical and reserved approach to musical phrasing, thereby producing a more delicate sound (think of "Lullaby and Goodnight," also known as "Brahms' Lullaby"). His life was dedicated to music and not much else, so that he, like Beethoven, never took a wife, although he was infatuated with the composer Schumann's wife Clara. Self-critical to the extreme—it ate at him if a piece he wrote was imperfect—he burned much of his work and sketches except about two hundred pieces. He died in 1897 at age sixty-three of consumption, an eating away from the inside that we now know as cancer. He was the first great composer to have his voice recorded on Thomas Edison's sound-recording device: Twenty seconds still remains of Brahms playing part of Hungarian Dance, Number 1.

MARLON BRANDO

Marlon Brando, born to two alcoholic parents, was the third actor to receive two best actor Oscars: *On The Waterfront* (1954) and *The Godfather* (1972). He turned down the second award in protest for treatment of Native Americans, as well as a reluctance to glorify the mafia. Toward the end of his days, his life became more of a drama than any he portrayed on screen: his self-imposed exile on Tahiti, his son's murder trial (where he refused to take an oath, claiming he was an atheist), and his growing size, obesity, and blindness. He died in 2004 at the age of eighty of lung failure owing to pulmonary fibrosis, excessive scar tissue in the lung. Brando said, "I don't mind that I'm fat. You still get the same money." He was paid $4 million for his ten minutes' performance in the movie *Superman*.

PEARL S. BUCK

Pearl S. (Sydenstricker) Buck was raised in China and was taught to write English only as a second language. She wrote her first novel in 1930 and her most famous, *The Good Earth*, in 1932, for which she became the first woman to win the Pulitzer Prize. After writing for only eight years, she became the first American woman to win a Nobel Prize for Literature, in 1938. She was more than prolific and went on to write over a hundred books, in addition to organizing causes for interracial adoption. She died in 1973 at age eighty of congestive heart failure.

ROBERT O'HARA BURKE

Australia's most famous explorers are the odd pair of Robert O'Hara Burke and William Wills. They were the first to venture across the continent in the hope of finding a legendary inland sea, motivated by prize money offered to any who could return with geographical information, which would make it possible to string a telegraph from Melbourne to the northern Gulf of Carpentaria. Burke, with no previous experience in exploration, along with Wills, a trained surveyor, believed they were capable of trekking where even experienced bushmen thought foolhardy. Burke, an impulsive and impatient fellow, figured he could beat the odds by putting together an overstocked caravan, packing two years' supply of food, dozens of horses and camels, eighty pairs of shoes, thirty hats, and over fifty buckets of beads to trade with the aborigines. However, when lugging such a supply proved slow-going, he abandoned much of his preparations to gain speed, forsaking caution in order to make it into the history books as the first. At the halfway point, it was Burke, Wills, and two men—Charles Gray and John King—continuing the rest of the way with six camels, one horse and twelve weeks' supply of food. They made it to the other coast, but within six months— by June of 1861—on their return journey, three of the four were dead: Gray had been beaten by Burke for stealing food from the supply train and soon after died from exhaustion. Burke died at age forty of starvation, and Wills was dead from scurvy at age twenty-seven. King was kept alive with the aid of aborigines and eventually he was rescued, though he died nine years later at the age of thirty-one.

GEORGE BURNS

Outdated vaudeville actors unable to break into motion pictures or those who had the acting talent for Broadway flocked to early TV. One such married couple, the radio team of George Burns and Gracie Allen made a successful transition with their TV debut in 1950, *The Burns & Allen Show*, playing themselves in comedy skits. The program was extremely popular and ran until 1958, when Gracie decided to retire. The famous line from the show, "Say good night, Gracie," happened for good in 1964 when Allen died at age sixty-nine of a heart attack. Cigar-smoking George Burns continued his straight-man comic act and starred in more than a dozen films, lasting until he actually played God at age eighty-eight in *Oh, God! You Devil* (1984). Burns died in 1996 at the age of one hundred of cardiorespiratory arrest, proving, at least in this case—regardless of his nearly century-long addiction to cigars—that longevity belongs to the lighthearted lead and rarely to the foil.

> "I don't believe in dying. It's been done."
> —GEORGE BURNS

WILLIAM BURROUGHS

William Burroughs made his name as the renegade man of letters. He was the vagabond gentleman junkie, an antiauthoritarian, who wrote the spooky novel *Naked Lunch*. Burroughs shot his second wife in the head during a William Tell horseplay stunt in 1951. Norman Mailer once said of Burroughs: "The only American novelist who may conceivably be possessed of genius." Burroughs died in 1997 at age eighty-three from a heart attack. He believed that his early years using opiates, when they were pure, preserved him.

RICHARD BURTON

Richard Burton has the Oscar distinction as the biggest loser: He was nominated over seven times but failed to take home the prize. Burton, despite his loss, was the highest-paid actor in Hollywood and worked toward the record of most married, a total of five times, twice to Elizabeth Taylor. A lifelong insomniac and notoriously heavy drinker, he smoked five packs of cigarettes a day, until he died suddenly of a cerebral hemorrhage at age fifty-eight in 1984. The most nominated female (six times) without winning was Thelma Ritter. She is remembered as the perturbed mom in *Miracle on 34th Street*, unable to find the toy Kris Kringle had promised her boy. In 1968 she had a heart attack on the set of the *Jerry Lewis Show* and died at age sixty-two, two weeks before her birthday.

CHILDREN FROM DIVORCED OR SEPARATED FAMILIES GREW UP TO SHOW A HIGHER RISK OF PREMATURE MORTALITY. MEN WHO HAD EXPERIENCED THE LOSS OF A PARENT ARE MORE LIKELY TO HAVE THEIR OWN MARRIAGES END IN DIVORCE. RICHARD BURTON'S MOTHER DIED WHEN HE WAS TWO, AND HE WAS SOON AFTER SENT TO LIVE WITH AN AUNT. HE BEGAN DRINKING AND SMOKING AT AGE EIGHT.

JOHN CABOT

Many believe the first maps of the New World were taken from notes made by explorer John Cabot, Italian-born Giovanni Caboto, who sailed under the English flag. There is no doubt that Cabot was one of the most experienced mariners of that generation who explored the North American shores in 1497 and possibly made it to the South American coasts in 1498. Cabot was killed by Spanish pirates while returning from his second voyage in 1499 at age forty-nine. His ship was scuttled, sunk, and his body was never found. Some say America should be named instead Giovannia or The United States of Cabotika. In fact, in the 1700s the name was nearly changed and was almost called the United States of Columbia in honor of Columbus.

ALBERT CAMUS

The youngest Noble Laureate in Literature to die was Albert Camus. The French author and philosopher received the award at the age of forty-three in 1957. His work was postulated on the inherent absurdity of life. Three years later, in 1960, he died in a car accident. Examiners found an unused train ticket to the same destination for which he was headed in his coat pocket. That train arrived safely. He once remarked that dying in a car would be meritless and a supremely absurd way to die.

> "All great deeds and all great thoughts have a ridiculous beginning. Great works are often born on a street corner or in a restaurant's revolving door."
> —ALBERT CAMUS

DALE CARNEGIE

The year 1948 made Dale Carnegie a household name after *How to Stop Worrying and Start Living* became a bestseller. He had written previous self-help books in the thirties, including *How to Win Friends and Influence People* (1936), but this one turned him into an industry. His techniques were used as the curriculum for a twelve-week course and are still used by employers to teach salesmen how to make higher earnings. Carnegie started out as a salesman for soap and lard before he turned the winning style he learned making customers out of everyone into a philosophy of sorts on how to succeed. His books have sold more than 30 million copies to date. He died of Hodgkin's disease in 1955 at age sixty-seven.

WILLIS CARRIER

Before air conditioning, productivity rates during the summer months in nearly every industry plunged 40 percent. Prior to its invention, attempts to cool buildings involved electric fans that were used to circulate chilled air produced from large blocks of melting ice. In 1902 Willis Carrier wanted to show his mother that she hadn't wasted her money sending him to college. When Carrier's first employer, a mechanical engineering firm was asked by a Brooklyn printer to find a solution to the heat and humidity that made ink run and stopped the presses, the more senior of his coworkers slipped the new rookie the assignment, certain he'd screw it up and get canned. Fresh out of Cornell University, twenty-five-year-old Carrier sweated; he feared having to tell his mother that he was fired only months after he began his new job. This fear motivated him to look at the problem as none before had. Within a few weeks he invented a new way to pass brine (saltwater) over coils and then redirect its cooler, evaporating air back into the room. Carrier's invention controlled the humidity and chilled the air better than a truckload of melted ice. He called it The Apparatus for Treating Air, which didn't have the marketing ring needed. Although his invention solved the printing company's problem, it was slow to catch on in other industries. Eventually, movie theaters, displaying blue ice cubes on the marquees, tried it. Congress was air-conditioned in 1928 and the White House in 1929. The first air-conditioned auto was the 1939 Packard. Carrier never saw the windfall from his invention. He stayed hot under the collar, financially, most of his life until he died in 1950, at age seventy-three, from a heart ailment. He left behind an invention that once prevented him from getting into hot water with his mother and in so doing kept the rest of the world cool.

When air ducts get wet from leaky roofs or from being too close to sweating plumbing pipes, numerous types of mold and bacteria easily fester. People living or working in indoor air environments cooled with compromised air-conditioning ducts feel tired and often develop persistent coughs and muscle aches, and they may develop tightness of chest, fever, or chills. Annually, over 6,000 premature deaths are attributed to bad A/C ducts, often cited on death certificates as hypersensitivity pneumonitis, an inflammatory lung disorder.

JOHNNY CARSON

The Tonight Show was hosted by comedian Johnny Carson from 1962 to 1992 and ranked as the leader in late-night TV for most of its reign. Johnny took over the show from Jack Paar whose adlibs during live commercials made sponsors angry. His classic was about a commercial for underwear, to which he added, for a laugh, "These fit so tight, it's like being hugged by a midget." Paar died after a triple bypass, arteriosclerosis, and a stroke in 2004 at age eighty-five. Carson, a lifelong smoker, died of emphysema at age seventy-nine in 2005.

GEORGE WASHINGTON CARVER

George Washington Carver was fascinated with wild plants when he was a slave and was known by the locals near the Missouri farm he was interned as the Plant Doctor. When slavery was abolished, he went to school and eventually became the first black student at the University of Iowa, where he studied agriculture. He devised ways for southern farms to use soil for crops other than cotton, in particular peanuts. In 1896 the Department of Agriculture gave him a job to study soil and farming practices at the Tuskegee University, where he remained until his death in 1943, which was caused by falling down a flight of stairs when he was approximately seventy-nine, since his date of birth was never recorded. Carver is known for inventing more than three hundred uses for the peanut, transforming what was once considered an exotic legume into the $5-billion industry it is today.

PEANUT BUTTER RANKS FIFTH BEHIND HOT DOGS, GRAPES, NUTS, RAW CARROTS, AND CELERY AS THE TOP FOODS THAT CHOKE PEOPLE TO DEATH.

MARY ANN SHADD CARY

Mary Ann Shadd Cary (1823–1893) was an educator and abolitionist. She was the first black woman to graduate from Howard University Law School and the first black woman to vote in a federal election. She helped President Lincoln enlist black men to fight in the Union and her house was frequently a safe haven in the Underground Railroad for slaves fleeing the South. After the war she became a school principal, and then a lawyer in Washington, D.C., at the age of sixty. She died in 1893 at age seventy from heart failure, with an estate valued at $150.

JOHNNY CASH

He sold 50 million albums in a fifty-year career, singing the songs of the outlaw and downtrodden. Known for his black suits—as he said, "I'd love to wear a suit of white, but not until the world is right"—Cash teetered on self-annihilation through years of alcoholism and drug abuse, though he walked back to the line of self-preservation after he married the love of his life June Carter. When she died during heart surgery at age seventy-three in 2003, her brokenhearted husband, "The Man in Black," officially died four months later at age seventy-one of respiratory failure due to diabetes. The performer, who opened each appearance with the simple "Hello, I'm Johnny Cash," said good-bye, buried, of course, in a black suit.

MUSICIANS' LIVERS & LIFESTYLES

In 1965 **Alan Freed** (Aldon James Freed), a DJ who was recognized as coiner of the term rock and roll (even though the Boswell Sisters did a song titled "Rock and Roll" in the forties), died of uremia (kidney failure) and cirrhosis at age forty-two, a few years after he pled guilty to taking payola, bribes to play certain songs. In 1972 **Clyde McPhatter** of the Dominoes died of liver failure at age thirty-nine. In 1973 **Ron "Pigpen" McKernan**, keyboardist for the Grateful Dead, took in more alcohol than his liver could handle and ultimately died of gastrointestinal hemorrhage at age twenty-seven. Although **Florence Ballard** sang "Stop in the Name of Love" while with the Supremes, she couldn't stop drinking for love or anything else and died as a result at age thirty-two in 1976, ultimately of coronary thrombosis. Pal and former roommate of Johnny Cash, **Waylon Jennings**, known for "I'm a Ramblin' Man," finally rested when diabetes took him out at age sixty-four in 2002.

When **Ray Charles** was four, his five-year-old brother fell into an outdoor bathtub. Ray was unable to pull him out before his brother drowned. Soon after, Ray Charles began to lose his sight and was totally blind by seven. Who

knew what "Georgia on My Mind" really meant to the popular singer, although a seventeen-year heroin addiction might have something to do with it. He died of liver failure at age seventy-three in 2004.

From gang member to "King of the Make-Out Song," **Barry White,** known for "Can't Get Enough of Your Love, Baby" and "You're the First, the Last, My Everything," couldn't keep from boiling over in passion. His chronic high blood pressure caused fatal renal failure at age fifty-eight in 2004. And in 2005 singer **Luther Vandross,** noted for the hits "Endless Love" and "Dance With My Father," died at age fifty-four. Luther struggled with his obesity most of his life, and in 2003 he went on a strict diet eliminating all carbohydrates. He lost over 100 pounds. It wasn't long before he suffered a stroke. Some say the pressure to look thin finally killed him; he died of a heart attack.

WILLA CATHER

Willa Cather taught English in a Pittsburgh high school before working as an editor at *McClure's* magazine. She won a Pulitzer Prize in 1923 for *One of Ours* and persisted with a style of writing considered "high art," influenced by Henry James. Despite the use of stilted language, she had a bestseller in 1932 with her novel *Shadows on the Rock*, about a Parisian widow and her daughter set in seventeenth-century Quebec. In her personal life she was a lifelong lesbian and had numerous affairs with influential women, though she remained mostly loyal to one Edith Lewis while living at Five Bank Street, Greenwich Village for over forty years. Cather died in 1947 at age seventy-three of cerebral hemorrhage.

A cerebral hemorrhage, or aneurysm, is when a blood vessel suddenly bursts in the brain. It is not always fast and often gives a warning that this has occurred by manifesting as a headache accompanied by a stiff neck, nausea, sudden irregularity in verbal skills, or difficulty swallowing. Approximately 50,000 people die in the United States from spontaneous cerebral hemorrhage each year.

SERGI CHALIBASHVILI

Diving is a daring and competitive sport. One, two, three running leaps and then the diver pounces on the edge of the board to become airborne. The greater the height, the better the chance to complete difficult turns and twists before plunging into the water. According to the Bureau of Labor Statistics that oddly keeps track of the death of athletes, two divers die each year and twenty or more suffer serious spinal injury. It usually happens as it did in the 1983 World University Games when Sergi Chalibashvili went so high to do his three-and-a-half reverse somersault that he smashed his head on the edge of the board on the way down. He lay in a coma for a week before he died at age twenty-one. He lives on in training videos that divers watch, cringing at the head impact part, but, hopefully, learning how to avoid a similar fate.

JOSHUA CHAMBERLAIN

General Joshua Chamberlain was in twenty-four battles and was wounded six times. He was chosen by Grant to receive the formal surrender of weapons and

colors (April 12, 1865) from Robert E. Lee at Appomattox Court House in Virginia. During the ceremony he saluted the Confederate soldiers, an action that caused uproar in the North but which he defended as an act of honor among warriors. After the war, he was elected governor of Maine by the largest majority in the state's history. He died at the age of eighty-five from the complications of battle wounds, apparently having taken quite some time for those previous six battle scars to do their damage.

THE CLAMPETTS

In 1963 when America was in mourning and glued to the TV watching the events of President John Kennedy's assassination, the most popular show was the *Beverly Hillbillies*. More people tuned in to see Jed Clampett (Buddy Ebsen) and Granny (Irene Ryan) than to see the Kennedy funeral procession. This sitcom shot to the top rating within weeks of its debut and baffled the critics who had panned it. It was the Horatio Alger story Americans so loved, told via slapstick and wordplay ("fancy eatin' table" for a billiard table and "fancy leather lunch box" for a briefcase). It was fun to watch as the likable hillbillies moved from Tennessee to Beverly "Hills, that is." Buddy Ebsen had his own real-life rags-to-riches story. He started out as a dancer on the vaudeville circuit after he came to Broadway from Orlando, Florida, in 1928 with less than thirty bucks in his pocket. He was originally slated to be the Tin Man in the *Wizard of Oz* but got sick from the silver body paint and was replaced by Jack Haley. He later lost another big chance when he was scheduled to play Davy Crockett in the Disney series, but lost out to Fess Parker. Success eluded him until he was cast as Jed Clampett, which eventually led him to another popular lead as *Barnaby Jones*. Off camera he had the same easygoing temperament that made him a likable TV personality. He attributed his longevity to downtime he spent at sea on his catamaran. He died in 2003 at age ninety-five owing to complications from pneumonia. For the cast of *Beverly Hillbillies*, five additional characters have made an appearance in the obituaries: Cousin Pearl Bodine, played by **Bea Benaderet** (who was also the voice of *Flintstones*' Betty Rubble), died of lung cancer in 1968 at age sixty-two. Cantankerous Granny, played by **Irene Ryan**, died onstage in 1973 at age seventy from a brain tumor while performing in *Pippin* on Broadway. Mr. Drysdale, played by **Ray Bailey,** died at age seventy-five of a heart attack in 1980. Mrs. Margaret Drysdale, played by **Harriet MacGibbon,** died in 1987 at age eighty-one of pulmonary failure. Jane Hathaway, played by **Nancy Kulp,** succumbed to cancer at age sixty-nine in 1991.

ROBERTO CLEMENTE
Roberto Clemente Walker was the first Hispanic American to be inducted into the Baseball Hall of Fame, even if it was posthumously. With a throwing arm like a catapult, he broke records as an outfielder during his eighteen years of major league ball and tallied up an impressive record with his bat, achieving a .317 lifetime batting average. Born into poverty in Puerto Rico, Roberto made it his life mission during off-seasons to go back to his island and help the poor. At age thirty-eight in 1972 he was en route to Nicaragua to fly in relief supplies to victims of an earthquake when the overloaded plane ditched into the Atlantic Ocean less than a mile after takeoff from San Juan airport. Although he was in perfect health, he often told his wife that he believed he was going to die young. Nevertheless, unlike some remembered for their bling or their outside-of-dugout flings, Clemente remains a hero to many, since he died trying to do good. His body was never recovered.

ONE BIG ERROR
Baseball players were admired for their skill on the field, but a few made headlines for actions out of uniform. In 1935 **Len Koenecke** was playing for the Dodgers, but he was sent home in midseason owing to a string of errors. While flying back to Buffalo, New York, he got drunk and started a ruckus on the plane. When he decided to try to take over the controls from the pilot, a violent scuffle ensued. To save the plane from crashing, someone bashed Koenecke's skull in with a fire extinguisher. He died at age thirty-one.

BASEBALL PLAYERS, DIED IN PLANES
September 20, 1956: **Tom Gastall,** catcher for the Baltimore Orioles, died in a plane crash in Maryland. November 27, 1956: St. Louis Cardinal catcher Charlie

Peete was killed in a plane crash in Venezuela. February 13, 1964: **Ken Hubbs** (twenty-three), Chicago Cubs second baseman and 1962 Rookie of the Year, was dead after his plane crashed in Provo, Utah. August 2, 1979: **Thurman Munson** (thirty-two), New York Yankee catcher was taking flying lessons when his plane crashed in Canton, Ohio. He died during a practice landing that touched down just short of the runway.

CLEOPATRA

Cleopatra was the last pharaoh of Egypt. She was not only beautiful but intelligent—according to Plutarch, "It was a pleasure to hear the sound of her voice, and she tuned her tongue like a many-stringed instrument expertly to whatever language she chose." She came to power by the age of seventeen and manipulated the laws preventing sovereignty to be held by a woman until her grasp on control was indisputable. When exiled, she presented herself to Julius Caesar rolled in a carpet with the gift of herself on the condition she be returned to power over Egypt. The current ruler of Egypt, her brother, Ptolemy, was promptly drowned in the Nile. When she bore Caesar a son, named Caesarian, he actually contemplated joint rulership but was assassinated on the Senate steps for even thinking such nonsense. Shortly afterward, Mark Antony, the most powerful leader in Rome, then set up a meeting with Cleopatra and fell instantly in love. When Mark Antony took his own life when he lost his bid for Rome, Cleopatra soon joined him and, according to legend, died from the bite of an asp, a poisonous snake. But this is highly unlikely, since Cleopatra, if nothing else, avoided pain and pampered her body like few women before or after. A North African asp bite would have caused convulsions, vomiting, and swelling. She did intend to die and laid herself out on a regal bed of gold, surrounded by servants. She knew snakes and liked their symbolism, reportedly laughing when she heard herself called the Viper of the Nile as a result of her ability to mesmerize men. It seems more probable that she drank a concoction that contained cobra venom, if a snake was involved at all, which would guarantee a quicker death, and had the baskets of vipers at her bedside for effect. She was thirty-nine.

DEATH ON THE MENU

Romans loved poisons. In the third century B.C. an entire village was poisoned when authorities believed an epidemic stemmed from its people. In 211 B.C. at least 20,000 Capuans (a village to the south of Rome) were poisoned. Records indicate that the Numidian queen, Sophonisba, was killed in 203 B.C. with a deadly concoction. The toxicity of poisonous insects, snakes, spiders, and scorpions was common knowledge, though this means was seldom used in homicide. Vegetable poisons were the favorites, including belladonna, deadly nightshade, and mandrake. Cicero wrote that hemlock and honey was a palatable smoothie for the doomed, as well as the autumn crocus, yew extract, and opium.

KURT COBAIN

In 1994, fresh out of rehab, Kurt Cobain, twenty-seven-year-old rocker of Nirvana, was found dead in his Seattle home, with a gunshot wound to his head. The autopsy shows that there was 225 mgs of heroin in his blood, three times the amount needed for a lethal overdose. The hardest-core junkie would be immediately incapacitated after shooting that much dope, unable to hold a shotgun or fire it, which leads some to believe his death, although listed as suicide, has more sinister overtones.

MUSICIAN SUICIDES

Ronnie Smith was chosen to replace Buddy Holly for the remainder of the 1959 rock tour after the singer died in a plane crash. Plagued by ghosts, Ronnie hung himself at age twenty-eight in 1962. **Joe Meek** (Robert George Meek) had some success with "Ridin' the Wind" but apparently not enough, since he shot his landlady then himself at age thirty-seven in 1967. **Mike Furber,** leader of Mike Furber and the Bowery Boys with the hit "Just A Poor Boy," believing, apparently, too much in negative self-talk, hung himself when he was twenty-five in 1973. In that same year Temptations vocalist **Paul Williams** shot himself at age thirty-four. In 1976 **Phil Ochs,** singer of "Draft Dodger Rag," hung himself at age thirty-five. In 1979 **Donny Hathaway,** known for the song "Where is the Love," had apparently never found it and jumped from the fifteenth-floor window of a New York City hotel at age thirty-three. In 1983 Badfinger's **Tom Evans** hung himself at thirty-six.

The Singing Nun, Sister Luc-Gabrielle (Jeanine Deckers), known for the song "Dominique," became a sensation after she appeared on the Ed Sullivan Show in 1964. She eventually left the Belgium sisterhood after recording a song in favor of birth control. After she was sued for back taxes, the Singing Nun at age fifty-one and her female significant other committed suicide together in 1985.

In 1986, forty-two-year-old **Richard Manuel** of the Band hung himself. In 1988 **Roy Buchanan,** a blues singer known for "My Baby Says She's Gonna Leave Me," apparently couldn't get over it, since he hung himself while in a county jail after an arrest for public intoxication at age forty-eight. In 1991 son of Willie Nelson, **Billy Nelson** (William Hugh Nelson, Jr.), who wrote "Put Me on a Train Back to Texas," hung himself at age thirty-three. In 1995, Pariah singer **Sims Ellison** with the hit "Nobody Listens," presumably believed it, since he shot himself at age twenty-eight. **Wendy O. Williams** of the Plasmatics proved she wasn't fooling when she sang "It's My Life," because she too shot herself at forty-eight in 1998. **Dave Blood** (David Schulthise) of the Dead Milkmen took the name of his group literally and committed suicide to give it authenticity at age forty-seven in 2004.

A NEW KIND OF MILE-HIGH CLUB

In 2006 sound engineer for some of the best bands, including Pink Floyd and Red Hot Chili Peppers, **Gerald Georgettis** was seated next to a crying baby on an airplane during a flight from Miami to Los Angeles. Unable to take the crying, among other things, he was somehow led to hang himself in the airplane's bathroom at age fifty-six.

NAT KING COLE

In 1948 Nat King Cole (Nathaniel Adams Coles) became a major player with the release of "Nature Boy," which sold a million records and made the singer an international celebrity. The song was written by a Brooklyn yogi, **eden ahbez** (who believed only divinities deserved names with capital letters) who left the lyrics tacked to Cole's stage door. Cole's velvet voice and impeccable stage presence earned him great success and the historic achievement of being the first African American to host a nationally televised variety show. Off the stage, Cole was not influenced by eden's advocacy of all things natural and continued to smoke cigarettes by the boatload until he died of lung cancer at age forty-five in 1965. On the other hand, eden ahbez might be considered the first original hippie who walked around in sandals and had long hair and a beard fifteen years before it was fashionable. He camped for years below the L of the Hollywood sign, sleeping outdoors with his family, eating vegetables, fruits, and nuts, and he studied Oriental mysticism. In 1966 he was seen in the studio with the Beach Boys, acting as a consultant. Rebel to the end, he died in 1995 after being struck by a car while jaywalking at age eighty-six.

COLT'S NEW MODEL ARMY METALLIC CARTRIDGE REVOLVING PISTOL.

The Drawing is one-half the size of the Pistol.
cal. .45 inch.   PRICE $20,00.

COLT'S METALLIC CARTRIDGE ARMY PISTOL, WITH ATTACHABLE STOCK.

SAMUEL COLT

In 1839 Samuel Colt patented the revolving-chamber pistol. As a teen he had worked as a sailor and had spent long hours staring at the ship's wheel. He used this principle to invent a gun that could shoot multiple bullets without reloading. He excelled at both invention and marketing and today would be considered a compulsive workaholic. He struggled with a way to produce his guns cheaply but was forced to find a method of mass production after he received an order from the U.S. government in 1847 for 1,000 revolvers. By the time he died of exhaustion at age forty-seven, Samuel Colt had produced more than 400,000 Colt .45 revolvers. At his funeral in 1862 it was said of the Colt .45 he invented: "God created man, but Sam Colt [the Colt .45] made them all equal."

MORE THAN 34,000 PEOPLE, WITH A DAILY AVERAGE OF 75 ADULTS AND 10 CHILDREN, WERE KILLED BY GUNFIRE IN THE UNITED STATES IN 2006. GUNS IN AMERICA KILL MORE IN ONE WEEK THAN DURING AN ENTIRE YEAR IN ALL OF EUROPE. OVER THE LAST TWO YEARS ALONE, MORE AMERICAN CIVILIANS DIED FROM GUNFIRE THAN ALL OF THE AMERICAN SOLDIERS KILLED DURING THE NINE YEARS OF THE VIETNAM WAR.

JOHN COLTRANE

John Coltrane was a jazz saxophonist who strove to create a new jazz sound. He is considered an avant-garde musical revolutionary, even though many casual jazz listeners say his later recordings sound like nothing more than disconnected noise. During the 1950s his jazz was more traditional and well received, although he was often unreliable due to his addiction to drugs and alcohol. In 1957 he sought a spiritual solution to the demons that plagued him. At the end, he thought that if he could find the universal language of music, it would be strong enough to cure illness. Nevertheless, he died in 1967 at the age of forty of a liver ailment, which appears to have been the Hepatitis C virus, often acquired from intravenous drug use. This was long before that disease was known.

CHRISTOPHER COLUMBUS

Few in Columbus's time really believed the earth was flat. The fear resulted from not knowing how immense the earth sphere was. Most knowledgeable sailors believed it was surely big enough for them to die of thirst and starvation long before reaching habitable land, if they sailed west instead of east to reach Asia. Columbus used calculations from Arabic and Greek texts that cited the possible circumference in miles, and he converted this into the shorter Italian mile. Believing the earth was nearly half the size it actually was. He was emboldened by his error in math to effect his plan. He was slightly above average height (5 feet 6 inches), with reddish hair that fell long from his friarlike bald head. He

had a light-skinned complexion that quickly flushed crimson when others called his ideas foolish. Nevertheless, Queen Isabella and King Ferdinand of Spain came to believe he was the best man to take the political gamble of exploration, necessary to keep abreast of their neighbors, and eventually they agreed to his terms to share in all profits of whatever he discovered—in part because they assumed he would never return. In 1492, Columbus landed in the Bahamas, and then sailed to Cuba and the Dominican Republic before returning to Spain a year later. He made four additional voyages but was arrested in 1500 and thrown into jail on complaints of incompetence as a governor. Eventually, the Spanish royalty set him free, though they reneged on giving him 10 percent of the profits. By then Columbus's years at sea, including a year shipwrecked on Jamaica, had bent his body from arthritis and weakened his eyesight by bacterial conjunctivitis. In addition, he claimed to hear divine

Isabella of Spain died at age fifty-five in 1504 of pancreatic cancer. She is remembered not only for sponsoring Columbus but for authorizing the most brutal Spanish Inquisition the Church ever conducted. She got a small taste of the torture inflicted on thousands as she wasted away. Her daughter, the last of Spanish-born royalty from her lineage, Joanna the Mad (Juana la Loca) was locked in a windowless room, probably suffering from schizophrenia, for over forty years until she died in 1555 at age seventy-four.

voices, and he began to wear friar's robes. At age fifty-five in 1506 he died in his apartment in Valladolid, Spain, from Reiter's syndrome, a condition of swelling joints caused by repeated bouts of food poisoning or prolonged venereal disease. At his death he was afforded the extra expense of excarnation, removing all the flesh from his bones to preserve his skeleton: Only people of high status and potential icons received this costly treatment. His bones—just as he had in life—moved a number of times from Spain to Santo Domingo; Havana, Cuba; and back to Spain. Thus, no one is certain where his true remains rest or if all of them are gathered in one place.

PERRY COMO

Perry Como (Pierino Ronald Como) first entered the charts in 1949 with "Far Away Places," a hit that ushered in a decade of nearly unrivaled popularity. America loved his cool-as-a-cucumber relaxed style, so much so that Como became the first artist to have more than ten records sell over a million copies. From his start as a crooning baritone barber, he went on to have his own TV show in the fifties and hosted a traditional Christmas special for forty-five years, through the early nineties. He died in 2001 at age eighty-eight owing to complications from Alzheimer's disease.

CONFUCIUS

Confucius was born as the result of an autumn-spring romance, his father seventy and his mother fifteen. When his father died, mother and child were cast into poverty. Eventually, Confucius acquired a lowly job in government, but because of his wisdom, he caught the ear of the ruling class and brought prosperity by his counsel. He left the position when he was displeased with the poor ethical behavior of the leaders, in particular an entertainment extravaganza display of one hundred dancing girls, which seemed particularly distasteful to Confucius. He then traveled around the country to teach, offering a philosophy of morality and a pragmatic way to live. In later years a set of rituals were added to his doctrines that are still practiced to this day. He died, in 479 B.C. at age seventy-two, of coronary disease, what they called then a natural death, considering himself a failure unable to bring about change and mistakenly believing that his teachings would be forgotten.

IN A.D. 762, THE CHINESE MYSTIC POET LI PO DROWNED TRYING TO EMBRACE THE REFLECTION OF THE FULL MOON UPON A LAKE.

CONSTANTINE

Constantine was the Roman emperor who ended Christian persecution and called for the Council of Nicaea in A.D. 325 to organize various branches and offshoots of Christian sects into one, establishing certain mythologies still followed in many aspects to this day. During his life Constantine still supported Roman deities and chose not to get baptized himself until he was near death. Constantine was a tall man with a hooked nose and a jutting jaw, regal in presence, posturing like the military general that he was foremost. His empire spread from Britain to the borders of Persia and, to keep it intact, he issued harsh laws that had to be followed to the letter: The poor were tortured if they were late in tax payments and were often forced to sell their daughters into prostitution to pay the bill. If a girl ran away with a lover, she was burned alive, and anyone who had assisted her had molten-lead poured down his throat. He did ban crucifixions and said that petty criminals should no longer be branded in the face but only on the hands or feet. He died in A.D. 337 of coronary disease at age sixty-five.

NICOLAS CONTÉ

In 1795 during an embargo that prevented obtaining writing "leads" from England, the only source of pencils, French portrait painter and soldier Nicolas Conté devised a way to bake clay and pour the molten mixture between two halves of wood, thereby inventing the first pencil as we know it. What kids still refer to as number 2 lead pencils have always been made out of carbon. Conté formed a business to market his invention, but he was cut short when he died at age fifty-one in 1805  of blood poisoning. The "leads" from England were actually made of graphite and contained no lead, whereas Conté's mix, turning claying into charcoal, did. It was Conté's passion to find an instrument to allow him to continue drawing in the time of war that killed him.

Lead poisoning acts slowly but has been determined to cause impaired reasoning and violent behavior. People of all ages can get lead poisoning, but children's smaller bodies absorb more lead than adults' bodies do. Lead poisoning does more harm to children during developmental stages of growth. Living in substandard housing, 890,000 preschoolers in urban areas, especially in the Northeast and the Midwest, continue to be exposed to lead poisoning. They have elevated blood lead levels, primarily from paint chips and plaster and not pencils. U.S. obituaries that were written because of deaths from lead poisoning since 1930: 49,212.

HERNÁN CORTÉS

Hernán Cortés defeated the Aztec of Mexico by impersonating a god. By the time Cortés was eighteen, he was already a veteran of battle, helping to conquer Cuba. In 1518 he tried to get permission to lead an expedition into Mexico but was not trusted and disobeyed orders to return with six hundred men in his charge. Upon arrival on the east coast of Mexico, he met a beautiful native woman who became his interpreter and mistress. Through her insider information he learned the whereabouts of the legendary kingdom of gold and marched to Mexico City to see the ruler **Montezuma.** A few battles ensued, but the Aztecs thought the Spanish were warrior-gods and fled more often than fought. Cortés managed to keep Montezuma alive and to rule the people through him, but when an uprising occurred, Cortés presented the deposed leader to calm the people, though they only stoned Montezuma to death for his failure. Shortly afterward, the Aztec empire fell and Spain colonized in earnest. Cortés then became governor and tried to establish peace, growing sugar. He was the first to import African slaves to the New World. His soldiers dismantled most of the Aztec empire, melted down the statues, and sent the treasures back to Spain. In the end, Cortés was accused of numerous crimes by others jealous of his power. Although he tried to have the Spanish court reimburse him for his expeditions and discoveries, he received little compensation. He died of a messy

*Without **Malintzin**, the woman the Spanish referred to with honor as Doña Marina, with whom Cortés fell in love and had a child, the conquest of Mexico would have been forestalled. She is considered both as traitor and as symbol of the mother of Mexican people with mixed blood, yet her museum in Mexico City and the house she supposedly lived in are avoided by many because of the rumors of ghosts and the faces of dead Aztecs seen in the opaque panes of glass. She died at the age of thirty-four in 1529 from neither love nor treachery but from a European germ, smallpox.*

and embarrassing case of diarrhea (some still call it Montezuma's revenge) and pleurisy, the lungs filling with fluid, at the age of sixty-two in 1547.

BOB CRANE

A silly sitcom *Hogan's Heroes* (1965–1971) featured GIs in a Nazi POW camp having a good time. What is possibly more bizarre than the notion that a death camp was funny was the secret life of main character Colonel Robert Hogan, played by Bob Crane. Once he was found murdered in 1978 at the age of forty-nine, an investigation revealed that while he was trading one-liners with Colonel Klink, he was living a secret life as a pornographer and sex addict. After he was bludgeoned with a tire iron, the production associate of Crane's newly formed XXX-film company was eventually arrested but never convicted. Just before his death, Crane made films with himself as the lead, porno-acting with a strange cast of women and partaking in orgies. Some say Crane had second thoughts about releasing the films. Authorities fingered his producer associate to have the best motive, though to date no one has been convicted of the crime.

McHale's Navy (1962–1966), another TV show that tried to put a funny spin on World War II, featured a wacky bunch of sailors running a wartime patrol boat in the South Pacific. Captain Wallace "Leadbottom" Binghamton, played by Joe Flynn, didn't like the water and prophetically so, since in real life he was found drowned in his Beverly Hills home swimming pool in 1974 at age forty-nine, apparently after suffering a heart attack.

THOMAS CRAPPER

Plumber Thomas Crapper did in fact invent the parts needed to make the first flush toilet in 1864 and held nine patents for water-closet improvements and the still much-valued ballcock (the thing inside a toilet tank that allows the water to rise but not overflow after each flush). Crapper proved how some given names predict a destiny of sorts, since now crap is both a noun and a verb, a rare distinction in the lexicon of toilet issues, even if the word was previously used to describe the dregs at the bottom of a beer mug. Crapper died in 1910 and not, as some urban legends believe, from obstructed bowels but from clogged arteries at age seventy-three.

JIM CROW

Beginning around 1830 the most popular mass market vehicle for live music delivery was the traveling minstrel show. It's a phenomenon hard for contemporary Americans to comprehend, since it centered on imitating slaves singing and dancing yet is the first entirely American form of entertainment. The man responsible for establishing this was **Thomas Dartmouth "Daddy" Rice.** He put together a song-and-dance routine, performing as a character wearing blackface (skin colored with burnt cork) that imitated an old crippled slave he dubbed Jim Crow. From

that point on, every minstrel show had a Jim Crow performer. Daddy Rice expanded his repertoire to include characters Sambo, Jim Dandy, and Zip Coon, which became equally popular and made Rice one of the wealthiest performers of his time. However, his love of partying and promiscuity left him penniless when he died in 1860 of "pox," now called syphilis, at age fifty-two.

MARIE CURIE

The first woman to be awarded a Nobel Prize was **Marie Curie** in 1903 for Physics. She became the only woman to receive two Nobel Prizes, when she was awarded the prize for Chemistry in 1911. Her work with radiation and the discovery of the elements radium and polonium opened the doors for many advances in science and medicine. Soon after Madame Curie won the 1911 prize, she was hospitalized for depression and kidney problems and suffered from ill health the remainder of her life. The dangers of radiation were not understood and she often worked unprotected with radioactive substances. She died in 1934 at age sixty-six of aplastic anemia, a bone marrow condition caused by radiation. In 1938 Marie's daughter, **Irene Joliot-Curie**, won a Nobel Prize for Chemistry for her work with neutrons, setting the stage for nuclear fission. She died of leukemia at age fifty-eight in 1956 as a result of being exposed to radiation while assisting her mother years before.

Radiation exposure alters cells and the normal means in which they divide. The type of illnesses it causes depends on the amount and duration of exposure. Bursts of radiation contact cause immediate burns, while slower long-lasting exposure stores itself in the body's soft tissue, including the brain. Measured in rems, it affects the body by forming either wildly growing tumors, cancers, or blood disorders. In the United States each person is exposed to at least 360 rems per year, a cumulative amount that never leaves the body's soft tissues. Once the body has 10,000 rems, cancer will form.

JOHN B. CURTIS

Chewing gum was invented by John B. Curtis in 1848. He'd seen Indians chew the sap from spruce trees and labored over a Franklin stove to develop the right formula. He chewed a variety of bitter concoctions before he opened the first commercial chewing gum factory in America, called the State of Maine Pure Spruce Gum Company, eventually employing over two hundred people. An avid chewer and sampler of his new product lines, he died from asphyxia caused by a lump of gum stuck in his throat.

MORE THAN 2,800 PEOPLE DIE EACH YEAR FROM CHOKING, YET ONLY 300 DIE FROM CHEWING GUM, USUALLY CHILDREN UNDER THREE YEARS OLD. THE AVERAGE AMERICAN EATS 1.8 POUNDS OF GUM EACH YEAR.

Walter E. Diemer invented the first bubble gum in 1928 by combining 400 pounds of latex, wintergreen, peppermint, vanilla, cinnamon, and the only food coloring he had on hand, a concoction of pink liquid, in a giant vat. He attributed his longevity and happy life to riding a tricycle and blowing bubbles like a kid. He died at age ninety-four in 1998.

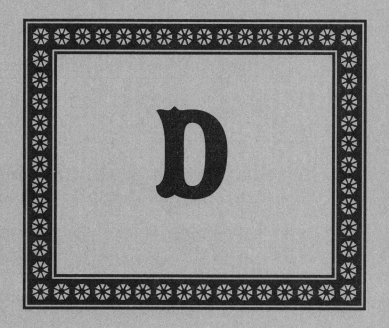

DOROTHY DANDRIDGE

Dorothy Dandridge was the first black performer ever nominated for a best actress Oscar for her lead in the musical *Carmen Jones* (1954), although she lost that year to Grace Kelly. Dandridge suffered an abusive marriage and was left in debt, subsequently touring in nightclubs to earn a living. She died of an overdose of antidepressants in 1965 at age forty-two. The first black performer to win an Oscar as best supporting actress was **Hattie McDaniel** for *Gone With the Wind* (1939). McDaniel had roles in more than three hundred films, although she received screen credits for only about eighty and often supplemented her income by working as a maid. When she died at age fifty-seven in 1952 of breast cancer, she had less than ten thousand dollars in her estate.

CLARENCE DARROW

Clarence Darrow's 1932 autobiography *The Story of My Life* was among the bestselling books that year, and it showed how people in the news then, as now, had a readymade platform for popular appeal. Darrow was the defense lawyer at the internationally infamous Scopes Monkey Trial in 1925, when a teacher was charged with violating a Tennessee state law that prohibited teaching the theory of evolution. Darrow went against well-known orator **William Jennings Bryan,** who believed anything other than divine creation as taught in the Bible was both irrational and immoral. In the end, Darrow lost the

case and the teacher **John Scopes** was fined one hundred dollars. (Scopes left teaching and went into the oil business. He died in 1970 at age seventy of a stroke.) Bryan died of a heart attack only five days after the trial ended, from the stress of his performance at age seventy-five. Darrow lived until 1938, when at age eighty he too succumbed to heart disease, the equalizer in the end to all three men involved, regardless of opinion.

BETTE DAVIS

Bette Davis won a best actress Oscar twice: *Dangerous* (1935) and *Jezebel* (1938). She was in over a hundred films and found a cult following for her manner of speech and affected acting. On the set she was supposedly combative and difficult to work with and accused of being equally so in her home life. Her daughter

B. D. Hyman published a book, *My Mother's Keeper*, which portrayed Davis as controlling and self-involved. Davis never again spoke to her daughter and disowned her for this attack. Ms. Davis then went about ordering the epitaph for her own tombstone, finding the perfect phrase she believed summed up her life: "She did it the hard way." Davis died in 1989 at age eighty-one of a stroke due to complications of breast cancer. B. D. Hyman is now a fundamentalist preacher.

MILES DAVIS
Son of a St. Louis dentist, this trumpet player was once considered a legend in his own lifetime. Miles Davis began playing the trumpet when he was thirteen and within two years played the instrument professionally. From the late 1940s through the 1960s Davis was the most innovative musician on the jazz scene, even though his irritable temperament, perfectionist-motivated mood-swings and hard-core addiction to heroin made it hard for him to keep a steady band. Davis, who once trained to become a boxer, physically exerted himself while playing as if he were in the ring with an uncompromising opponent. Some compared the music Miles Davis played during this period to pure genius, noting that his trumpet's sound resembled a singing voice. By the mid-1970s he was worn-out and suffered from serious ailments, including two broken ankles after a car accident in 1972 that forced him to retire. He did play occasionally through the 1980s until his death at age sixty-five in 1991, after a long bout with pneumonia and a stroke.

EACH YEAR 500,000 CASES OF PNEUMONIA ARE REPORTED AND RESULT IN ABOUT 61,000 DEATHS IN THE UNITED STATES. PNEUMONIA IS AN INFECTION IN A PERSON'S LUNGS CAUSED BY BACTERIA CARRIED IN DROPLETS THROUGH THE AIR VIA COUGHS, SNEEZES, OR, LIKELY IN THE CASE OF MILES DAVIS, BY SHARING OR INADEQUATELY CLEANING A TRUMPET'S MOUTHPIECE.

JAMES DEAN
James Dean was the only actor to be nominated for an Academy Award twice while dead, one for *East of Eden* (1955) and another for *Giant* (1956). According to his death certificate, Dean died of a broken neck in a two-car collision on September 30, 1955, at 5:45 P.M. at age twenty-four. In fact, his head was nearly severed. Three hours before the accident he had been given a speeding ticket, though he continued to gun the sports car close to 90 mph. The Porsche 550 Spyder that Dean was driving was sold and continued to cause death and injury to a variety of owners until the car mysteriously vanished in 1960—although it has been supposedly spotted roaring down California Route 46, the site of Dean's accident, without a driver.

STEPHEN DECATUR
Stephen Decatur was the most noted hero of the War of 1812, a captain of war frigates who ultimately surrendered his ship and was imprisoned on Bermuda until the war ended. Nevertheless, by 1816 he was named naval commissioner and hobnobbed with the social elite of Washington, D.C.: Because of his good-

SYMPTOMS OF A DUEL.

looks and chestfull of medals, he quickly became the toast of the town. At one such social gathering he ran into another wartime associate, Commodore James Barron, who had been disgraced when Decatur sat in on the court-martial of Barron years before. Decatur was challenged to settle the question of honor with a duel. Decatur took the whole matter lightly, believing himself the invincible hero people said he was. The morning of the duel Decatur went to breakfast at Beale's Tavern near the Capitol and ate his normal breakfast, consisting of Hamburg chicken stuffed with mashed potatoes and vegetables, followed by assorted breads, cold meats, and some Dutch sweet cakes fried in deep fat. He washed it all down with a few glasses of rum and was presumably ready for a nap instead of a duel at 9:00 A.M. In addi-

tion, he agreed to shorten the normal distances of 12 paces taken, or approximately 36 feet, before the pair turned to shoot at each other, to 8 paces, in order to give the older Barron with his poorer eyesight a better chance. On March 22, 1820, he and Barron met on the dueling grounds in Maryland and promptly shot each other. Decatur received a mortal wound in the abdomen and died later that evening at age forty-one at his home one block north of the Capitol on H Street. His last words: "I did not know that any man could suffer such pain!"

*The most famous duel occurred in 1804 when **Alexander Hamilton** paced off with Aaron Burr. Although Hamilton was successful in fourteen previous duels, it was the same underestimation of his opponent that Decatur had suffered that got Hamilton killed at age forty-nine. Hamilton supposedly fired above Burr's head and snapped a tree branch, certain that Burr was a bad shot and would miss him. He was wrong: Burr's slug penetrated his liver, causing intense pain until Hamilton died the next day. In total, seventeen elected U.S. politicians died in duels.*

ED DELAHANTY

Bad behavior by ballplayers is nothing new. In 1903 the hitting star Ed Delahanty (twenty-six) of the Washington team of the American League was found at the bottom of a bridge near Niagara Falls missing his left leg. A *New York Times* sportswriter, Robert Smith, described Delahanty: "He was a handsome fellow, although there was an air about him that indicated he was a roughneck at heart and no man to temper with." Delahanty had been on route home from Detroit to New York when a train conductor ejected him for drunkenness, brawling, and threatening other passengers with a razor blade. Left in the middle of nowhere, he started to walk across the tracks when he came to an open drawbridge. The watchmen tried to stop him, but Delahanty cold-cocked the guard and proceeded. According to the Pullman Railway Company, he tumbled into the gorge below. His body wasn't discovered for six days and was found stripped of cash and jewelry. Nearby, the body of a dead young woman was also discovered. Since railway men were tough characters in those days, it's more probable that Delahanty was taken off the train and taught a lesson. The dead woman was a witness. The missing leg resulted from the floating body's getting in the way of a passing boat propeller.

DOUBLE HEADER

In 1942 pitcher **Gordon McNaughton** (thirty-two) used to beat his girlfriend, Eleanor Williams, and often accused her of cheating. He had met her while doing his favorite off-hours activity of playing dice, though he finally ended the affair when she miscarried their baby. However, dice-girl Williams refused to let go. When she knocked on his hotel room door and found him with another woman, all hell broke loose. Williams came armed with a gun she had stolen from a policeman she was seeing. After a loud argument, McNaughton said, "I'm a coward. Go ahead and shoot me. I'm tired of arguing." Williams obliged and shot him in the heart. She served fourteen years in prison. When the policeman got his stolen revolver back two months later, he used the same gun that killed McNaughton to commit suicide.

The weirdest death in baseball history belongs to outfielder James Phelps, who died after suffering a bite by a poisonous snake. In 1909 he was playing for a Louisiana team when he went out deep to catch a fly ball. He felt something snatch at his leg but paid it no attention. He finished the game but died shortly after from the venom of a snakebite.

EARLE E. DICKSON

The Band-Aid was invented by Earle E. Dickson because his new bride cut her fingers frequently while cooking. In 1927 he took a piece of hospital gauze, cut a small square and adhered it with a piece of surgical tape. Earle made a bunch of these pre-cut strips with gauze in the center for his wife to use while she attempted to master wound-free food preparation. At the time he worked at Johnson & Johnson as a cotton buyer and had an in to present his idea for a new product to the main of-

fice. They liked it and made the first adhesive bandages by hand. By the time of Dickson's death in 1961 at age sixty-eight of cardiac arrest, and not from a cut he didn't cover with a Band-Aid, as some urban legends believe, his invention reached sales of more than $30 million annually. Although the medical supplier rewarded Dickson with the position of VP until his retirement, his widow and heirs got sliced out of the windfall of royalties.

DIONYSIUS

In 399 B.C. Dionysius the Elder of Syracuse observed his young son using a spoon to shoot a pea at another sibling sitting at the far end of the table during dinnertime. Instead of fuming, as was the standard mindset of this clerk who had by then become supreme military commander, noted for his vindictiveness and ruthless tactics, he had the idea of creating a military weapon, namely the catapult. He quickly set about constructing a device that could hurl 350-pound boulders or other flaming projectiles well over 300 feet. His use of a cog-held wooden arm sprung in place by a strap of leather changed warfare and remained the standard in heavy artillery through Roman times until the use of gunpow-

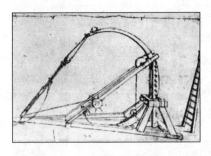

der in the Middle Ages. His invention killed untold millions, yet, on the other hand, fortification of cities with his device also allowed pockets of civilization to flourish against the onslaught of any number of barbarians. During his use of the catapult Syracuse became the most powerful city in Greece. Dionysius the Elder died eighteen years later in 367 B.C. at the age of sixty-five, poisoned by his own physicians in a plot instigated by his son, the pea shooter, also known as Dionysius the Younger, who then became ruler in the elder's place and was an equally cruel tyrant.

WALT DISNEY

Walt Disney, an animator, film producer, showman, and innovator in theme park design, who built an entertainment empire with current annual revenues topping $30 billion, holds the record with fifty-nine Academy Award nominations. In his personal life, the creator of Mickey Mouse was a chain-smoker, which contributed to his death in 1966 at age sixty-five of cardiac arrest due to lung cancer. According to his death certificate, his body was cremated two days after his death at Forest Lawn Memorial Park, Glendale, Cali-

fornia. Rumor persists that his body was supposedly frozen (cryonics) for future resuscitation and reanimation, housed under Disneyland's attraction "Pirates of the Caribbean." The only fact on the issue remains the certified signature of the alleged cremator, since Disney's funeral services were held in secret. To further dissuade those seeking Disney's frozen crypt, official press releases emphatically insist his ashes were scattered at sea. Incidentally, Disney's neighbor, Dr. James Bedford, a seventy-three-year-old psychologist from Glendale, California, was indeed frozen after his death in 1967. (Dr. Bedford holds the record as being the longest-suspended patient [and is still being held] in cryopreservation.)

Cryonics is a freezing process in which a person is preserved until medical advancements will someday reach a state that would allow the resituated body to be cured of whatever killed them and regain a healthy life. In short, it is the belief that death is merely a condition for which medicine has yet to find a cure. It costs on average one hundred thousand dollars to preserve a whole body this way indefinitely. According to David Pascal of Cryonics Society, *there are currently 1,443 signed up to become cryonicists in the United States. There are 150 persons currently in suspension.*

HOWDY DOODY

Howdy Doody was the first children's program presented live for one hour every Saturday morning, featuring a freckle-faced boy marionette. When kids across the country began yelling "It's Howdy Doody Time!" it marked the beginning of the first generation of kids to be reared on TV. The program ran until 1960 and spawned a few other children's programs from characters in the ensemble. "Buffalo" **Bob Smith**, who was the host and the voice of Howdy, died in 1998 at the age of eighty of pneumonia. The original Clarabell the clown was played by **Bob Keeshan** who later became Captain Kangaroo and the host of his own show in 1954: Keeshan died at seventy-six in 2004 of respiratory failure. **Lew Andersen,** who took over the job as Clarabell, died in 2006 at age eighty-four of prostate cancer. Kids thought Howdy Doody was real, and in 1952 he received over a million write-in votes to become president. When the show ended, Howdy spent many years locked inside a dark trunk in a cold and lonely vault. In 2000, after a lengthy court battle deciding ownership, Howdy was finally freed, though currently hangs lifeless, on display at the McPharlin Puppetry Collection in the Detroit Institute of Arts.

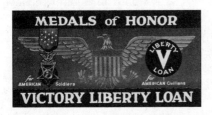

DESMOND DOSS

One man received the Medal of Honor for refusing to fight. During wartime conscientious objectors are often looked upon as cowardly, especially if patriotic sentiments are running high. Those who objected to using violence for any reason and refused to serve in the military were historically executed or imprisoned. During World War I, two thousand conscientious objectors refused to accept any part of military service and were subsequently placed under arrest.

TWO AMISH OBJECTORS, MICHAEL HOFER (TWENTY-FIVE)
AND JOSEPH HOFER (TWENTY-FOUR) DIED DURING TORTURE
ADMINISTERED AT LEAVENWORTH PRISON IN 1918.

The military policy of World War II gave the option for objectors to perform other duties, so when twenty-three-year-old 5-foot-6-inch Desmond Doss was drafted and refused to carry a gun due to religious convictions, he accepted a tour as a medic. He was ridiculed and considered a disgrace to the uniform, and he was regularly kicked in the head whenever he kneeled to pray. But when the time for action arrived, he proved himself a hero by any standards. As part of the 77th Infrantry, he singlehandedly saved the lives of more than seventy-five men and demonstrated awesomely brave actions, attending to fallen soldiers in the midst of ferocious enemy fire. Despite mortar shells, grenades and gunfire whizzing past his head, he bandaged the wounded and carried them one by one to cover. He became a symbol of gallantry without ever firing a shot. Doss himself spent six years in the hospital recuperating from tuberculosis and gunshot wounds. He was finally discharged, almost completely deaf. President Truman awarded him the Medal of Honor in 1945. When Doss died in 2006 at age eighty-seven of edema in the lungs, five hundred people showed up for his funeral.

UNSUNG HEROES
MORE THAN 75,000 VIETNAM VETERANS HAVE COMMITTED SUICIDE
SINCE THE END OF THAT WAR AND MORE THAN 11,000 GULF WAR
VETERANS HAVE NOW DIED FROM VARIOUS AILMENTS AND INJURIES.

EDWIN DRAKE

Edwin Drake was a laid-off railroad worker when the Seneca Oil Company hired him to prospect the hills of Pennsylvania for a wage of $2.83 per day. Instead of using handpicks to search for pools of underground fuel, Drake invented a method of drilling straight down. In 1859 he hit upon a subterranean ocean of oil and established the world's first oil well. Within months, vast fortunes were made, revolutions in industry and transportation took place, and men like J. Paul Getty and John D. Rockefeller became billionaires. The oil company didn't want Drake to file a patent so they fired him and kept the techniques he invented for themselves. Drake received no royalties and no severance pay or pension, even though he was crippled by the hard work of drilling. When he died in poverty twenty years later, his death certificate cited his cause of death as "Invalid."

MICHAEL DUNN

Michael Dunn played the 3-foot–10-inch villain Dr. Loveless on *Wild Wild West*, and in many other roles both in film and TV, he never settled for the cute roles assigned to many other dwarf actors. Toward the end of his life, his physical deformities, including a malformed spine and irregular lung capacity, kept him in constant pain. But he was determined to keep going and took more and more pain medications, including two different prescribed narcotics and a barbiturate. In 1973 at age thirty-eight he ingested too much at one time and stopped breathing. Despite the large quantities of narcotics in his blood at the time of death, the coroner decided to deem the cause of death as congenital chondrodystrophy, or dwarfism.

*Another Little Person, **Hervé Villechaize**, was popular to viewers for his role as 3-foot–10-inch Tattoo in the television series* Fantasy Island *(1978–1984), but on the set he was constantly arguing with the producers and forever propositioning women. After the show was canceled, he sat each night in a dark room playing reruns of* Fantasy Island, *while drinking and screaming curse words at the screen. Although he took up the cause of charity work for abused children, he cared nothing for the causes of those with his same smaller stature and insisted everyone call him a midget, not the politically correct "little person." In 1993 he finally shot himself during one of his rages and died at age fifty in his home.*

JEANNE EAGELS

In 1929 Jeanne Eagels was nominated for a best actress Oscar for *The Letter* after she died earlier that year at age thirty-nine from alcohol and heroin complications. Eagels had started as a Ziegfeld Follies girl, but her talent and beauty soon moved her from the chorus line to center stage. Tabloids of the time followed her progress and her secret marriage to a Yale football star, and they especially liked her temper, her no-shows, and her quitting plays whenever she felt like it. At one point she was banned from appearing on stage by Actors Equity, which had

forced her to move to Hollywood to make the "talkie" *The Letter*, one of the first films that showed the true dramatic possibilities of audio in cinema. In the fall of 1929 she checked into a private drying-out hospital in New York City a week before the stock market crashed; unfortunately she left via the morgue.

During the 1920s heroin was used with impunity on Broadway, and many actors made their daily runs to the thriving heroin shops operating in New York's Chinatown before and after every performance. By 1929 there were 200,000 heroin addicts in the United States. The prevailing treatment at the time consisted of treating the drug addict with more drugs, particularly more potent morphine derivatives, which often caused fatal overdoses.

AMELIA EARHART

Amelia Earhart was the first female aviation hero. She was a likable, slender woman with an independent mind. Determined to do anything a man could do, despite the obstacles, she drove a truck and worked at the telephone company to earn the money needed for her first flying lessons. She had the right image and was photogenic enough to be asked to make a sponsored, first female-copiloted flight across the Atlantic. Publisher George Putnam was going to do a book on this and met the young woman to determine her candidacy. Apparently, she was more than photogenic because this meeting ultimately led to their "open marriage" and a relationship that Earhart agreed to only if the "medieval code" of fidelity by either party was not followed.

At the age thirty-nine in 1937 she attempted to circumnavigate the globe. Similar to Magellan's fate, she got only three-quarters of the way when her plane ran out of fuel and crashed into the Pacific Ocean. What really happened to her is unknown, with theories ranging from being captured by the Japanese and treated as a spy, to her living a life of solitude on a deserted island with a native fisherman. However, it is most probable that no sign of her body was ever recovered because she was eaten by sharks.

GEORGE EASTMAN

George Eastman developed the handheld camera and various photographic processes. Photography before Eastman required a camera bigger than the monitor of a personal computer and used a cumbersome tripod stand for support. The photographer covered his head under a tent, regulating light exposure on glass plates to be dried and developed later. It required an alchemist's knowledge of chemicals. Eastman, with his small and instant cameras, extended the skill of photography to the public; 65 billion photographs have been taken with the process Eastman invented. Despite vast wealth, Eastman disliked having his own picture taken and preferred solitude, never marrying. At the age of seventy-seven in 1932 he invited a few friends over for dinner and excused himself after dessert. He went up to his room and wrote in a steady hand: "My work is done. Why wait?" In a very un-"Kodak moment," he then took a revolver and shot himself once in the heart.

MISTER ED

Talking horse *Mister Ed* starred in a tremendously popular TV show from 1961 to 1964, and for many years after in syndication. Mister Ed was a palomino by the name of **Bamboo Harvester** who died at the age of nineteen two years after the show was canceled. Without fanfare he was put down after developing arthritis. **Allan Lane,** who was the voice for Mister Ed, died of cancer in 1973 at the age of sixty-four.

THOMAS EDISON

The incandescent lightbulb was Thomas Edison's illuminating idea, although he didn't actually invent it; rather, he modified previous attempts until he de-

vised the longest-lasting filament to make electric light economically feasible. A master at both invention and marketing, Edison also invented and improved many other things, including the phonograph and the motion-picture camera. He said, "Genius is one percent inspiration and ninety-nine percent perspiration." He died of Bright's disease at age eighty-four, in 1931, but before doing so, he breathed his last gasp of air into a bottle. Before technology allowed bodies to be frozen, he hoped his essence could be captured this way. The sealed bottle is still on display in Menlo Park, New Jersey.

EACH YEAR 500 PEOPLE IN THE UNITED STATES DIE AT HOME OF ELECTROCUTION, 50 FROM FAULTY WIRING, 150 FROM LARGE APPLIANCES, AND THE REST FROM SCREWING IN A LIGHT BULB.

VINCE EDWARDS

TV shows about doctors and hospitals are perennial and change stations, time slots, and casts like real doctors making rounds. The first programs to make big primetime success in this genre were *Dr. Kildare* and *Ben Casey* in the 1960s.

Vince Edwards played Ben Casey, the idealistic surgeon-hero, held in check by wise Dr. David Zorba, played by **Sam Jaffe**. Edwards (Vincent Edward Zoino III) was an Italian kid from Brooklyn whose father was a bricklayer. He was sent off to a vocational school but didn't have the hands for it and finished his studies in theater. He was an excellent swimmer with a well-defined athlete's physique, which from the beginning led to his being cast more for his appearance and less for his talent. It served him well, and he became a national heartthrob for both sexes by age thirty. Unfortunately, Edwards got his fill of real-life doctors after a long bout with pancreatic cancer which caused his death in 1996 at age sixty-seven. Sam Jaffe kept a few steps ahead of the medical pack until age ninety-three when he died of cancer in 1984.

CODE RED

In the seventies *Medical Center* was a popular doctor show that ran for seven seasons and ended in 1977. One year later, the star, Dr. Paul Lochner, played by **James Daly**, died at age fifty-nine of heart failure. The 1980s' big medical dramas were *St. Elsewhere* and *Doogie Howser, M.D.* Dr. Westphall on *St. Elsewhere* was played by Ed Flanders who in 1995 at age sixty shot himself. He left no note. *ER* began in 1994 and was still on the air in 2007. During the series, four TV doctors have died: In 1999 med student Lucy Knight was killed by a psych patient; Mark Greene died of a brain tumor in 2001; Dr. Romano was killed by a helicopter blade in 2003; and Dr. Michael Gallant was blown up by a roadside bomb in Iraq in 2006.

ALBERT EINSTEIN

Albert Einstein was a physicist and mathematician who won a Nobel Prize for the theory of relativity: $E=mc^2$, a concept that changed the viewpoint on energy. Although a pacifist, his ideas pointed to the possibility of making an atomic bomb. He died in 1955 at seventy-six when an aorta in his stomach exploded. He requested that his body be cremated and his brain be removed for study. It was discovered that Einstein thought in images and not numbers. He had a greater amount of glial cells per neuron in the brain, cells that needed and used more energy, a link, some believe, to his own internal gastronomic meltdown. Einstein's brain had been preserved like pickles in a glass container for years and transported across the country for research.

GRAVITATIONAL ANOMALIES

In 2000 physicist and astronomer Dr. Jeffrey Willick, considered an expert in the workings of the universe, was about to answer his hypothesis "Did structure in the contemporary universe emerge from the very nearly uniform primordial distribution of matter solely via the process of gravitational instability?" when he was killed at age forty in a freak accident. While he was sitting at a Starbucks in Englewood, New Jersey, working on his laptop, a car crashed through the window killing him. The coffee chain fended off a wrongful death lawsuit filed against them by indicating that parking lot barriers are not universally required. Technically, Willick didn't die from gravitational instability but from random unsteadiness of reckless drivers. Each year more than 250 people die when cars breach sidewalks and kill unsuspecting diners.

DUKE ELLINGTON

Duke Ellington (née Edward Kennedy Ellington) composed over two thousand songs and is credited with making jazz, once considered music of the poorer class, a respected American sound. Before his death of lung cancer in 1974 at age seventy-five, the Duke was awarded the Presidential Medal of Freedom in 1969. (His death certificate cites pneumonia as the cause of death.)

> "It's like an act of murder; you play with intent to commit something."
> —DUKE ELLINGTON

FRANK EPPERSON

The Popsicle was invented by a kid, eleven-year-old Frank Epperson, who in 1905 left a glass of soda water with a mixing stick outside on the porch during one cold spell and woke up the next morning to find it frozen. He never forgot it and made the frozen pop-stick regularly as a giveaway for trade shows he hosted to boost his real estate ventures. He finally patented the idea in 1924 and called it the "Epsicle—a handled, frozen confection or ice lollipop." The name was changed because kids simply asked for Pop Epperson's icicle or Pop's cicle. Epperson ran into trouble after the Crash of 1929 and was forced to liquidate his assets; he sold the rights to the frozen dessert that still ranks as the number-one ice cream novelty. Before he died of pneumonia in 1983 at age eighty-nine, Epperson said, "After the sale of the Popsicle patent, I never did get back on my feet."

DANIEL FAHRENHEIT

Daniel Fahrenheit, a German scientist, was out in the cold winter measuring the effects of freezing on his own body. He sought to measure temperature to find a range that was livable for humans. During one experiment, while shivering in short sleeves outside in a blizzard, he thought he was about to die when a mark he had calibrated with an alcohol measuring device hit 32 degrees. In the summer he felt near death at 100 degrees and determined that a piece of paper would begin to burn at 212 degrees. Eventually, he replaced alcohol with mercury in his thermometer, a decision that would make thermometers most accurate for centuries to come but a choice that resulted in his early death. A careful scientist, he was cautious about the foods he ate and mindful not to ingest chemicals he worked with. (Both his parents had died from eating poisonous mushrooms.) But he didn't know how chemicals, particularly mercury, are absorbed in the skin. He died of blood poisoning at age fifty in 1736.

TODAY, MERCURY IS STILL USED IN THERMOMETERS AS WELL AS IN WASHING MACHINES, MOTION-SENSITIVE DEVICES, SUMP PUMPS, SPACE HEATERS, AND IRONS. IN ADDITION, MOST FILLINGS USED BY DENTISTS CONTAIN MERCURY. U.S. DENTISTS PUT 44 TONS OF MERCURY INTO PATIENTS' TEETH EACH YEAR. ANNUALLY, 6,500 PEOPLE ARE HOSPITALIZED AND 500 DIE FROM MERCURY POISONING.

PHILO FARNSWORTH

Television was Philo Farnsworth's brainchild, when at age twenty-one he experimented with what he called an "image dissector," flashing light into an etched-glass plate. In 1927 the first image seen on his experimental TV screen was, prophetically, a dollar sign. Farnsworth, for the rest of his life, remained in unsuccessful legal battles to collect due royalties for his invention. Before long he faded into obscurity. He did appear on a TV program *I've Got a Secret* and received eighty dollars and a carton of cigarettes when game-show participants failed to guess his identity as the inventor of TV. He went on to file over three hundred patents for things such as enhanced vision for telescopes and infrared lights used in night-vision devices but sunk into depression and alcohol abuse after doctors suggested he use alcohol to curb his obsessively inventive mind. He died from the complications of alcohol in 1971 at age sixty-four. According to his son, Kent, TV was not allowed in their home while growing up; Farnsworth said, "I created kind of a monster, a way for people to waste a lot of their lives."

WILLIAM FAULKNER

William Faulkner was a southern writer known for experimental fiction, an American version of Irish writer James Joyce, using stream of consciousness and the meandering run-on sentence that seemed to go nowhere but ended up telling the agonies of the human heart and man's enduring spirit. Spirits, in fact, were big for Faulkner because he made no secret of his indulging in a lot of them; he practically celebrated his alcoholism. Reportedly, he was a binge drinker, going on sprees that lasted from days to months, most often after he finished a book, yet ceasing during these periods only when he passed out. Subsequently, his homelife was often bleak: William Faulkner would allow neither a radio nor music to be played in his home, and a museum in Oxford, Mississippi, where he lived, displays the mechanical guts he once ripped from a phonograph purchased by his wife and daughter. Nevertheless, by the time he died of a heart attack in 1962 at age sixty-four, he had left behind an astounding body of original work.

> "I can remember how when I was young I believed death to be a phenomenon of the body; now I know it to be merely a function of the mind."
> —WILLIAM FAULKNER

GEORGE FERRIS

The symbol of the Chicago World's Fair of 1893 was a giant 250-foot steel wheel, designed and erected under the supervision of **George W. G. Ferris, Jr.** It had 36 wooden seats that allowed 1,440 to ride at a time, taking them 25 stories above the fair at a then-exorbitant price of fifty cents apiece. The wheel was considered a wonder of technology and made Ferris, a former bridge inspector, a famous and a wealthy man during its heyday. But by 1896 he was worried about where future money would come from and, some believed, because of stress

contracted typhoid fever. He died five days after its onset at age thirty-seven. Reports suggested that it was suicide, since his wife had left him three months before and he was apparently heartbroken and depressed. The wheel was moved and reassembled in New Orleans for the 1904 fair. However, two years later, what many felt was the American Eiffel Tower was dynamited, its rusted spokes buried in a landfill. Ferris's name still stands on thousands of rides as a legacy—ironic that, since no one ever came to claim his cremated ashes.

FRED FISHER

In 1922 the song "Chicago" was written by composer Fred Fisher and became an instant hit. It was a smash again for the Dorsey Band in the thirties, a million-disc seller for Frank Sinatra in the fifties, and the theme song for the wildly popular Broadway musical of the same title during the nineties and today. Fisher committed euthanasia on January 14, 1942, in New York City. Police found him hanging with an electric extension cord around his neck at his penthouse apartment at 617 West End Avenue and officially classified his death a suicide. He left a note: "No one is responsible for my death." This was seen by his friends as a premeditated way to end a fatal illness he wrongly believed he had acquired. His songs all had upbeat catchy tunes with well-defined endings; he may have believed his own life should conclude in a similar fashion. In 1949 a fictionalized biographical film musical *Oh, You Beautiful Doll* portrayed his life from rags to riches.

ELLA FITZGERALD

Ella Fitzgerald, known as the First Lady of Song, grew up in an orphanage and was discovered on the Apollo Theater Amateur Hour in New York City in 1934 at the age of sixteen. She started out making $12.50 a week touring with a band, which culminated in $1 million a week for her 1974 Caesars Palace performance. Although Ella sang about love, she married three times with disastrous results—two of the three husbands were convicted as drug dealers and hustlers. Sadly, she later went blind, had both her legs amputated, and eventually died at seventy-eight in 1996 from complications of diabetes.

DIABETES DEATHS WORLDWIDE APPROACH 3 MILLION ANNUALLY. IT IS ONE OF THE ONLY MAJOR DISEASES, WHICH STEMS PREDOMINANTLY FROM OBESITY, WITH A RISING DEATH RATE.

F. SCOTT FITZGERALD

Although F. Scott Fitzgerald never made the bestseller list, he was considered by many to be the literary winner, epitomizing the Roaring Twenties as the greatest period writer. He published *This Side of Paradise* (1920), *The Beautiful and the Damned* (1922), and *The Great Gatsby* (1925) while living the partying, flamboyant life he described as no other. Despite being an alcoholic from an early age, periods of financial stress, and the static relationship with his equally famous schizophrenic wife, Zelda, he was the rage of the artistic scene. Fitzgerald's death also mirrored the fate of many that lived in excess during the period. He died at age forty-four, officially of cardiac arrest, suffering two heart attacks in a two-month period. However, reexamined medical records indicate that he most likely died of a hemorrhage as a result of advanced liver disease, a death which to observers seems no different from heart failure.

ALEXANDER FLEMING

Antibiotics are likely the most important invention of the twentieth century. The idea that germs could be used to kill germs was explored in the 1700s with the use of fungi. However, it wasn't until Scottish bacteriologist Alexander Fleming proved it possible with the accidental discovery of penicillin in 1928. He was known as a brilliant researcher, but he had no desire for housekeeping, and consequently allowing old experiments to linger in the lab, many of them growing moldy and fungi-ridden. When he finally got around to cleaning up, he noticed how one Petri dish of forgotten staphylococcus shriveled in the presence of a growing penicillin mold. This, or one man's lack of cleanliness, laid the groundwork for the first and best antibiotic known to kill a vast array of illnesses that had cut longevity short since the beginning of time. Although it was

Howard Florey and Ernst Chain who devised a means of isolating the powdery penicillin mold Fleming found and used it in an inoculation formula for human use, Fleming is credited as the discoverer. He died of a heart attack in 1955 at age seventy-three.

HENRY FORD

The first steam-powered car was built in 1771; it had three wheels and could reach speeds of 3 mph. It would take over a hundred years before German engineer **Karl Benz** developed a gas-powered protégé of the combustible engine that reached 10 mph. The end of the nineteenth century had many other versions, but it remained largely a curiosity until Henry Ford found a way to mass-produce it. Ford, a high school dropout, built his first automobile in 1896 called the Tin Lizzie, a car without a reverse gear or brakes, when he was thirty-three. He eventually went on to perfect the assembly-line method of production. By 1920 his Detroit factory could make ten thousand cars every twenty-four hours. Ford was credited with putting over 20 million cars on American roads by 1931. Once successful, Ford became obsessed with politics and was tied to a number of anti-Semitic causes; he even received a Nazi-awarded Service Cross of the German Eagle in 1938. After being sued for libel, he recanted his position and in 1947 died of a cerebral hemorrhage at age eighty-three. Karl Benz, of Mercedes-Benz fame, died age eighty-four in 1929 of bronchitis.

IN 2006 THERE WERE 62 MILLION REGISTERED VEHICLES IN THE UNITED STATES AND 6.4 MILLION UNREGISTERED AUTOS STILL CRUISING, ALL TOLD CAUSING 6,394,000 POLICE-REPORTED MOTOR VEHICLE TRAFFIC CRASHES, 3,189,000 INJURIES, AND 43,000 DEATHS.

STEPHEN FOSTER

Stephen Foster was the first full-fledged American composer, born, no less, on the Fourth of July, 1826, near Pittsburgh. Anyone who ever sat for a piano lesson has played his favorites, including "Oh! Susanna" (1848), "Old Folks at Home" [aka "Swanee River"] (1851), "Jeanie with the Light Brown Hair" (1854), and "Beautiful Dreamer" (1862). By the age of twenty-five Foster had published twelve original songs and had engaged in earnest as a professional composer. He labored to make his songs appeal to the sentiments of his contemporary America, and he is considered the country's first pop artist. However, the struggle to get paid for his work was the thing that did him in. Foster attempted to keep an exact accounting and even wrote out the first semblance of a royalty contract with the publisher, but he couldn't prevent another sheet music company from printing and selling his songs royalty-free. Nor did he receive anything for performance rights. For a lifetime of labor he earned $15,091.08, all the while composing, bickering to get paid, and drinking. Drinking he did with equal passion so that by the age of thirty-seven he was holed up in a cheap hotel room in New York City's theater district suffering from fever induced by alcoholism and liver failure. The exact cause of his death was laceration to his head. When he tried to get out of bed, he fell and shattered a porcelain washbasin, suffering a deep gouge. It took three hours before he was taken to the hospital, where he died three days later in 1864. He had thirty-eight cents in his pocket.

SAINT FRANCIS

Italian Giovanni di Bernardone, nicknamed Francesco by his wealthy father and later known as Saint Francis of Assisi, grew up a rich kid, carousing and partying with the other young spoiled merchant crowd living off their fathers' money. After years of excess, he began to get physically sick and decided to go on long fasts to heal his body. In one fast-induced hallucination he saw a statue of Christ come down from a crucifix and speak to him. He began to do things sure to enrage his father and even went to help lepers, an act of insanity in a time when that disease was highly contagious and fatal. The father beat him and brought him to the bishop, but before his father could cut him off financially, Francis took his own vow of poverty, stripped off the garments his father had paid for, and stood naked, saying he wanted nothing, not even the clothes on his back. He then went on to preach, favoring work with the poor above all else. In addi-

tion, he was not beyond preaching to inanimate objects and animals. Once he stopped on the road when he saw a flock of birds in a tree. He preached to the feathered congregation to be thankful for their gift of flight, perhaps reminiscent of his flight from his father. Nevertheless, after that he was always portrayed as a saint with birds perched on his arms and animals at his feet. In fact, it seemed his spiritual philosophy was geared to doing everything exactly the opposite of what his father believed. Toward the end of his life Francis went up to a mountain for a private retreat, and when he returned, he told his followers that an angel had visited him. His wrists, feet, and side were gashed open in the same places that Jesus received his fatal wounds on the cross. This was the first example of what was later deemed a *stigmata*. The wounds bled regularly, causing him to die at age forty-four in 1226.

Stigmatics: Eight saints have had stigmata, in addition to more than 1,000 non-canonized cases since Saint Francis.

This condition is apparently on the rise, with more than 500 ordinary people afflicted in the twentieth century alone. However, many of the newer stigmatics have wounds in the wrong places, such as on their palms, whereas Christ had them on the wrists. A few researchers attribute the unexplained phenomena to the mind's ability to exert physical effects on the body. Scientists point to Munchausen syndrome, a mental illness that causes the afflicted to fabricate or induce illnesses for attention. **Saint Catherine of Siena**, who fasted for long periods of time and survived by eating only the Eucharist wafer, believed she was actually married to Jesus. She died in 1380 at age thirty-three from stigmata. For some reason, she is currently the patron saint of fire prevention.

GEORGE A. FULLER

The contractor who figured out how to practically build soaring skyscrapers was George A. Fuller, perfecting the method of using steel frames and lightweight materials that enabled skyscrapers to achieve unlimited heights. In 1902 his firm built New York's first skyscraper, the Fuller, or Flatiron Building, at Broadway and Twenty-third Street, a triangular, twenty-one-story building that still remains impressive. From the air, it resembles an arrowhead pointing to a riddle yet to be solved. Fuller died in 1900 before it was completed at age forty-nine of mysterious circumstances. It was rumored he had been shot by an actress, Sadie Dean, while visiting her flat. Fuller's son-in-law, Henry Black, finished the building. Most biographical records of George A. Fuller have been shredded.

EVA GABOR

Eva Gabor was most famous for her role as Lisa Douglas, the die-hard, daahling Manhattanite, seen in the TV sitcom *Green Acres* (1965-1971). She was the youngest of three sisters originally from Budapest who made names for themselves for their romantic liaisons and many marriages. Eva made a few movies as well, but she acquired most of her fortune by using her glamorous persona to market a wig company. Later in life, she was seen shopping in Dollar Stores. Nevertheless, her death fits a similarly odd pattern of many other actors who spent time on TV shows that espoused clean country living: After suffering a fall and a broken hip, Eva died in 1995 at age seventy-six from pneumonia. From *Green Acres*, Mr. Haney, played by **Pat Buttram**, died in 1994 of pneumonia and kidney failure at age seventy-eight. **Eddie Albert** (Edward Albert Heimberger), known to most as Oliver Wendell Douglas, sang that show's theme song and put out an album during the show's heyday. "Keep Manhattan, give me that countryside" became lyrics Albert took to heart, eventually becoming an advocate for environmental issues. He suffered from Alzheimer's disease, and he, too, died of pneumonia at age ninety-nine in 2005. From *Petticoat Junction*, a crossover show, with many of the players from *Green Acres* appearing in this sitcom as well, Uncle Joe Carson, played by **Edgar Buchanan,** died of pneumonia at age seventy-six in 1979. The anomaly, Billy Jo, sexy in a *HeeHaw* sort of way, played by **Meredith MacRae**, died of brain cancer in 2000 at age fifty-six. For other contemporary country shows, namely *Mayberry R.F.D.*, a crossover from the *Andy Griffith Show*, had Aunt Bea, played by Frances Bavier, who died in 1989 at age eighty-seven from complications of pneumonia. And **Don Knotts**, who played Barney Fife, died in 2006 at the age of eighty-one from pulmonary and respiratory complications, demonstrating that actors partaking in country shows, even if it's canned air and the farmhouse is built on a set, have a good chance of living long and dying of pneumonia.

GALILEO

Many believe Galileo Galilei invented the telescope, although he actually only modified the designs described by Netherland inventors to make the first one that actually worked. His observations, and the teachings of astronomer Nicolaus Copernicus whose hypothesis that the sun rather than the earth is at the center of the solar system, nearly cost him his life when he was called to the court of the Catholic Church. He agreed not to teach the doctrine to forestall his execution but was then placed under house arrest for the remainder of his life. Despite the hardships, Galileo went on to map the heavens, and he was the first to see the Milky Way. He discovered the basic principles of relativity that Einstein expanded. He invented an early version of a water-filled thermometer, a microscope, a tomato picker, and a comb that doubled as a fork. He died, blind, from debility at age seventy-seven in 1642. In 1992 the Roman Catholic Church pardoned Galileo and conceded that the earth does indeed revolve around the sun.

JULIO GALLO

Julio Gallo didn't invent wine, but he was the first to mass-produce it and sell it for cheap. He was noted as the inventor of the Skid Row favorite—the fortified wine called Thunderbird. Gallo was the son of an immigrant Italian grape grower, who with his brother Ernest, transformed their father's vineyards into the world's biggest winery. In 1993 at age eighty-three he died while surveying his vineyard in Modesto, California, after his Jeep overturned when it hit a ripple in the road. (Ripple was another Gallo brand once popular with the alcoholic, the destitute, and college students.) In the end, as for so many who drank the label's cheaper vintages, Gallo expired from blunt-force trauma.

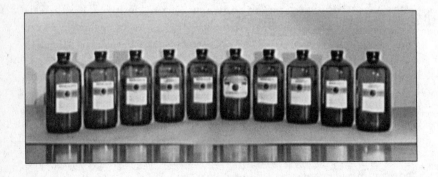

On the TV series Sanford & Son, *Ripple was Fred Sanford's favorite beverage. Off set, Sanford, played by Redd Foxx, preferred pricey cocaine to Ripple and even wore a golden coke spoon and chain around his neck to prove it. In 1991, when Foxx died on the set of a new sitcom,* Royal Family, *the rest of the crew thought he was pulling a stunt when he fell down clutching his chest with a fatal heart attack at age sixty-eight.*

VASCO DA GAMA

Vasco da Gama, out of Portugal, went the sensible way to the Indies via Cape Horn, Africa, in 1498 and helped establish his country as the leader in trade for the next three hundred years. Considered a practical man, da Gama went to school for navigation and reportedly seldom smiled. If alive today, he would use the phrase, "What's the bottom line?" often and with all seriousness. Once, to get the ruler of India's merchant cities to sign a trade agreement with him and stop trading with the Arabs, he captured a ship containing Muslim pilgrims and burned it, with 380 people aboard, refusing to let even women or children escape the sinking inferno. Eventually, da Gama was noted on the high seas as the "fixer," a man who found solutions to problems. When there was trouble brewing in the newly established Portuguese India trading posts, he was sent back there to take over as viceroy. But within three months, he contracted malaria. It was a bite from one small mosquito in the vast land he helped colonize that killed him in 1524 at age fifty-five.

THE MOSQUITO HAS KILLED MORE PEOPLE WORLDWIDE THAN THE COMBINED TOTALS OF ALL WARS OR CATASTROPHES IN HISTORY. EACH YEAR 2.7 MILLION PEOPLE DIE OF MALARIA, 75 PERCENT IN AFRICA AND INDIA, THE SAME AS IT WAS IN THE TIME OF DA GAMA: TWO DEATHS PER MINUTE.

JUDY GARLAND

Judy Garland (Frances Ethel Gumm) had a hit in 1939 with "Over the Rainbow" when she was only sixteen years old, and was featured in the movie seen by more people than any other film ever made, *The Wizard of Oz*. Performing since she was two years old, Judy went on to star in thirty-two movies, record a hundred singles, a dozen albums, and give over two thousand live performances from the vaudeville stage, to television, to Carnegie Hall. Despite her petite height of 4 feet 11 inches, she lived life in a whirlwind, never stopped performing or marrying—five husbands all told—and in her later years turned to alcohol and Benzedrine to keep it all together. In 1969 at age forty-seven she was found dead in her bathroom from an overdose of barbiturates.

DAVE GARROWAY

Starting in 1952 NBC's *Today* show became the first and longest-running morning show, and second of all TV shows behind *Meet the Press*. The first hosts were Dave Garroway (1952–1961) and a chimpanzee named J. Fred Muggs. Garroway disliked having to share the stage

with a monkey and allegedly spiked the chimp's orange juice with Benzedrine in order for the monkey to misbehave and get fired. Garroway killed himself by gunshot in 1982 at age sixty-nine. Muggs is still alive and living in Citrus, Florida. The second host was John Chancellor (1961–1962): He died at age sixty-eight of stomach cancer in 1996. Frank McGee co-anchored with Barbara Walters from 1971 to April 1974, and he died of bone cancer at age fifty-two in April 1974. The remainder of *Today*'s hosts are currently alive.

SIDDHĀRTHA GAUTAMA

Siddhārtha Gautama, known as the Buddha, was born into wealth in what is now Nepal, reared in luxury, married, and lived the life of a prince for twenty-nine years. On one venture outside his palace he saw a crippled old man and a decaying corpse. He decided that to achieve immortality he had to cast his material trappings aside and live the life of a monk. He learned how to meditate and by the age of thirty-five found the answer, what he called the Middle Way. Of course,

the full doctrine of his teachings is more complex than this. He nevertheless attracted many with his demeanor and quest for answers in a world that offered none. At the age of eighty he told his followers he was about to leave his earthly shell behind. He then accepted a meal of pork and mushrooms given to him by a blacksmith. Devotees say the last meal had nothing to do with his death, yet mushrooms and pork were extremely dangerous meals to eat in ancient times because of trichinosis (parasites) in the meat and toxins in the mushrooms. Mushroom tea was often given as a poison. Some say this was euthanasia; nevertheless, he died shortly after in 483 B.C. and was cremated.

LOU GEHRIG

Yankee Lou Gehrig, who held the reputation as the Iron Horse, was noted for his stamina of never missing a game, playing 2,130 in a row, and for dying young. Despite the first signs at age thirty that he was suffering from amyotrophic lateral sclerosis, a neurological disorder that eventually turns muscle function to that of a newborn infant, he only worked harder to compensate, unaware that a disease was causing his diminishing strength. Instead of medical tests, he relied on pushing himself harder and following a number of pregame rituals. Ballplayers follow many myths and superstitions not to break their winning streak, and Gehrig believed eating pickled eels made him hit better. Many recipes for eels contain a high dose of glutamate and its salt derivative MSG. Studies now show ALS patients have higher levels of glutamate in the serum and spinal fluid, which may be the cause of this motor neuron degeneration. The exact quantity of eels Gehrig ingested is unknown, though it must have been considerable to have a lifetime batting average of .340, 350 home runs, and 1,500 RBI, one of only seven players in the history of the game to do so. Before he died at age thirty-seven in 1941, he said, "[Today] I consider myself the luckiest man on the face of the earth." He referred to his illustrious career and the opportunity to play with other greats and, presumably, not to his superstition about eating eels.

EACH YEAR, FIVE THOUSAND PEOPLE IN THE UNITED STATES ARE DIAGNOSED WITH ALS, ALSO KNOWN AS LOU GEHRIG'S DISEASE. THERE IS NO CURE AND THE DISEASE WILL USUALLY CAUSE PARALYSIS AND DEATH IN TWO TO FIVE YEARS.

Of all the saints, Jerome has a reputation as the one with the worst temper. Considered the most learned man of his times, he translated the Greek Bible into the colloquial language of the fourth century. Yet contrary to what is expected of saints, he had a venomous tongue and a poison pen for those spouting frivolity. Eventually he wound up living alone in a cave, dying at age seventy-five in A.D. 420. His body is in a church in Rome, and his head is a relic in a cathedral in Madrid.

GERONIMO

Geronimo waged war for twenty-five years against both U.S. and Spanish armies to protect his tribal lands. Born with the name Goyathlay, he had a violent life from the beginning with the death of his father during a war, followed by the murder of his first wife, three children, and mother during a raid by Spanish soldiers. "St. Jerome!" is what the Spanish settlers yelled when they saw Geronimo preparing to attack, asking for help of the patron saint of translators, for some reason. Some linguists believe that is how "Geronimo," the derivative of Jerome, became a name synonymous with a wild assault. He and a band of thirty-eight remained the very last to elude U.S. troops, until he finally surrendered in 1886 and was sent to a reservation. Toward the end of his life he embraced his celebrity status and appeared at county fairs to sign autographs and even rode in President Teddy Roosevelt's inaugural parade. He died of pneumonia in 1909 at seventy-nine. His grave was allegedly robbed by members of Yale's Skull & Bones Society, and Geronimo's skull is used today in initiation rituals of the secret club to which both Presidents George W. and George H. W. Bush once belonged.

GEORGE GERSHWIN

"Rhapsody in Blue" was written by George Gershwin in 1924 at the request of bandleader Paul Whiteman. As the concert to which the song was to be performed approached, Gershwin remembered his promise and hastily composed what would become a jazz piano concert classic, effectively moving jazz from the speakeasy to the concert hall. Whiteman's orchestra sold a million copies in six months and subsequently brought Gershwin great wealth and worldwide recognition. The man, a high school dropout who also wrote the opera *Porgy and Bess*, was never idle, his mind constantly whirling in song. He died at thirty-eight in 1937 of a brain tumor.

ANDY AND MAURICE GIBB

In 1988 Bee Gee's Andy Gibb, known for "I Just Want to Be Your Everything" was dead soon after he turned thirty of myocarditis, an inflamed heart, partially due to years of drug abuse. The youngest of the Bee Gee brothers, Andy seemed the most talented, at least the most handsome of the four. Even after family intervention for his drug addiction, he continued his downward spiral with heavy alcohol consumption. His death by myocarditis is caused by a viral infection, rampant during that period owing to alkaloids that were used to "step-on" cocaine, a process that adds cocaine lookalikes to make street sales of the drug even more profitable. These additives were cumulative and often more harmful than cocaine itself. After Andy's death, brother Maurice, nine years older, continued to lead the trio, which sold over 180 million records throughout their career. The disco era and especially their hit "Saturday Night Fever" catapulted the Gibbs brothers into fame and riches. At age twenty-one Maurice owned six Rolls-Royces and as many Aston Martins, all the while partying heavily until he became an alcoholic. Shortly after Andy's death, Maurice cleaned up and became a regular at the extremely nonglamorous Miami's Little River AA group. In 2003 Maurice Gibb, despite living the cleanest life of them all, at least for more than a decade, developed a rare twisted-bowel obstruction disorder known as ischemic enteropathy, which caused a fatal heart attack at fifty-three.

MUSICIANS WITH COMPLICATIONS

In 1957 the Be-Bop Boy and His One-Man Band star **Joe Hill Louis** (Lester Hill) cut his thumb on a guitar string and died of tetanus infection at age thirty-five. In 1968 Spanky and Our Gang guitarist **Malcolm Hale,** known for "Sunday Will Never Be the Same," died on a Sunday at age twenty-seven from carbon-monoxide poisoning due to a bad heating system. In 1971 **Gene Vincent** died from an unhealed wound acquired in a car accident eleven years earlier, killing the singer of "Be-Bop-A-Lula" at age thirty-six. In 1976 **John Persh,** bass guitarist and singer of "I Just Want to Celebrate" while with Rare Earth, did anything but sing that song when he learned he had a staph infection that killed him at age thirty-four. In 1982 **Tommy Tucker** (Robert Higginbotham), known for "Hi-Heel Sneakers," died of carbon tetrachloride poisoning (stripping-agent fumes) while refinishing his wood floors at age forty-eight. In 1982 the song "We've Only Just Begun" by **Karen Carpenter** was forever rejected as a slogan for dieting programs after she died of heart failure due to anorexia nervosa at thirty-two. In 1988 larger-than-life disco queen and overweight transvestite **Divine** (Harris Glenn Milstead) died of sleep apnea at age forty-two. In 2000 Blue Oyster Cult singer **Helen Wheels** (Helen Robbins), who sang "Room To Rage," was beyond pissed-off when she died of a staph infection after a routine surgery at age fifty, and "Constipation Blues" singer **Screamin Jay Hawkins** (Jalacy J. Hawkins), who was famous for performing while sitting in a coffin, had surgery on his bowels and died of an aneurysm at seventy.

GILLIGAN'S CASTAWAYS

"Just sit right back and you'll hear a tale, a tale of a fateful trip . . ." opened *Gilligan's Island*, a comedy that ran from 1964 to 1967, making ninety-eight episodes about the improbable group of castaways that have played eternally over and over in syndication. **Bob Denver**, who played the beatnik Maynard G. Krebs in *The Many Lives of Dobie Gillis* (1959–1963) before playing bungling Gilligan, appeared to many to be taking more than a toke or two of wacky weed on and off the set. He was busted in 1998 when a parcel of marijuana was delivered to his house, allegedly sent by the actress who played Mary Ann on *Gilligan's Island*. Police also found a cache of water pipes and pot-smoking paraphernalia on the premises. Remembered by many as the Skipper's Little Buddy, Denver died in 2005 at age seventy from complications of treatment for throat cancer. The Skipper, **Alan Hale, Jr.**, didn't care about typecasting after cancellation and opened a popular restaurant where he greeted guests with a tip of his sailor's cap: He died in 1990 at age seventy-one of cancer of the thymus. **Natalie Schafer** played Mrs. Howell and died in 1991 at age ninety of cancer. The millionaire, Mr. Howell, was Jim Backus of *Mr. Magoo* fame.

*Mister Magoo, the near-blind spokesman for GE lightbulbs, who got in and out of precarious situations despite his handicap, became a popular cartoon through the 1960s. The voice of Mr. Magoo was **Jim Backus** who got into his final hair-raising debacle at age seventy-six, and died of pneumonia in 1989 after years of Parkinson's disease. The cartoon's creator, **John Hubley**, died during a heart surgery at age sixty-two in 1977. Due to the sensitivity to persons with disabilities, it's unlikely Mr. Magoo will be resuscitated from his current moribund status anytime soon.*

JACKIE GLEASON

The fifth highest-ranked comedy of the twentieth century was *The Honeymooners*, a sitcom about working-class bus driver Ralph Kramden, played by Jackie Gleason with his wife "one of these days" Alice, played by **Audrey Meadows**. The show wasn't that big a hit while it aired but found a loyal following in syndication that turned it into a classic. Roly-poly Gleason appeared in fifteen films cast as everything from a deaf-mute janitor in *Gigot*, a redneck sheriff in *Smokey & the Bandit*, to a pool shark in *Hustler*, a role that earned him a nomination for an Oscar. He came from humble origins. He was abandoned by his father at age eight and supported by a mother who left him aching for attention while she worked long hours as a token collector in the New York City subway system. He had a desire to be loved and was known as a big tipper, always acting as if on-stage wherever he went. He cared little about his weight, saying that a comedian could "get away with more as a fat man," and was known to hold lavish dinners, easily devouring five lobsters at one sitting. He was widely recognized as a heavy drinker, nicknamed the Jolly Juicer by his drinking buddies. However, Gleason never considered himself an alcoholic because, he rationalized, he had the will-power to refrain from drinking until after a performance. Understandably, he developed diabetes and ultimately died in 1987 at age seventy-one of cancer of the liver. His mausoleum in Miami, Florida, bears the inscription "And Away We Go." *Honeymooners* co-star Audrey Meadows, a lifelong chain-smoker, died of lung cancer at age sixty-nine in 1996.

JOSEPH GLIDDEN

Barbed wire doesn't seem like such an important invention today, but it once played an integral part in the development of the American West. Joseph Glidden's 1873 invention closed down the open ranges and placed cattle on well-defined lots of private land. By the 1890s most of America's plains and wide-open country was cordoned off with spikey wire, which effectively ended the era of the cowboy. Glidden, through barbed wire, became one of the richest men of his time. However, he died from an infection from an unhealed cut, much the way his invention had injured many handling it and the animals caught in its web. Upon his death, his body was shipped in a special ice-cooled train coach. His final wish was that he be buried far from the dusty plains where his Texas headquarters were located to lie eternally like a gentleman in a gravesite in New York.

Before antibiotics were invented, getting a simple cut, especially from handling barbed wire, was the cause of many fatalities. One treatment for a gangrenous wound involved the use of fly maggots, which in theory fed only on dead flesh and allowed the still living flesh to heal. This, however, created more dead flesh, now called necrosis, which in effect set off a cascade of worsening conditions, including inflammation that wreaked havoc on the immune system. Although it seemed that many died from a small cut, it was most likely any number of diseases, even the common cold, that proved fatal to the individual's compromised immune system.

GOLDEN OLDIES

The 1950s is rightly associated with the birth of rock 'n' roll, but during that decade some of the most popular recordings, according to *Billboard*'s list of the top one hundred songs for the decade, included many hits by the crooners, as well as a few big band remnants:

> **Bobby Darin** scored the number-four spot in the decade with "Mack the Knife." He died in 1973 at age thirty-seven of complications during heart surgery (*See also* Mack the Knife). **Guy Mitchell,** born Al Cernik, was a pop singer who had the 1950s number-five song with "Singing the Blues." He died of surgical complications in 1999 at age seventy-two. The number-ten spot was held by **Tennessee Ernie Ford** (Ernest Jennings Ford) for "Sixteen Tons." Seriously alcoholic, he died of liver

failure in 1991 at age seventy-two, exactly thirty-six years to the day that "Sixteen Tons," a song about coal miners, was released. **Johnny Horton** had the decade's fifteenth most-sold song with "Battle of New Orleans," which was also named as one of the best songs of the century by the Grammy committee. He died in 1960 at age thirty-five in a car accident, after a head-on collision with a drunk driver. **Nelson Riddle**, a big-band leader, had number eighteen with "Lisbon Antigua." He died in 1985 at age sixty-four of heart failure. **Dean Martin**, born Dino Paul Crocetti, placed number nineteen with "Memories Are Made of This." He died in 1995 at age seventy-eight on Christmas morning of respiratory failure due to emphysema. Number twenty-two was **Tommy Edwards'** "All In The Game." A brain aneurysm killed him in 1969 at age forty-seven. **Domenico Modugno**, Italian singer and composer, had the twenty-sixth place with "Volare." He died of a heart attack at age sixty-six in 1994.

Number seventy-two belonged to Alvin & the Chipmunks with "The Chipmunk Song" sung by **David Seville**. He died in 1972 of a heart attack at age fifty-two (Alvin, Simon, and Theodore are reportedly still alive). The seventy-ninth spot was orchestra leader **Hugo Winterhalter's** "Canadian Sunset." He died in 1973 at age sixty-three of cancer. Perez Prado (aka the King of the Mambo) placed ninety-three with "Patricia." Prado died at age seventy-two in 1989 of a stroke. Country singer **Marty Robbins** (Martin David Robinson) was the most famous country-singer at the time, who capped the list for best songs of the decade at one hundred with "A White Sport Coat (and a Pink Carnation)." He went by way of surgical complications trying to mend his heart after the third attack at age fifty-seven in 1982.

Sheb Wooley (Shelby F. Wooley), primarily an actor, came up with the novelty hit "The Purple People Eater" that made the list at number thirty-five for most popular songs of the 1950s and has since sold over 100 million copies: He died at eighty-two of cancer in 2003, never having revealed if the song was about a purple monster who ate people or a monster who ate purple people.

CHARLES GOODYEAR

Before Charles Goodyear came up with the right formula, all rubber products eventually melted, and the "rubber fever" of the 1800s ended in a mess. Goodyear became the classic obsessed inventor, dedicating his life to perfecting what he called "elastic wood." Despite being in and out of jail for debt, he kept his backyard kettle going, boiling Brazilian waterproof gum, kneading and working the steaming experimental globs hour after hour, adding everything he could think of to make it work. He dressed in rubber hats, suit jackets, rubber ties, and rubber pants, forever trying to promote the joys of rubber. He envisioned a world made entirely out of rubber. He begged and borrowed to raise funds to build a rubber pavilion at the 1855 World's Fair in Paris, where roofs, floors, doors, furniture—everything was made out of his rubber. After spending so much to partake in the event, meanwhile overlooking the small detail of

SIMPLY MISS AMERICA

Seventeen-year-old **Ruth Malcomson** from Pennsylvania took first place in 1924. By this time the event received national media coverage on radio and in print. It drew a crowd of more than 300,000 viewing 87 contestants from around the country. Amateurs, married women, and professional models entered. Fashioning the latest in swimwear, they were often paid by top designers to participate. Norman Rockwell the painter was a judge that year, in addition to designer Annette Kellerman, who was arrested in 1907 for indecent exposure when she tried to have women wear her one-piece bathing suit designs instead of bloomers. Ruth Malcomson nearly lost to Mary Katherine Campbell until they came up with a rule not to allow the previous year's winner to take the title in any consecutive year. They also made a rule not to allow married women to enter. Ruth bowed out of the limelight after her win, saying, "The simple life is for me." She died in 1988 at age eighty-one.

protecting his patents, Goodyear was seriously broke and $200,000 in debt. Dyspeptic and gout-wracked, he went back to his workshop, standing on crutches over his rubber cauldrons, still wearing his rubber skullcap and rubber clothes until he died in 1860 at the age of sixty. Charles Goodyear and his family were never connected to the Goodyear Tire & Rubber Company, the leader in an industry that employs 300,000 and earns $6 billion a year.

MARGARET GORMAN

The first Miss America contest began in Atlantic City, New Jersey, and was staged to keep tourists in town longer than the Labor Day weekend in September. Contestants were judged by 50 percent applause and 50 percent judges' approval. In these early years the bathing suit competition was the main event. The winner received a three-foot-high golden mermaid statue, a handshake, and a kiss on the cheek. In 1921 the first winner was Margaret Gorman, a sixteen-year-old girl from Washington, D.C. She was invited to join the competition after

winning the Most Beautiful Bathing Girl in America the year before. She entered the contest for the next eight years but never won again. She died of pneumonia in 1995 at age ninety.

KIRBY GRANT

From 1951 to 1962 rancher-pilot *Sky King*, played by the accomplished aviator Kirby Grant, with the help of his real-life nephew and niece "Skipper" and "Penny," battled against a slew of corny bad guys. It was a wholesome show that always had Sky King swooping in at the last minute to rescue the needy, using his Cessna T–50, a wooden-winged airplane. By 1985 Grant was too old to fly and instead decided to drive to Cape Canaveral, Florida, where he was to be honored for encouraging air flight during the launch ceremonies prior to liftoff of the Space Shuttle *Challenger*. He died in a fatal car crash miles from the launch pad at age seventy-three. Two months later, the same Shuttle would explode at takeoff, killing all seven astronauts on board.

JOHANNES GUTENBERG

Of equal importance as the transmission of knowledge via the computer was the invention in the Middle Ages of printed books in 1456. Johannes Gutenberg is cited as the first in Western culture to invent a system of movable type that eventually allowed books and knowledge to become accessible to everyone. Previously, hand-written works that often took a lifetime to inscribe were only in the possession of the libraries of royalty and of the Church. Gutenberg was a goldsmith who modified machines used in olive oil presses and in woodcutting techniques to devise the first printing process. Since he didn't have enough money, he found a partner to finance the operation. Unfortunately, it took a long time to come out with his first product that was sure to be a bestseller, the Bible. The partner dragged the inventor into court and seized his equipment and printed books. Gutenberg never made a dime from his invention. Within no time, the technique was adopted throughout Europe and credited as the single-greatest invention that moved civilization from the Dark Ages to the Renaissance. Gutenberg eventually became homeless and destitute, dying of malnutrition at the age of sixty-eight in 1468.

WOODY GUTHRIE

Woody Guthrie, best known for his song "This Land Is Your Land" (1940), was born in Oklahoma in 1912. His music was greatly influenced by the Dust Bowl era and the poverty and suffering it caused. He achieved his fame via a Los Angeles radio station that featured "hillbilly music" and traditional folk songs. He became increasingly political and directed his songs to address topical ills of the day. By the late 1940s his alcoholism exacerbated his fragile health and signs of Saint Vitus' dance (abnormal involuntary-movement disorder) and schizophrenia curtailed his playing. From 1956 to 1967 he was institutionalized in various psychiatric hospitals until his death October 3, 1967, of Huntington's disease at age fifty-five.

NATHAN HALE

At age twenty-one Nathan Hale was captured, even though he was disguised as a schoolteacher toting a phony Yale diploma while operating behind enemy lines in British-occupied Manhattan. To get information, he frequented bars, as taverns were always the best places to listen in on conversations of both soldiers and civilians. However, Hale divulged his true loyalties to British Major Robert Rogers, who was also undercover and pretending to be a patriot; Hale had one stein of ale too many and told Rogers everything. Hours later Hale was arrested and presented to the British commander-in-chief, General Howe, for interrogation. Howe tried to bribe Hale into joining the British side, offering him a prestigious position as an officer in the king's infantry. When Hale refused, he was tried as a spy and hanged at the corner of what is now Sixty-sixth Street and Third Avenue in Manhattan. Although Hale's intentions were noble, it could be said that his drinking habit is what really killed him, becoming America's first deceased undercover agent. Once caught, Hale made an impression on the British soldiers who witnessed his hanging. He was composed and dignified as the noose was placed around his neck, saying "I regret I have but one life to lose for my country." The colonial army and armies to come used Hale as an enticement for recruitment. Hale's body is believed to be buried close to the Forty-fourth Street entrance to Grand Central Station where a hotdog cart is currently parked.

HANNIBAL

The Roman Empire began in 510 B.C. and went through various stages, or republics as the governments were called, before its fall in A.D. 476. During those nearly one thousand years of recorded history, only a few names are remembered by nonhistorians. The first was the relentless general Hannibal from the north of Africa who nearly defeated Rome. He is most famous for his daring attempt to cross the towering

Alps in 218 B.C. He started out with 75,000 footsoldiers, 9,000 cavalry, and 37 war elephants but lost over 20,000 men and all but a few elephants in the effort. For nearly twenty years he lived off the land and war spoils while circling Rome and pounding at its door. Even after a truce of sorts, Hannibal was eager to fight Rome anywhere he could, never forgetting the promise he made to his father as a boy to "bring steel and fire against Roman destiny." But in the end he was finally cornered and took a vial of poison he had carried around his neck since his first days of war in a hollowed-out elephant-tusk pendant. He died by his own hand at age sixty-three in 183 B.C. rather than be captured.

HAPPY FACE

Everyone knows of the smiley-face symbol. But few know that one man was responsible for making it a cultural icon; Mr. **B.A. "Hap" Day** was a major figure in New York City's "Have a Nice Day" campaign of the early 1970s. He vigorously campaigned to make the happy smiley-face part of everyday life. But on August 19, 1996, "Hap" was found dead. According to Reuters: "Behind a public toilet at First Street and Avenue C in lower Manhattan Mr. Day was discovered by a maintenance man, facedown in a shallow puddle, with a hypodermic syringe dangling from his neck. Death was due to an acute overdose of heroin, methadone, barbiturates, and Drano." Eyewitness John Newmeyer observed: "If that wasn't enough, he wore a Shirley Temple dirndl, a long blond wig, a girdle, and six-inch spike heels when his body was found."

WILLIAM HENRY HARRISON

William Henry Harrison was elected president in 1840. Some thought he was too old at age sixty-eight to handle the job. To show he had stamina and was a skilled orator and public speaker, he persisted and delivered a nearly three-hour speech during the March inaugural celebration, despite a driving, freezing rain. Harrison caught a cold and died thirty-two days later, becoming the first U.S. president to die in office.

*In 1923 at age fifty-seven, President **Warren G. Harding** died of a heart attack while in San Francisco preparing for a speech. At the time, Harding was implicated in the Teapot Dome scandal, an investigation into monetary irregularities in the Veterans' Bureau. Not only was the president accused of overlooking his attorney general's corrupt dealings, but newspapers also discovered he had a mistress and an illegitimate daughter. Although officially Harding died suddenly of a heart attack, some believe the president died from poison, administered by himself or his wife.*

FRANK HAYES

In 1923 jockey Frank Hayes died of
a heart attack in the middle of a race.
Nevertheless, his horse, Sweet Kiss,
came in at first place at Belmont Park
racetrack in New York on June 4 of
that year. Hayes had begged owner
A. M. Frayling to let him ride; it was
only the second time thirty-five-year-
old Hayes had been wearing riding

silks. The *New York Times* stated, "It was his second, last and only victory." Even
though he became the only jockey to ever win a race dead, he never knew it. At
the end of a race the winning jockey has to get weighed. They reportedly carried
Hayes's corpse and heaped him on the scale. Bettors scrambled to the window
to collect their winnings, and not much was made of the jockey's passing. Other
jockeys were not too eager to ride this horse, and Sweet Kiss never won another
race. From then on, the term Sweet Kiss of Death entered the lingo of dying.

ERNEST HEMINGWAY

Ernest Hemingway was furious that
his archrival Faulkner won the Nobel
Prize before he did. (Faulkner said
of Hemingway: "He has never been
known to use a word that might
send a reader to the dictionary." And
Hemingway said of Faulkner: "Poor
Faulkner. Does he really think big
emotions come from big words?")
The larger-than-life man known as
Papa was a wordsmith who hammered out each of his carefully
crafted sentences as if made of a fragile stone. Although he wrote other
books of merit, *The Old Man and the
Sea*, a slim novella, earned him a Pulitzer (1953) and a Nobel Prize in 1954.
When he won the award, he said that "Writing, at its best, is a lonely life." In
fact, everything other than the solitude required to write was anything but
lonely for Hemingway, always surrounded by wives, children, and adventure
seekers like himself. A near-fatal plane crash in Africa made the Nobel committee hurry up and honor Hemingway while he was still alive. After he received
the award, his lifelong alcoholism began to take its toll and he became obsessed with the notion that the IRS was after him. Soon after being subjected
to electric shock treatments to cure his alcohol-induced depression and para-
noia, he returned to his estate in Ketchum, Idaho, and shot himself in the head
with a shotgun on a cool summer morning, two days before the Fourth of July,
in 1961 at age sixty-one.

JIMI HENDRIX

James Marshall Hendrix, legendary rock guitarist of "Foxy Lady" and "Purple Haze" fame, died at the age of twenty-seven from a barbiturate overdose, ultimately a victim of the wild man image he portrayed onstage. Before that final night, Jimi took a "black bomber," a capsule containing amphetamines and sedatives. He also snorted some LSD at 8:30 P.M. on September 17, 1970, and didn't return to his flat until 3:00 A.M. He ate a tuna sandwich and took nine sleeping pills. During the night he vomited but was too comatose to turn on his side. Subsequently he choked on the partially digested tuna. At 11:30 the next morning he was pronounced dead of asphyxiation.

MUSICIANS GAG

Tommy Dorsey, trombonist and dance-band-leader died in his home at age fifty-one in 1956 from choking in his sleep. **George Nelson,** the apparently not so long-winded baritone of the Orioles, with the hit "Baby Please Don't Go," fatally gagged during an asthma attack at age thirty-three. In 1964 **Rudy Lewis,** who sang "Up on the Roof" and was the lead singer for the Drifters, died the night before he was scheduled to record "Under the Boardwalk." Under still mysterious circumstances, asphyxiation (choking on food) was cited as the cause of Lewis's death at age twenty-eight. Another singer quickly filled his shoes. In 1973 **Steve Perron,** who wrote ZZ Top's "Francine," died of the inhalation-of-own-vomit-from-heroin-overdose routine at age twenty-eight. In 1980 another rocker who made a song he had to live up to was **Bon Scott** with "Highway to Hell" when he choked at age thirty-three on his own vomit after a binge.

"Mama" **Cass Elliot** (Ellen Naomi Cohen) of the Mamas and the Papas has unjustly been known to have died choking on a ham sandwich, when in fact it was a heart attack that took her at age thirty-two in 1974, as a result of fluctuating weight gain and diet regimes.

KATHARINE HEPBURN

When it came to winning an Oscar, Katharine Hepburn outdid all females and males alike, winning four times. She was called arrogant during her heyday, refused to sign autographs, wore no makeup, and preferred to wear pants in public, despite her studio's wishes, and was known to treat the press in an offhand manner. Some say her independence was born when as a child she found her older brother, whom she adored, hung by his own hand from a rafter. She was made to keep up the story that her family wished to believe, saying his death was

caused by a magic trick he attempted that had gone awry. Her lifestyle—married only for a few weeks, though known for illicit affairs with many powerful Hollywood men, including the married Spencer Tracy for many years, and never having or adopting children—Hepburn admitted was due to her selfishness, which she believed contributed to her long and fruitful years. She died at age ninety-six on June 29, 2003, at 2:50 P.M. of cardiac arrest, pushing the cause of longevity belonging to the winners to the extreme.

> "Life is hard. After all, it kills you."
> —KATHARINE HEPBURN

HERON

Heron was a Greek geometer who discovered how heat and steam could move objects but employed this scientific breakthrough only as a toy, using steam from a pot to spin a ball. He also invented the first vending machine, which dispensed a dab of holy water for a coin. The bulk of his writings about the principles of geometry were lost in the 1850s, and only a smattering of his true genius is  known through lectures he gave while teaching at the Museum of Alexandria. Heron apparently died three times. He was spotted in 150 B.C., again in A.D. 62 and another eyewitness account places his existence at circa A.D. 250. Some say he may have found the ultimate formula for immortality and could very well be currently living the life of some absentminded math teacher among us.

ALFRED HITCHCOCK

Alfred Hitchcock Presents was perhaps the only true horror show on TV, an anthology of both mysteries and melodramas that debuted in 1955 and aired through 1962. Hitchcock had already made thirty films and used his rotund profile in silhouette as a trademark, himself offering a drooling introduction to the show that was about to follow. At the end of each episode Hitchcock again returned to center stage to inform the audience that the dastardly criminal or sociopath presented was dutifully apprehended and currently

receiving appropriate punishment, as he said "as a necessary gesture to morality." Despite a lifetime devoted to the most ghoulish, strange, and murderous endings conceivable, he viewed his own final illness as a terrible inconvenience and intolerably mundane. At age eighty Sir Alfred Hitchcock struggled through the indignity of dialysis after renal failure. He died of chronic congestive heart failure only four months after he was dubbed a knight by Queen Elizabeth II in 1980. Upon his request, he preferred not to deal with the untidiness of a dead body and was promptly cremated.

ADOLF HITLER

Hitler's mother and father were cousins, and their marriage was not recognized as a legitimate one. He went by his mother's last name Schicklgruber for the first thirty-nine years of his life, until he decided to adopt his father's name, even though he was beaten by the elder on a near-daily basis throughout his childhood. How this man went from copying scenes from postcards and selling his hand-painted reproductions to tourists to becoming the leader of the Nazi party—responsible for killing 11,283,000 homosexuals, gypsies, and Jews, in addition to the 45 million people dead from the war he raged—is ultimately a story of coincidences. Hard to fathom how it occurred at all. Nevertheless, when this megalomaniac with an inferiority complex was certain he was defeated he chose to commit suicide. While sequestered in a bunker with his mistress Eva Braun, propaganda minister Joseph Goebbels, Goebbels's wife and six children, and a few remaining staff, Hitler intended to use prussic acid, a form of cyanide, as the poison of choice to kill himself. To make sure the poison capsules were still potent, he first tested them on his favorite dog, Blondi. He then sat for his last meal of spaghetti with light sauce. In his private chamber within the bunker, he and Braun took the poison, but Hitler preferred not to wait for it to take effect and shot himself in his right temple with a 7.65mm pistol ten days after his fifty-sixth birthday in 1945. Their bodies were then taken outside and doused with gas, but the complete burning of their corpses was interrupted by bombing. Goebbels then fed his own six children the cyanide capsules and went outside with his wife, knelt down, and ordered an SS soldier to shoot them both in the back of the head before burning their bodies. The Soviets, who eventually overran the bunker, found the remains of Hitler and performed an autopsy. Some said a portion of Hitler's skull was given to Stalin to use as an ashtray, though all his remains were eventually burned to ash and dumped in the Elbe River.

CYANIDE SALT IS THE FAVORITE CHOICE OF SUICIDE PROPONENTS SEEKING A FAST-ACTING, NONREVERSIBLE COMPOUND TO KILL THEMSELVES. CYANIDE PREVENTS CELLS FROM RECEIVING OXYGEN, AND DEATH OCCURS ON A CELLULAR LEVEL, PAINFULLY CAUSING EACH OF THE BODY'S 10 TRILLION CELLS TO SUFFOCATE IN UNISON.

DEAD DICTATORS

In 1945 at age sixty-one, when Italian dictator **Benito Mussolini** knew his time was up, he tried to escape by putting on a private's uniform over his general's outfit and hid in the back of a German truck retreating toward Austria. However, he was recognized and captured by Italian partisans, shot in the heart, then hung upside down on meat hooks for display.

Joseph Stalin was dictator of the Soviet Union from 1922 until his death at age seventy-three in 1953, when he was poisoned by what Russian papers called his doctor-assassins to mimic a stroke. It was Nikita Khrushchev, Stalin's successor, who shared a bottle of wine with Stalin the night of his death and ordered Stalin's bodyguards to bed. No doctors were summoned for thirteen hours until he was dead. Stalin had killed tens of millions of his own people and noted coldly, "One death is a tragedy; a million is a statistic."

FELIX HOFFMANN

In 400 B.C. Hippocrates wrote of a concoction he made from the bark of a willow tree that reduced fever and eased the pains of childbirth. The exact formula for the first aspirin was lost until a number of chemists in the nineteenth century dug deeper and discovered the pain-relieving ingredient of willow bark to be salicin. Most remedies using salicin were too harsh on the stomach until a young chemist, Felix Hoffmann, found a way to synthesize the compound to be more palatable. He hoped to create an acceptable prescription to treat his father's worsening arthritis. Eleven days later, in 1897, Hoffmann devised the formulas for aspirin and heroin, both of which were patented by the German dye manufacturer Friedrich Bayer & Co., the firm in which he was employed. Aspirin was considered to have minor marketing potential, taking a back-burner to heroin, which Bayer touted aggressively, at first believing heroin was healthier than aspirin. Once the addictive properties of heroin were discovered, the company went on to push aspirin to great success. Aspirin was first sold as a powder, and then made into tablet form in 1915; Bayer stopped producing heroin in 1913. Not much fanfare was given to Hoffmann during his lifetime, and he retired into obscurity in 1928, at which time there were more than 200,000 heroin addicts in the United States alone. Hoffmann never again duplicated his two-week span of pharmaceutical genius. He died in 1946 at age seventy-eight of cardiopulmonary arrest.

Hippocrates, known as the Father of Medicine, was the first to disregard superstition in favor of examining the patient's diet and physical vital signs to determine the cause of sickness and to prevent illness. He died in 377 B.C. at the extremely old age of eighty-

three from an imbalance of humors, a term he used to describe what he believed to be the four sustaining and life-giving elements of the body.

WILLIAM HOLDEN

William Holden was once dubbed Hollywood's golden boy, remembered for parts in many films—from the washed-up screenwriter in *Sunset Boulevard* to the ill-fated prisoner in *The Bridge on the River Kwai*. For TV he starred in the cop drama *The Blue Knight* in the seventies. In 1981 Holden was alone in his Santa Monica apartment drinking until he was beyond intoxicated. He slipped on a throw rug, gashed open his forehead on a coffee table, and died at age sixty-three. His body was discovered four days later.

BILLIE HOLIDAY

Billie Holiday (Eleanora Fagan Goughy) once worked in a brothel and was arrested for prostitution before she tried her luck on the club circuit in 1932 when she was seventeen. It wasn't until 1939 with the release of "Strange Fruit," a song about lynching, that she made a mark at the Café Society, an intellectual and interracial club in Greenwich Village, New York City. From then her career took off, though not so her personal life. Her sultry voice and melancholy songs of unrequited love transformed her into a popular well-paid artist. Simultaneously, she attached herself to men who mistreated her, at the very least. As she descended into heroin addiction and alcohol abuse, by the 1950s she had lost most of her money and the earlier quality of her unique voice. In a classic case of life imitating art, she lived the sad songs she sang. She spent her last days handcuffed to a bed rail with a police guard standing sentry while she died of cirrhosis of the liver in 1959 at the age of forty-four with $750 taped to her leg and seventy cents in her bank account.

CHRONIC LIVER DISEASE IS THE TENTH LEADING CAUSE OF DEATH IN THE UNITED STATES, WITH OVER 25,000 DEATHS ANNUALLY. ANOTHER 4 MILLION PEOPLE HAVE HEPATITIS C, PREDOMINANTLY FROM DRUG USE. MANY OF THEM WILL EVENTUALLY DIE OF CIRRHOTIC LIVER DISEASE.

HOMER

Homer lived in the eighth century B.C. His epic poems *The Iliad* and *The Odyssey* are considered the oldest-surviving examples of Western literature. Homer was blind and because of this handicap chose to scribe his words rather than travel about reciting them orally, as did most poets of the time. It is believed that many of the adventures and histories recorded in these documents were originally of an oral tradition and that Homer, with possibly the help of his daughter, took the time to transcribe them. Homer died in his eighties near the sea when he stepped in a pool of soft sand that submerged him up to his neck. Two boys fishing nearby heard his distress call, and although they didn't recognize who he was, they used one of the riddle-type questions Homer made famous in his poems to see if the old man was worthy of their aid. Homer asked the boys to help so he could marvel at what they had caught in that day's nets. Supposedly, the boys posed

this riddle to Homer for him to solve: "What we caught we left behind; what we did not catch we brought with us." Homer couldn't answer the riddle and drowned with the rising tide.

*The poet **Aeschylus** died in 456 B.C. when an eagle mistook his bald head for a stone and used it to smash open a turtle shell.*

VILLARD DE HONNECORT

From sundials to liquid clocks that used drips of measured water to indicate the hour, to mechanical pendulums employing gears, man found it essential to know the time of day. Commerce depended upon it. Villard de Honnecort was an architect for cathedrals, and although he cannot be associated with any one in particular, he was a great sketch artist. In 1250 he left the first rendering of a mechanized clock that worked with weights

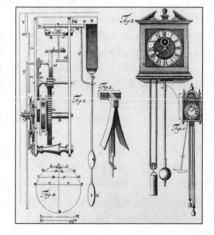

and gears, thus supplying a blueprint for how clocks would be built for the next seven hundred years, called the perpetuum mobile. Honnecort probably didn't invent the clock. There is dispute among experts whether he was indeed an architect or simply a traveling artist. Although he was born in France, the exact date of his birth is unknown. Evidence indicates he was probably in the wrong place, at the wrong time, and was murdered by highwaymen during a trip to Hungary at the approximate age of forty.

HOUDINI

Harry Houdini, born Erik Weisz, by age twenty was already a professional magician. At first he focused on card tricks. Next was a vanishing act, such as when he made a full-grown elephant disappear from the stage by dropping it into a hidden swimming pool. Later he perfected his escape-artist stunts, which made him famous. By the age of twenty-five Houdini was a worldwide sensation, escaping from jails, prison vans, handcuffs of all makes, and straitjackets. When imitators began to steal his audiences, he added submersion, suspended himself upside down in water tanks and inside safes—any stunt that would add "the thrill of death" if he failed. Houdini later went on to make movies and actually worked as a spy for Scotland Yard and for U.S. intelligence-gathering operations. During his heyday he said he accomplished his feats by dematerializing, but actually he had the ability to swallow keys and regurgitate them at will or dislocate his shoulder to get free from a straitjacket. Toward the end of his life he devoted his energies to debunking spiritualists, though many believed he himself had learned the secrets of communicating with the dead. After a performance in Montreal, a jealous college student sucker-punched Houdini while he reclined on a sofa. Houdini developed a gangrenous appendix within a week, which became too serious for treatment. Houdini couldn't escape his hospital bed and died on Halloween in 1926 at the age of fifty-two. He promised his wife that he would contact her from beyond the grave a year later. She kept a candle burning next to his picture for ten years before she finally blew it out. The man who punched Houdini, **Jocelyn Gordon Whitehead,** despite advanced degrees, became a derelict and died of malnutrition in 1954.

*Amateur magician **Joe Burrus** was going to outdo his idol Houdini. He was handcuffed and chained, placed in a plastic coffin, and buried under seven tons of soil and concrete. However, as the concrete poured from the cement mixer, the sudden weight crushed the lid of the plastic coffin. Attempts at excavation were unsatisfactory, and Joe drowned in mortar mix in 1990 at age thirty-two.*

ROCK HUDSON

Born Roy Scherer, Jr., Hudson was a reclusive kid growing up in the Depression. He tried to help his single mom put bread on the table by acting in plays, but he had trouble remembering his lines. When he went to Hollywood, he was signed on for his good looks, 6-foot–4 and broad-shouldered. Reportedly, he took thirty to forty takes just to repeat one line. In the fifties and sixties he became a romantic idol, making sixty-two films. He was considered the top box-office draw of his generation, adored by swooning women of all ages. Although he was married for three years in the 1950s, it was no secret in Hollywood that he was gay. It was a shocker to the public, though, and ultimately drew attention to AIDS, when he died of complications from the disease in 1985 at age fifty-nine. He made this last public statement: "I am not happy that I am sick. I am not happy that I have AIDS. But if that is helping others, I can at least know that my own misfortune has had some positive worth." One person who found scant nobility in his final "coming out" was Hudson's young male lover, Marc Christian; when Hudson knew that he had the disease, he didn't tell Christian and continued the relationship. When Hudson died, Christian was awarded millions from the Hudson Estate.

*A few other TV actors who died of AIDS: **Rene Enriquéz** (fifty-six) played Lt. Ray Calletano on* Hill Street Blues; *and although pancreatic cancer was cited as the official cause, he succumbed to the disease in 1990.* **Franklyn Seales,** *who starred as Dexter in* Silver Spoons, *died at age thirty-seven in 1990.* **Peter Kevin Hall,** *who played Harry the Bigfoot in* Harry & The Hendersons, *died in 1991 at age thirty-five.* **Robert Reed,** *the Dad of* The Brady Bunch, *went out with the disease at age fifty-nine in 1992, though he had colon cancer listed as the cause.* **Ray Sharkey** (forty) *of the* Wiseguy *perished by it in 1993.*

HUMAN FLY

As skyscrapers rose above the urban landscape, a number of daredevils saw the new concrete skyline as a vertical challenge. They called themselves *builderers,* though dubbed human flies by the press. The first and most prolific was **Harry H. Gardiner** who climbed over seven hundred buildings from 1905 through 1923, including the Flatiron Building in New York City and the Capitol in Washington, D.C. A small man who wore round, frameless glasses, he climbed the walls of skyscrapers in ordinary clothes and without the aid of ropes, suction cups, cables, or nets. He thrilled spectators by dangling from cracks in the bricks

and swinging one-handed to another ledge, swaying like a pendulum to reach for a crumbling cornice. It was President Grover Cleveland who dubbed him the Human Fly after witnessing Gardiner scale a 150-foot flagpole as if it were a stick lying on the ground. Many others got into the act and most of the urban climbers made a good living since the events were usually tied to advertisements, such as Gardiner's scaling of the Bank of Hamilton building in Ontario where he reached in the window on the eleventh floor to buy a life insurance policy the bank was marketing. In 1923 New York City passed the nation's first ordinance banning urban climbing after human fly **Harry F. Young** fell from the side of the Hotel Martinique at the ninth-floor mark. After that, Gardiner sailed to Europe to continue his stunts. Exactly what happened to him remains a mystery. A man fitting his description, with the same name, and known age of fifty-seven, though without mention of his climbing career, was found beaten to death at the foot of the Eiffel Tower in 1928.

STONEWALL JACKSON

During the Civil War the South viewed General Thomas Jonathan "Stonewall" Jackson as its greatest hero. He carried two books everywhere he went: The Bible and Napoleon's *Maxims of War*. He acted like more of a mystic, putting his ear to the ground and his eyes to the heavens before deciding on a mili-

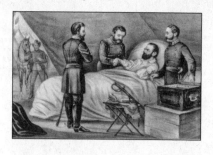

tary stratagem. He was mistakenly shot by his own men on May 2, 1863. Doctors then amputated his left arm, but a fever set in from infection and he died at age thirty-nine eight days later. Soldiers had taken the amputated arm and buried it near a battlefield to bring them good luck, but it was eventually exhumed in 1929 and reburied closer to home at Jackson's family plot in Spotsylvania, Virginia. His last words, either from the delirium of fever or from an otherworldly vision, were "Let us cross over the river, and rest under the shade of the trees."

DAVID JANSSEN

The Fugitive (1963–1967) was a crime drama about a man wrongfully accused of killing his wife, who escapes en route to prison. He plans to hunt down the real killer, a one-armed man, while the police hunt him. The falsely accused Dr. Kimble was played by seldom-smiling David Janssen, who in real life was a smoker and a heavy drinker. He died of a sudden heart attack at age forty-eight in 1980. The one-armed man was **Bill Raisch,** who died of lung cancer in 1984 at age seventy-nine. The voiceover narrative for each episode was provided by **William Conrad** (later a star of his own police show *Cannon*). He died in 1994 of congestive heart failure at age seventy-three. Although the show's creator denied any similarity, most people thought the plot had to do with the **Sam Sheppard** case. In 1954 Sheppard was accused of killing his pregnant wife, Cleveland doctor Marilyn Sheppard, found murdered in their home. Sheppard's trial received as much publicity as the O. J. Simpson trial thirty years later. Sheppard was sent to prison, though he maintained he was innocent, saying he was attacked by a wild white-haired man. Eventually he was released by the Supreme Court on a technicality in 1966. Once out of prison he tried his luck as a pro wrestler, going by the moniker The Killer. This venture was curtailed by excessive drinking; he died in 1970 of liver failure at age forty-six.

JESUS

Jesus of Nazareth started Christianity. His adult life has been the cause of more writings and interpretations in the last two thousand years than that of any other person in history. Using New Testament accounts, forensic specialists have recently examined the circumstances of his death. At age thirty-three Jesus was scourged with a spiked lash that caused very deep lacerations. These wounds caused tremendous blood loss, nearly one-fifth of his total volume, which produced a condition known as hypovolemic shock. After he was forced to carry a wooden yoke, part of the crucifix called the patibulum, causing more blood

JESUS NAILED TO THE CROSS.
JESUS POSTO EM CRUZ.

loss, nails one inch in diameter were hammered through his wrists, fixing him to this crossbeam. This piece was attached to the vertical upright portion of the crucifix called the stipe. His feet were nailed to the stipe, most likely through the instep, the portion of foot between the toes and the ankle, such that the soles of his feet rested flat against the wood. Being hung in this fashion caused critical respiratory distress. He died of asphyxiation and hypovolemic shock before the final thrust of a spear pierced his side. His last words were "It is finished. Father; into your hands I commit my spirit." If he had died in any other way, many believe, his legacy might have been forgotten.

DEFINITION OF CRUEL AND UNUSUAL PUNISHMENT

In Roman times crucifixion was reserved only for the lowest class of criminals. Middle-class or merchant criminals were executed by the sack. The condemned were placed in a leather pouch along with an animal, anything from a rooster, dog, cat, and sometimes even an ape, if available. The sack was thrown into a river and the person died thoroughly shredded, bitten or pecked to death long before he drowned. The wealthy could be beheaded, drink poison, or run onto their own sword.

Joan of Arc Saved France

W.S.S. WOMEN OF AMERICA SAVE YOUR COUNTRY
Buy WAR SAVINGS STAMPS
UNITED STATES TREASURY DEPARTMENT

JOAN OF ARC

A fifteenth-century French woman known as Joan of Arc began to hear voices. To her, God had a message of insider military information, instructing her to drive the English out of France. She dressed for battle and showed up for war, and by her conviction (others called it madness) she rallied the troops and achieved a long-sought victory of a key occupied city in just nine days. French King Charles VII, his own lineage rife with frequent bouts of insanity, dubbed her and her family nobility. A year later she was captured by the English, tried for heresy by the clergy of the Inquisition, and burned at the stake at age nineteen in 1431. Charles VII made no effort to free her. Five hundred years later she was canonized a saint.

Between 1450 and 1600, records indicate at least 30,000 were burned or executed as heretics or witches. The torture devices used during this period go beyond what the cruelest of masochistic minds could imagine, including water torture, racks, fingernail pullers, skull-and-limb-crushing vices, burning feet machines, and metal chambers shaped like statues of the Virgin lined with spikes in which the accused was enclosed to elicit a confession of heresy. The instruments were blessed prior to use; however, in 2002, Pope John Paul II issued a general apology for this and for the "errors of his church for the last 2000 years."

HENRY JOHNSON

In World War I the U.S. army was still segregated. Blacks who joined the effort were assigned to the labor service. One black group of National Guard known as the Harlem Hell-Fighters were finally allowed to fight under the French flag. They were provided with French helmets, though they continued to wear the U.S. uniform. One soldier, Sgt. Henry Johnson, a former redcap or luggage carrier, became, as Teddy Roosevelt remarked, "one of the five bravest men" of that conflict. While he was on sentry duty in 1918, a German raiding party caught Johnson and another soldier in an ambush. Johnson prevented his downed buddy from being captured and fought the

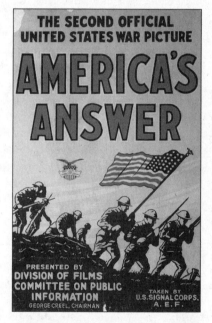

Germans off in hand-to-hand combat, using only the butt of his empty rifle and a knife. He received twenty-one wounds from the fierce melee. When Johnson returned from war, there was a parade down Fifth Avenue and a huge celebration in Harlem. Shortly after the confetti was broomed away, he tried to return to the old luggage job at the Albany Union Railroad Station but was unable to do the work. He received no pension from the army and became a wino on the streets, speaking of war exploits that no one believed. Penniless and estranged from wife and family, he died alone in a Veterans hospital bed at age thirty-two from liver failure. In 2003 Johnson posthumously received the Distinguished Service Cross.

BLIND WILLIE JOHNSON

Blind Willie Johnson is the unknown hero of American music, a traveling singer and guitar picker who greatly influenced both blues and rock. Beyond five recording sessions between 1927 and 1930, each of only one day and yielding thirty tracks, there is little known of this icon whose songs were sung and reworked by such names as Bob Dylan, Led Zeppelin, Muddy Waters, The Rolling Stones, Eric Clapton, and the Grateful Dead. He sold no more than a few hundred records during his lifetime. The only reliable biographical details of his life are found on his death certificate, which reveals that he was born in 1895 in Texas and died in 1945 in Texas of malarial fever, with syphilis and blindness listed as secondary causes. What is also known is that he traveled throughout Texas, the Mississippi Delta, to Maine and back. Most of his life he sang on street corners or in churches (sometimes played on church radio programs), or at whatever venue would have him. It is believed that he went blind at age seven when his stepmother threw lye in his face to get back at his father who had just given her a beating. Afterward, his father took him into town every Saturday, with a tin cup around his neck, where he played the guitar he had taught himself, using a pocketknife as a slide. Solace for the singer came in playing and composing blues-type music with religious and spiritual overtones. In 1993 a collection of his recordings was released but sold less than fifteen thousand copies.

ANISSA JONES

Anissa Jones played the cute-as-a-button pigtailed girl Buffy on *Family Affair* (1966–1971). When the show ended, she partied at night and worked in the day at a local doughnut shop, waiting until she turned eighteen to get hold of her TV earnings. A few months after she received $70,000 from the trust fund for her stint on *Family Affair*, she indulged in even more serious party-girl behavior. In 1976 at eighteen years and three months, she died of an overdose after ingesting Quaaludes, phencyclidine, cocaine, and liquor. Adding more of a foretelling irony to the title of the show, **Brian Keith** (Uncle Bill), also of *Family Affair*, shot himself in 1997 at age seventy-five, two months after his daughter, **Daisy Keith**, an actress who played alongside her father, committed suicide.

KID ACTORS

Carl Switzer, known as Alfalfa of *The Little Rascals*, was shot to death in 1959 at the age of thirty-one. Switzer had tried to start a big-game hunting expedition company after the acting roles dried up. He was shot by his partner over an argument of who-owed-whom fifty bucks. **Rusty Hamer** was the funny, wise-cracking child star of popular TV show *Make Room for Daddy* in the fifties and sixties. When the show was over, Danny Thomas, the star of the show, offered to send Rusty to college. But Rusty took a job on an offshore oil rig, then became a waiter in a Louisiana café. In 1990 at age forty-two, with the limelight a distant memory, he shot himself in the head with a .357 Magnum. **Dana Plato** played the humorous Kimberly Drummond in the TV comedy *Diff'rent Strokes* (1978–1984). Afterward, she slipped quickly into drug and alcohol abuse and even tried her hand at pornography flicks to jump-start her career. When it all backfired, she felt the only way out was to commit suicide with an overdose of painkillers and Valium in 1999 at age thirty-four.

BRIAN JONES

Brian Jones invited Mick Jagger and Jagger's boyhood friend Keith Richards to try out for the blues band he was putting together, called, on a fluke, The Rollin' Stones. (A track, "Rollin' Stone Blues," from a Muddy Waters album happened to be lying on the floor when a bar owner asked Jones the name of his band while booking the group over the telephone.) Jones was born rebellious, unable to sit still in school, and he was caned often by teachers, though he was able to score high grades with little effort. The rise of the rock era made his naturally unruly personality a charismatic draw. It was Jones who struggled to get the group gigs and who invented the stage persona, rather than Jagger, strutting across the stage, and he was the first to wear the outrageous fashions later associated with rock stars. However, as the group's popularity grew and a manager, former publicist of the Beatles, honed their image, Jagger and Richards moved to center stage, with their rock style winning over Jones's tendency toward traditional blues and jazz. The Stones shot to the top, reaping fame and fortune, though Jones, despite success, felt more and more alienated from the group he had formed, retaliating by meanspiritedness against the other band members and an untoward use of drugs and alcohol. The final insult came when Richards screwed Jones's girlfriend while Jones was laid up in the hospital recuperating from yet another binge. It wasn't long before Jones was asked to leave the band, with Jones issuing a statement: "They stole my love . . . and my music." A month after a new guitarist took his place, Jones was found floating in his swimming pool, dead in 1969 at age twenty-seven, from what the coroner listed as Death by Misadventure. Neither Jagger nor Richards attended his funeral.

MUSICIAN DROWNINGS AND OCCUPATIONAL HAZARDS

In 1964 teen idol **Johnny Burnette,** with his song "You're Sixteen," drowned after a boating accident at age thirty. In 1983 inebriated Beach Boy **Dennis Wilson** jumped off his boat to retrieve sentimental photos he had just tossed overboard and drowned at age thirty-nine. In 1984 thirty-seven-year-old **Candy Givens** of Zephyr drowned in a hot tub. In 1997 gentleman jazz man **Zachary Breaux** was thirty-six-years-old when he died trying to rescue a drowning woman off Miami Beach, Florida. In 1997 **Jeff Buckley,** known for "Last Goodbye," was thirty years old when he drowned in the Mississippi River. In addition, at least three rockers died when water and electric guitars mixed: In 1972 **Les Harvey** of Stone the Crows touched a live wire onstage with wet feet (though wet with what remains a mystery) and was electrocuted. In 1973 **John Rostill** of the Shadows was another musician to be electrocuted by an electric guitar and permanently riffed at age thirty-one. In 1976 **Keith Relf** of the Yardbirds was rumored to have played his electric guitar in the bathtub but was actually doing so in his damp basement when he died by electrocution at thirty-three.

MISADVENTURE REDEFINED

"All I Wanna Do" was written for Sheryl Crow by **Kevin Gilbert,** who might have had other things on his mind when it came to his idea of fun when he penned the lyrics "All I wanna do is have a little fun before I die." Gilbert died from autoerotic asphyxiation at the age of twenty-nine in 1996.

SCOTT JOPLIN

Black performers of the 1800s didn't look on minstrel shows as negatively as one might imagine, since it was the only venue for their music. In fact, "Ragtime" was a spinoff of the fast-paced act that minstrel shows required to keep audiences enthralled. The idea was to "rag" (as in to cut up and alter) a traditional piece of music by changing the rhythm and tempo, and replace the counterpoint harmonies of classical music with syncopated African percussion harmonies. Some said they were "jazzing up" the sound. The craze began with the publication of Scott Joplin's "Maple Leaf Rag," followed by "The Entertainer," in addition to sixty other well received compositions he published. For the "Maple Leaf Rag," Scott Joplin was supposed to receive a one-cent royalty, though he collected only a fraction of this sum, netting $360 in 1900. Nevertheless, Joplin persisted and began work on the first opera written by an African American, *Treemonisha*, produced in 1911 with disappointing commercial results. Soon after, dementia from syphilis began to take its toll, and he wrote only phrases of music during brief interludes of lucidity. Scott Joplin died of the complications of syphilis in 1917 at age forty-nine, in obscurity and without even a notice of his death or obituary to be found anywhere. The rage of ragtime was gone as jazz took over as the *in* sound. Joplin's music remained relatively unknown until the movie *The Sting* (1973) gave it new life. In 1976 his opera *Treemonisha* won a Pulitzer Prize.

HELEN KELLER

Helen Keller was a pioneer for rights of the disabled. In 1891 when she was nineteen months old, she fell ill from scarlet fever, which left her not only blind but deaf as well. At seven years old she was taken to Alexander Graham Bell, an expert on hearing and speech, who encouraged her parents to enroll Helen in the Institute for the Blind in Boston. There, in her frustration to communicate, she would seem wild, thrashing about and was at first considered to have no mind capable of understanding—in short, an imbecile. Helen's father found a live-in private tutor, twenty-year-old Anne Sullivan, who taught Helen how to finger-spell, as Braille was then called. She learned the code for W-A-T-E-R, but never knowing light or sound, Helen couldn't correlate the words to the liquid these letters spelled. Anne thrust Helen's hand under water flowing from a pump, followed by the

Ondine syndrome is a medical term used to explain why people without other known ailments go to sleep and never wake up. Recently, researchers have focused on neurotransmitters in the brainstem that control breathing: A person can suddenly hyperventilate without reason and die, not able to control his breath. Some believe that the amount of involuntary breaths each person is arbitrarily allocated in life becomes "used up."

letters for water tapped into her hand. Suddenly Helen realized that the cool substance coming from the pump had a name and quickly learned how to read, write, and eventually speak. With Anne Sullivan's continued friendship, Helen became the first blind and deaf person to graduate from college in 1902. In 1915 the two women founded Helen Keller International, a nonprofit organization that worked to prevent blindness. Not only did Helen become an international speaker, writing twelve books, she also starred in a silent movie and tried her hand at a vaudeville tour. She died of Ondine syndrome during a nap in 1968 at age eighty-seven. Anne Sullivan also had a visual impairment, caused when doctors rubbed cocaine on her eyes before performing a procedure to treat pink eye when she was a child. By 1935, a year before her death, she too was totally blind. She died at age seventy of coronary artery disease.

GRACE KELLY

Grace Kelly's Oscar win brought her new status and subsequently attracted the attention of European royalty. When she married Prince Rainier III of Monaco in 1956, she was dubbed Her Serene Highness The Princess of Monaco and became the first Oscar winner to become a real princess. In 1982 she had a stroke while driving and crashed her car. She died the next day of brain trauma hemorrhage at age fifty-two.

JACK KEROUAC

Jack Kerouac was a poet and novelist known for rejecting the values of the 1950s looking for a new meaning from life. He is cited as the intellectual fuse that set off the explosion of the counterculture generation of the 1960s. Born in French-speaking Canada, Kerouac learned English at age six, eventually becoming a high school football star, which led to a scholarship at Columbia University. Before long he broke his leg, dashing his hopes of becoming a professional athlete. Yet when that bone snapped, so did the impetus to fulfill another lifelong dream—to write—begin. When the scholarship was lost, he shacked up with a girlfriend to stay in New York and there met the future stalwarts of the Beat Generation, including Allen Ginsberg, Neal Cassidy, and William Burroughs. During World War II Kerouac signed up with the Merchant Marines but was given a psychiatric discharge, citing "indifferent disposition." His first novel, featuring a traditional format, was published in 1950. But it would take another seven years to find a publisher for his experimental style, which would make him famous. Once *On the Road* was in print and hailed by the *New York Times* as the new voice of the generation, it was as fateful as the broken bone in his college days. His ambiguity over his fame and notoriety led him to drink even more. Instead of having an "indifferent disposition," it could be said he possessed a temperament of internal and ultimately fatal contradictions: He studied Buddhism yet called himself a Catholic; he lived the life of the hippies, nomadic and unattached to possession, yet disdained the movement, identifying more with improvisational jazz; he traveled the country and Mexico yet never had a driver's license. In 1969 at age forty-seven he died of a stomach hemorrhage caused by chronic alcoholism and cirrhosis of the liver with ninety dollars to his name. Today his estate is worth over $20 million.

The hep jive language admired in On the Road *can be traced to singer and radio personality* **Bulee "Slim" Gaillard,** *who became a sensation after his release of a recording "The Flat Foot Floogee" in 1938, followed by "Tutti Frutti." Slim's nonsensical voice and jive-talk pronunciation was exciting to some and confusing to others, to the effect that many of his songs were banned from radio as being too degenerate, with sexual innuendo, even if few understood what the songs were really about. Slim was later quoted by Ronald Reagan, had his "Floogee" song buried in the 1939 World's Fair time capsule, and is now considered by many as the father of Rap music. Despite making Kerouac's list of cool hipsters, he was unable to find a following for his music and faded from the scene, turning to acting, landing parts in a few TV shows, including the TV mini-series* Roots. *Eventually, in 1982, Dizzy Gillespie found him running a motel in San Diego and persuaded Slim to return to music. Before long Slim developed a cult following that led the way to a BBC special,* The World of Slim Gaillard *in 1989. Although dying from cancer, he rallied to make it back into a recording studio in 1990, though succumbed to the ultimate "switcheroony" (one of his jive words) from life to death in 1991 at age seventy-four.*

FRANCIS SCOTT KEY

"The Star-Spangled Banner" was written in 1814 by Francis Scott Key, a thirty-five-year-old aristocrat, lawyer, and amateur poet. He actually wrote only the lyrics and put them to a popular English song, "To Anacreon in Heaven," after witnessing the British bombardment of Baltimore. He circulated a handbill with the lyrics under the title, "Defense of Fort M'Henry," which at once became a popular patriotic number. Key died of pleurisy (when the lungs fill up with fluid) at age sixty-three in 1843. Not until 1931 did the song become America's national anthem.

THE AVERAGE AMERICAN LIFE SPAN IN 1850 WAS FORTY-ONE. IN 2006 LIFE EXPECTANCY REACHED SEVENTY-SEVEN.

JOHN MAYNARD KEYNES

In 1920 John Maynard Keynes's *Economic Consequences of Peace* was a bestselling nonfiction book. The British economist's views presented in his tome were ignored, which ultimately allowed the stock market crash at the end of the decade. Yet his theory that governments should intervene to forestall recessions, inflations, and other economic occurrences has since been adopted and is still in use. He died in 1946 at age sixty-two of the biological consequences of a ruptured heart valve.

"In the long run we are all dead."
—JOHN MAYNARD KEYNES

GENGHIS KHAN

Temujin, known as Genghis Khan, united nomadic Mongol tribes to form the largest landmass under one ruler before or since, subjugating over 100 million people, though killing at least 30 million in the process. Although he was born into a ruling stratum of a Mongolian nomadic tribe, when Temujin was nine his father was poisoned, and this forced his mother and siblings into impoverishment. At age twelve Temujin killed his brother for a bigger piece of fruit. When his mother scolded him, he showed absolutely no remorse. His impulsive violence, he learned, could help make him the leader of his small unit. A few years

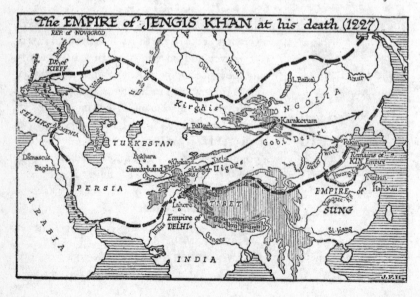

The EMPIRE of JENGIS KHAN at his death (1227)

later he was captured and treated harshly as a slave. Poverty, homicide, and cruelty proved an unavoidable combination, which formed him into one of the most vicious military leaders of all time. Once he invaded a city or enemy stronghold, he massacred every single person except a select few who were allowed to run ahead to the next city to tell of what happened when they resisted. Women, only if considered beautiful, were raped before they were murdered, the best chosen by Genghis Khan himself. It was this policy that caused his death. In 1227 he had finally beaten a long-resistant enemy and chose one lovely princess for his bed. When the time came for her rape, she pulled a knife from under her robe and castrated him. Although she was diced and quartered into a thousand pieces, the injury made it difficult for Genghis to ride a horse. In August of that year he fell off his saddle and died at age sixty-three. His body was buried in a secret location. To prevent the whereabouts of his final resting place from being found, everyone in the funeral procession was murdered. The exact site of his burial still remains a secret.

AS BIG AS HIS EMPIRE

Kubla Khan, the last of the great Khans and grandson of Genghis, was made famous by opium smoker Samuel Coleridge's poem "Kubla Khan": "In Xanadu did Kubla Khan / A stately pleasure-dome decree: / Where Alph, the sacred river, ran / Through caverns measureless to man / Down to a sunless sea." Kubla Khan was no stranger to warfare, attempting, unsuccessfully, to invade Japan twice, but he favored sitting on the royal throne rather than in the saddle, as his grandfather preferred. Toward the end of his life he grew heavier and heavier, preferring to dine on only animal organs. He was known to devour two large tiger livers for breakfast alone. He got so huge that he needed six elephants to carry him around on his throne. The symptoms of his fatal illness resemble gout, a condition that increases iron and uric acid in the bloodstream, and was exacerbated by his diet of organs. His joints became too swollen to move, and he died of sleep apnea, unable to catch his breath after a glutton-induced slumber at age seventy-eight in 1294.

VICTOR KILLIAN

Victor Killian played Pap in the 1939 version of *Huckleberry Finn*. He later had roles in many fight scenes, including one in *Reap the Wild Wind* with John Wayne in 1942, during which a stunt gone wrong caused him to lose one eye. During the 1950s Killian was brought to testify before the House Committee on Un-American Activities and was subsequently blacklisted. However, between 1976 and 1978 he was cast in the sitcom *Mary Hartman Mary Hartman* and played

Mary's grandpa the Fernwood Flasher. While he was watching TV in his Hollywood apartment in 1979, home invaders burst in. After what appeared to be a valiant struggle, Killian's body was found the next morning clubbed to death. He was eighty-seven. Five days later in the same Hollywood neighborhood eighty-three-year-old **Charles Wagenheim,** who played supporting roles in many crime dramas and is best

remembered as the thief in *Diary of Anne Frank* (1959), suffered a home invasion in his apartment. At age eighty-three he too was beaten to death. Three months later, a twenty-four-year-old nurse was arrested for the crimes.

*In 1953 **Philip Loeb** was playing the star role of the patriarch Jake in a popular television show called The Goldbergs when he was accused of being a Communist. He was promptly fired and could find work nowhere. In 1955 at age sixty-three he committed suicide with an overdose of barbiturates. He left a note that read: "Died of a sickness commonly called the blacklist."*

TED KNIGHT

Mary Tyler Moore was a household name from the sixties after she starred as the sexy wife Laura Petrie in *The Dick Van Dyke Show*. In the seventies, at the dawn of feminism, she returned as a spunky career woman that made hilarity then out of issues not so funny now, such as if a woman should ask a man out for a date. Ted Knight (Tadeus Konopka) made it big when he was cast as Ted Baxter, the not-so-bright anchorman who always got a laugh with his un-hip faux pas of peeing in his shoes. Knight was a C-list actor who couldn't pay his rent before he made it to the *Mary Tyler Moore Show*. After the show became a hit, he admitted to cheering himself up by hanging out at a local supermarket in the hopes of being recognized. He died at sixty-two in 1986 of cancer of the urinary tract. Before he died, Knight left wishes that his private funeral be fun, and he asked his long-time friend Ed Asner to send him off with a laugh track, reminiscent of the show's imaginary Chuckles the Clown. In the TV version of Chuckle's funeral Mary achieved a classic moment of comedy when she tried desperately to stifle her giggles to no avail. In real life, after Mary's only son died from a self-inflicted gunshot wound, officially deemed accidental in 1980, she saw no humor in funerals. Since then, the city of Minneapolis has erected a bronze statue of Ms. Moore in a carefree pose tossing her hat into the air. Knight got a star on the Hollywood Walk of Fame.

Barbara Colby starred in Phyllis, a Mary Tyler Moore spin-off that ranked in the top ten highest rated shows for 1975. She played Julie, Phyllis' boss at the photography place. In mid-season Barbara Colby was jumped while heading to her car in a parking lot near Broadway in New York City. Colby offered no resistance, though was shot anyway by the assailant. She died on the scene at age thirty-five. The shooter was never caught.

ERNIE KOVACS

In 1955 Ernie Kovacs (*The Ernie Kovacs Show*) exhibited how far-out the TV variety show could go, offering a zany combination of humor that is a direct predecessor of *SNL* and *Late Night with David Letterman*. Ernie Kovacs was the first to take the camera off the stage and point it behind the scenes, called "breaking the fourth wall," that only TV could do efficiently and with humor. Kovacs was extremely popular in the fifties and sixties with everyone except the IRS, since he didn't believe in taxes and refused to pay. In 1962, after drinking way beyond today's standards of what's acceptable to operate a car, he got into his Corvair (a car Ralph Nader later said was unsafe at any speed) to drive home on a rainy night. At the first turn he lost control when he tried to light a cigar, and he smashed head-on into a telephone pole. He was ejected from the car and died instantly, only one week before his forty-third birthday.

OTHER COMICS' UNFUNNY ENDINGS

In the sixties *Rowan and Martin's Laugh-In* gave the viewers even zanier skits to the beat of the psychedelic and bell-bottom culture that was emerging. **Dan Rowan** died in 1987 at age sixty-five of lymphoma cancer. Comedian **Flip Wilson** appeared on that show and later hosted his own variety hour, *The Flip Wilson Show*, becoming the first black American to have his name in the title of a primetime show. But his "working for the man" mindset made him ask for higher and higher raises until the program became overbudgeted and was canceled in 1974. Wilson took solace in the bottle and died of liver cancer in 1998 at age sixty-four. The longest-running variety show *Saturday Night Live* began in 1972 and has had a smorgasbord of actors and comedians pass through its gates. The dead of that cast include: **John Belushi,** of alcohol and drug abuse at age thirty-three in 1982; **Gilda Radner,** of ovarian cancer in 1989 at age forty-two; **Chris Farley,** of alcohol and drug abuse in 1997 at age thirty-three; **Phil Hartman** (forty-nine) was shot and killed by his wife in 1998; **Charles Rocket** (Charles Claverie) cut his own throat, committing suicide in 2005 at age fifty-six.

RAY KROC

Ray Kroc was the slap-on-the-back, glad-hand, milkshake machine salesman who made American cuisine and fast food synonymous. Kroc opened the first

store of the McDonald's Corporation in 1955, although there were nine previous nonfranchised McDonald's Kroc had co-owned with founders **Dick and Mac McDonald,** who perfected the simplified menu of burgers, fries, and shakes in San Bernardino, California. McDonald's now has over 30,000 stores in 120 countries and claims to serve more than 50 million people a day. A new McDonald's reportedly opens somewhere in the world every seven hours. Kroc was said to have eaten the company food on a regular basis and attributed his longevity to that, even if, for everyone else, America's fast-food diets are a contributing factor in 910,000 U.S. heart disease–related deaths annually. Kroc's most famous saying, which he used at sales meetings was "Are you green and growing or ripe and rotting?" This applied to his own life and his death when in 1984, as soon as the 50-billionth hamburger was sold, he succumbed to heart failure at age eighty-one. Mac died in 1971 at age sixty-nine of cancer, and Dick died in 1989 at age eighty-nine of respiratory failure.

Since 1954 ninety-five murders have occurred in McDonald's restaurants, not including parking lots or those waiting on drive-through lines. The worst occurred in 1984 at a San Diego McDonald's when a forty-one-year-old former security guard said, "Society had its chance." This deranged individual decided to hunt for humans and figured the fast-food restaurant the best place to find them. He killed twenty-one. Incidentally, McDonald's Corporation tore down the building and donated the land to the city as a memorial park.

MICHAEL LANDON

Bonanza made its TV debut in 1959 and was a smash hit for fourteen years, ranking only second as the most popular western of all time after *Gunsmoke*. The story centered on a father raising three sons on the Ponderosa ranch, a huge spread on the shores of Lake Tahoe in Nevada. Ben Cartwright, the father, was **Lorne Greene**: He died from an ulcer at age seventy-two in 1987. Two of the three sons died young: The middle son, Hoss, played by **Dan Blocker**, a 6-foot-3, 300-pound, good-natured guy on and off screen died in 1972 at age forty-three of a pulmonary embolism after routine gall bladder surgery. The youngest son, Little Joe, played by Michael Landon, later went on to star in *Little House on the Prairie* and *Highway to Heaven*. Landon died at age fifty-four in 1991 of pancreatic cancer. Married three times, with nine children, he is remembered most for how he publicly faced news of his fatal illness with an unusual frankness. Blocker's type of embolism and Landon's cancer are often caused by exposure to chemicals, frequently from too much contact with butoxyethanol, a chemical in many household cleaning products. It seems likely that both actors breathed air or had skin contact with the chemical while on the set of *Bonanza*. The family cook, Chinese immigrant Hop Sing, played by Victor Sen Yung also died from exposure to chemicals, this time from his real-life kitchen: He died in 1980 at age sixty-five due to carbon-monoxide poisoning, stemming from a gas leak in a household appliance.

EVERY YEAR 32,000 AMERICANS DIE FROM CANCER OF THE PANCREAS AND MORE THAN 500 DIE FROM UNINTENTIONAL CO POISONING.

RODE OFF INTO THE SUNSET

The three top television westerns were *Gunsmoke, Wagon Train,* and *Have Gun Will Travel. Gunsmoke* featured Marshal Matt Dillon, modeled on Wyatt Earp. **Howard McNear** played morbid Doc Charles Adams: He died of a stroke in 1969 at age sixty-three.

Georgia Ellis was the prostitute Kitty Russell on *Gunsmoke*: She died in 1988 at age seventy-one of AIDS, acquired after she married a bisexual younger husband.

Wagon Train was a weekly drama portraying a clean-cut version of post–Civil War America's journey westward, featuring **Ward Bond** as Major Seth Adams. He died in 1960 at age fifty-seven of a heart attack. *Have Gun Will Travel* was about a professional gunfighter named Paladin, played by **Richard Boone** and Kim "Hey Boy" Chan by **Kam Tong**: Boone holstered his six-shooter for good as a result of cancer in 1981 at age sixty-three. Tong bowed out at sixty-two, going in 1969 of heart failure.

LAO-TZU

Lao-Tzu, a Chinese sage who wrote the *Tao Te Ching*, translated as *The Book of the Way*, subsequently founded Taoism. Lao-Tzu was a clerk in the Zhou dynasty court. Why he began collecting old axioms and sayings and transcribing these into a book with his unique style of presentation is uncertain and surely not one of his official jobs. People asked him to clarify his message, but he refused, not wanting to create a formal dogma; the use of ambiguity, paradox, and analogies found in the text allowed for broad and personal interpretation. Lao-Tzu is believed to have been reincarnated twelve times, each time working as a clerk in the court, living in total nine hundred years, until he was capable of writing all he learned into the *Tao*. Before he was last seen riding a water buffalo out of town into the wilderness, he was asked if he was leaving the city to die in solitude. He answered, "Life and death are one thread, the same line viewed from different sides."

LASSIE

The original Lassie was a male Collie named Pal, used in the first 1943 movie *Lassie, Come Home*. The owner hired a dog trainer by the name of Rudd Weatherwax to get the Collie (three years old at the time) ready for the movie, but when the owner couldn't pay the exorbitant training bill Weatherwax presented, the original owner had to turn over his best friend Pal as payment. Weatherwax then bred Pal and produced hundreds of Lassies, with nine of the original dog's direct male descendants featured in TV and movies. Lassie was awarded a star on the Hollywood Walk of Fame and died at age nineteen in 1959 of old age. The Lassie called Baby, seen in the TV series with Timmy, died at age nine of cancer in 1963.

*Another famous animal actor was **Flipper**, a female dolphin whose actual name was Mitzi. She was trained and kept at the Dolphin Research Center in Grassy Key, Florida. She died of a heart attack at age fourteen in 1972 and was buried under a leaping dolphin statue on the front lawn of the research center. Life expectancy of a wild dolphin is twenty-five years.*

ROBERT E. LEE

Robert E. Lee was a graduate of West Point, though he sided with the South and became its most celebrated general. After the war his mansion and its surrounding grounds that overlooked Washington, D.C., were turned into Arlington National Cemetery as a sort of payback, making his plantation unusable for anything but hallowed ground for dead northern soldiers. He narrowly escaped a war tribunal that wished to hang him as a traitor. He asked for a pardon during the national period of amnesty, though it was never granted until President

Jimmy Carter did so posthumously in 1981. Lee became president of Washington College in Lexington, Virginia, a year after the war and remained in that position until his death at the age sixty-three in 1870 of a stroke and complications from pneumonia.

VIVIEN LEIGH

Vivien Leigh won two Oscars, one for *Gone With the Wind* (1939) and another for *A Streetcar Named Desire* (1951). Her bipolar disorder made many consider her hard to work with because of extreme mood changes. She succumbed to tuberculosis in 1967 at age fifty-three.

Tuberculosis (TB) is a bacterium that has been on the planet since before the dinosaurs and has killed humans since their arrival. Preserved tissue of Egyptian mummies has been known to contain tuberculosis still capable of regenerating and infecting people in modern times. Spread by sneezing, coughing, and spitting, fear of this disease's contagious nature was the cause for the first U.S. law in 1910 prohibiting upchucking in public, except in designated spittoons. In 2006, 15 million people had TB and 1.5 million died, usually after suffering a high fever in conjunction with blood-filled vomit spasms.

SINCLAIR LEWIS

Sinclair Lewis was the first American to win the Nobel Prize for Literature, in 1930, particularly because his writings portrayed critical views of American culture and capitalism: "When fascism comes to America it will be wrapped in a flag and carrying a cross." He started by publishing fairy tale novels until he hit his mark with his more famous works, including *Main Street* and *Babbitt*. He died from the complications of alcoholism in 1951 at age sixty-five.

LIBERACE

Wladziu Valentino Liberace was a flamboyant entertainer, a classical pianist by training, who had a hugely popular show in the 1950s. During his heyday he commanded $50,000 a week for his Las Vegas appearances, and had over 150 fan clubs comprised of millions of middle-aged women totally ga-ga over his precisely coiffeured hairdos and extravagant costumes. His trademark number, "I'll Be Seeing You," was the song he always chose as the closing theme for his television and public performances. Liberace's love of the song seemed to haunt him in an ironic way, especially after a botched plastic surgery prevented him from fully closing his eyes. After his death at age sixty-seven in 1987 due to complications of AIDS, it was impossible for his estate to sell the house he purchased for $3 million. The fear then that the disease could be acquired by touching his furniture was so great that the lavish, chandelier-decorated property eventually sold at public auction for a mere $325,000.

MUSICIANS WITH AIDS

In 1985 **Ricky Wilson** of the B–52s at age thirty-two dies of it; **Tom Fogerty** of the Creedence Clearwater Revival at forty-eight in 1990; **Freddie Mercury** of Queen in 1991 at age forty-five; **Ray Gillen** of Black Sabbath at age thirty-four in 1993; Rapper **Eazy-E (Eric Wright)** at thirty-one in 1995; **Lonnie Pitchford**, Mississippi blues guitarist, dead from it at age forty-three in 1998; and **Robbin Crosby** of Ratt was forty-two in 2002, dead from AIDS.

ABRAHAM LINCOLN

Abraham Lincoln was the sixteenth president of the United States from 1861 through 1865 during the nation's most critical event, namely the Civil War. He kept no one happy during his term and was routinely criticized from all sides, though in the end he prevailed in abolishing slavery and keeping the Union together. On April 14, 1865, four days after General Lee had surrendered, Lincoln was scheduled to attend a play, *Our American Cousin*, at Ford's Theater. He nearly stayed home when his wife Mary Todd came down with a tremendous migraine, but she insisted she could bear it and squeezed Lincoln's hand when bolts of pain became too unbearable. John Wilkes Booth had first intended to kidnap the president in exchange for prisoners, but he decided at the last minute on assassination. When the funniest line of the play was delivered, with hopes that laughter would drown out the noise of his gunshot, he crept into Lincoln's balcony box and fired a single-shot, round-slug .44 at point-blank range that penetrated the skull and rested six inches inside Lincoln's brain. The president lingered in a coma for nine hours before expiring at age fifty-six. Twelve days later, Booth, at age twenty-four, was cornered and shot in the neck by Union soldiers. His body was locked in a prison warehouse and released four years later to the Booth family to be buried in an unmarked grave at the Greenmount Cemetery in Baltimore. Abraham Lincoln's body went on a 1,700-mile train ride around the country before he was buried. People lit bonfires near the train route and lined up for miles along the tracks in cold rain with bowed heads.

ASSASSINATED U.S. PRESIDENTS

At age forty-nine **James Garfield** was shot in Washington, D.C., on July 2, 1881. He died two months later on September 19.

At age fifty-eight **William McKinley** was shot in Buffalo, New York, on September 6, 1901. He died on September 14 of internal bleeding before the procedures of blood transfusion were known.

At age forty-six **John F. Kennedy** was assassinated in Dallas, Texas, on November 22, 1963.

SONNY LISTON

Sonny Liston grew up as the twenty-fourth of twenty-five children fathered by an abusive Arkansas sharecropper; dirt poor and uneducated, he ran away to live with his mother in St. Louis when he was thirteen. With the move to the city, Sonny quickly got into a different kind of trouble, gravitating toward the underworld and finding work as a leg-breaker for the Mafia. After a two-year stint in prison he was paroled to a boxing promoter with known ties to organized crime, and for the rest of his career his contracts were managed and owned by Mafioso kingpins. Sonny had a closed fist that measured fourteen inches—getting hit by one of his punches was like getting whacked in the face with a shovel. In 1962 he beat the well-liked Floyd Patterson and became the world champ, though he was considered a malevolent force in the sweet science of boxing. Most boxers have records stating their wins and losses (50 wins, 39 by knockout, and 4 losses), Sonny's records always includes mention of his 19 arrests. Two of those boxing losses continue to stir debate among sports fans, namely, his apparent lay-downs to young Cassius Clay, soon to be Mohammad Ali. According to his wife, Geraldine Liston, she claimed that Sonny had told her he was going to win big by losing to Ali in the first round. By 1969 at age thirty-seven, Sonny had retired and moved into gambling and had a propensity for drink and apparently some drug dealing. On New Year's Eve, 1970, in his Las Vegas home, he injected himself with heroin and died of an overdose. When his body was discovered five days later, the police found a balloon filled with heroin on the bathroom counter near where he had fallen. Autopsy reports stated that he died of cardiac arrest. Others (who might not understand the grip of heroin addiction) say someone must have put a gun to his head and forced him to take a "hot shot," since former associates claimed Sonny had always been fearful of hypodermics. Perhaps, as theories go, he was talking too much and the Mafia wanted him put down. Nevertheless, the barefoot kid who had punched his way into sports history and who had lived a life as a raging tornado was dead at age thirty-eight.

DAVID LIVINGSTONE

DISCOVERY of the SAGE of CHAPPAQUA by H.M. STANLEY.

In 1871 the *New York Herald* commissioned journalist **Henry Morton Stanley** to find the African explorer and lost missionary Dr. David Livingstone. Livingstone had been exploring Africa for thirty years, and even after Stanley found him, he used Stanley's supplies to keep at it. Livingstone died in his boots, found dead of dysentery in a kneeling position at the foot of his cot at age sixty. The natives buried Livingstone's heart in Africa and sent his body back to London. Henry Morton Stanley was most famous for uttering the words "Dr. Livingstone, I presume." After he fought in the Civil War on the Confederate side, Stanley became a journalist covering frontier expansion. He turned many into legends with stories he published in *Harper's Magazine*, including the exploits of Wild Bill Hickok. Stanley, despite his Woodward and Bernstein journalistic fame, stayed in the Congo and eventually became the first to develop the region and open it up to commerce. At age sixty-three in 1904 he caught a chill that developed into pneumonia and pleurisy. He died in London.

SCREW 'EM

Few women choose their hero path via exploration. One notable exception was **May French-Sheldon**, a wealthy American woman who became known as the first woman explorer of Africa. In the 1890s, with an entourage of 130 Zanzibarian men, she explored East Africa and the Congo. The press at the time called her a raging madwoman, but she didn't care. She went on to lecture for many years about her travels, stressing—way before it was fashionable—that a "woman could do anything a man could." She died of pneumonia in 1936 at age eighty-nine.

VINCE LOMBARDI

Vince Lombardi at first studied to be a priest until he found football to be a greater passion. After ten years as a second-string coach at West Point, he signed on to be head coach of the then-worst team in pro football, the Green Bay Packers. Through his methods of discipline he turned the team into a winning force and watched as the Packers beat the New York Giants 31–0 in 1961 for the National Football League championship, considered one of the more memorable upsets in football history. Lombardi continued to win throughout the sixties, again making football history as the coach of the Packers in the first Super Bowl in 1967, when his team beat the Kansas City Chiefs, 35–10. His view on winning, losing, and life in general was so succinct that his philosophy became incorporated into American culture. Lombardi's quotes are treated by many with the reverence accorded religion. His one-liners are used not only in sports but in business and in motivational trainings: "Once you learn to quit, it becomes a habit" and "It's not whether you get knocked down, it's whether you get up" are but a sample of his long list of musings. When he died at age fifty-seven in 1970 of colon cancer, 3,500 attended his funeral. Many in the crowd—steely-faced football players among them—wept openly. Although the cancer that killed him is often caused by inherited genetic mutations, high-glycemic foods that drastically jump blood sugar levels have also proved to be a major contributing factor. These include the sideline staples during football games—candy bars and orange juice. In addition, during his heyday, Lombardi regularly smoked cigarettes while pacing the sidelines. He never latched on to someone else's slogan: "Hang tough; Don't puff!"

DEADLY SPORTS RITUALS

After the University of Nevada football team's last game ended in a winning season, the coach **George Allen** had a celebratory cooler of ice-cold water dumped over his head. The next day he came down with bronchitis, which soon developed into pneumonia. The former NFL coach of the Rams and Redskins died five weeks later in 1990 at age seventy-two. However, his death certificate does not state death by Gatorade-dousing but lists heart spasm caused by arrhythmia, an irregular heartbeat, as the final penalty flag.

LONE RANGER

Clayton Moore played the masked cowboy riding high on his horse Silver in the TV favorite *The Lone Ranger* during the early fifties. With the help of the wise, quiet Indian Tonto, played by Jay Silverheels, the duo went about righting injustices in over one hundred episodes. Moore had the odd fate for an actor of wearing a mask onscreen so that even during the fame of the show, he was hardly

recognized. Perhaps for this, there is no other actor who clung to his role so diligently, regularly donning the mask and costume to go out in public, some say even while in his car at a drive-through for fast-food. He was seen wearing his Lone Ranger costume shortly before his death of a heart attack in 1999 at age eighty-five. Silverheels took much less affinity to his role as Tonto and passed away quietly, though coughing laconically, at age sixty in 1980, of pneumonia.

JACK LORD

Hawaii Five-O aired from 1968 to 1980, featuring cops in pursuit of thugs and organized criminals tainting the beautiful landscape of the Hawaiian Islands. This show has been syndicated into more foreign languages than any other show and still plays regularly throughout the world. "Five-O" is currently street slang for any police. Jack Lord (John Joseph Patrick Ryan), who played the incorruptible Steve McGarrett, was noted for his famous line "Book 'em, Danno! Murder One!" He died of congestive heart failure at the age of seventy-seven in 1998. Chin Ho Kelly was McGarrett's reliable Hawaiian sidekick. Played by Kam Fong, he died at age eighty-four of lung cancer in 2002. Kono was played by Zulu (Gilbert Frances Lani Damian Kauhi). He suffered from diabetes, had a kidney transplant that was rejected, and died in 2004 at age sixty-six. Jack Lord was originally sought to play *Star Trek*'s Captain Kirk, but he lost out to William Shatner because he wanted a percentage of the royalties. Off set, Lord lived a reclusive life in his mansion on Hawaii and was known to consider himself very cultured, giving impromptu poetry readings while on the set of his cop dramas. He left an estate worth $40 million.

LOSING LOTTERIES

> "We must believe in luck. For how else can we explain the success of those we don't like?"
> —JEAN COCTEAU

By definition, every contest requires a winner, in addition to an even larger crowd of losers. It's been said victory is sweet, yet the ill, or sour, aspects of winning are often not realized until much later. The word lottery comes from the Italian *loto,* meaning destiny or fate.

During the American Revolution Ben Franklin offered a lottery to pay for cannons, and George Washington conducted one to build roads. By the late 1800s lotteries were everywhere, creating a huge class of gamblers and debtors. By 1905 the Supreme Court effectively banned lotteries, and games of chance remained underground until 1964 when the State of New Hampshire offered the first government-run lottery called

The Sweepstakes. Today, thirty-nine states have lotteries.

In 1988 a Maine cab driver **Michael Allen** won $5.8 million. He split the winnings with his roommate at the time for his help in reminding Michael to purchase the ticket. After he won, this generosity continued and earned him the nickname Megabucks Mike by those who frequented the gay clubs where he partied. He also had a reputation as a risk taker a was described by bar employees as skittish and insecure, "quick to buy a round of drinks and a round of friends." In 1997 at age thirty-four he was beaten to death in a Lewiston, Maine, hotel room. Two young men in their twenties were arrested for the crime in a California YMCA weeks later.

In medieval and colonial England the idea of winning the lottery was more than hoping for good luck because if a person was in debt and needed the winnings to pay off a creditor, losing was practically a death sentence. Then, anyone who owed money was thrown in prison until the creditor was repaid. Once in jail, the imprisoned were expected to pay for their food and clothing, which inevitably increased their debt even further. Debtors died of starvation and exposure. The punishment, in theory, reimbursed the creditor with the knowledge that the accused would have a slow, agonizing, and undignified passing. "Gaol fever," using the Old English word for "jail," was the usual cause of death cited; it was probably typhus.

In June 1997 **Billie Bob Harrell, Jr.**, a former Home Depot stock boy, won $31 million in the Texas state lottery. He went out and bought a fashionable home and gave away money to acquaintances and strangers alike. Twenty months later, at age forty-nine, with the stress of giving and with dwindling cash, he lost fifty pounds before he locked himself in his bedroom, stripped naked, and shot himself in the chest with a shotgun.

> "Shallow men believe in luck. Strong men believe in cause and effect."
> —RALPH WALDO EMERSON

After fifty-eight-year-old former carpenter **Philip Alan Kitchen** won the lottery, he hired a caretaker and a cook, but all he wanted to do was be left alone on his sofa and drink. In 2002, by the time he died of pneumonia, he hadn't eaten any solid food for six weeks. He was found surrounded by cases of beer and whiskey, slumped over in soiled clothes amid his own feces.

In 2002 a lottery winner in England, **Dennis Elwell**, at age forty-eight killed himself by drinking cyanide seven months after his win. He tried to rekindle a romance with his wife, but when things didn't work out, he went back to the job as a factory worker and told a co-worker of the fatal dose he had just ingested. He was too far gone to be saved.

In 2004 **Oscar Cordoba**, a New Jersey lottery millionaire, stabbed his wife and killed his mother-in-law with a knife. And by that same year, Jack Whittaker, the biggest lottery winner in history, who walked away with a lump sum of $113 million in 2002, had racked up a litany of bad luck: He had been repeatedly robbed of more than a half million in cash, slipped Mickeys, and beaten.

He was also banned from numerous bars and allegedly threatened to kill the managers of the establishments from which he was banned. In 2004 when a teenager died in his house, he was sued for wrongful death. This was soon followed by news that his granddaughter Brandi Bragg (seventeen) was missing. The young girl was found three days later wrapped in a tarp, dead from a drug overdose.

In 2004, seventy-three-year-old **Carl Atwood** of Elwood, Indiana, was a lottery winner killed by a truck while he was walking to the grocery store, the same one where he had bought the winning ticket days before.

In 2005, seven years after **Gerald Muswagon** won a $10-million lottery jackpot, he had spent every last cent and hung himself in his parents' garage at age forty-two. And in that same year **Jeffrey Dampier, Jr.**, an Illinois lottery winner of $20 million, was kidnapped, robbed, and shot to death, allegedly by his twenty-three-year-old sister-in-law and her boyfriend.

"Everybody dreams of winning money, but nobody realizes the nightmares that come out of the woodwork."
—BANKRUPT EX-LOTTERY MILLIONAIRE WILLIAM "BUD" POST III, WHO WENT THROUGH $16 MILLION OF A PENNSYLVANIA LOTTERY WINNING BEFORE HE DIED OF RESPIRATORY FAILURE IN 2006

MACK THE KNIFE

Born Walden Robert Cassotto, **Bobby Darin** was one of the most popular teen idols of the fifties and was versatile in rock 'n' roll as well as in many other musical genres. Raised in poverty in the Italian slums of the Bronx, where a cardboard box served as his crib, he lacked medical care as a child and fell ill with numerous bouts of rheumatic fever, a disease that eats at the heart valves. Toward the end of his life he needed oxygen in order to sing. The song that won him a Grammy in 1959, "Mack the Knife," possibly presents some of the most bizarre lyrics of any popular song: "A-there's a tugboat ... down by the river don'tcha know Where a cement bag's just a'droopin' on down." Hardly anyone who sang the Darin version on the radio knew what it meant, although they could sense there was murder and mayhem about. The original Macheath, Mack the Knife, named

in the song, was a character in playwright **John Gay**'s *Beggar's Opera*, and he appeared onstage as a murderer, arsonist, and rapist. **Bertolt Brecht** adapted the play for a German audience, called *The Three Penny Opera* in 1928. In the 1950s **Marc Blitzstein** made it into a popular jazz number, using a list of names in the lyrics that were characters in the opera. John Gay died in 1732 at age forty-seven of "fever." His epitaph penned by himself is a classic: "Life is a jest, and all things show it, I thought so once, and now I know it." Brecht died of a heart attack in 1956 at age fifty-eight. The lyricist Marc Blitzstein died in 1964 at age fifty-eight soon after he was robbed and beaten by three Portuguese sailors after a sexual liaison gone bad on the island of Martinique.

FERDINAND MAGELLAN

Ferdinand Magellan was a captain in the naval service of Portugal, but he was stripped of his title and pension for disobeying orders and for trading with the Moors on the side. Queen Isabella of Spain then financed Magellan to find the legendary kingdom of John Priest. This fabled leader supposedly ruled a virtuous Christian kingdom somewhere in the heart of Asia, which held the Fountain of Youth, the actual key to the Gates of Paradise, as well as a very cool magic mirror that allowed the owner to view every kingdom on Earth at the same time. As farfetched as this sounds, everyone believed this John Priest actually existed. The question of his reality wasn't dispelled by scholars until the 1700s. In August 1519 Magellan left with 270 men, crossed the equator to Brazil, and crept down the coast to the tip of South America. From there he sailed northwest and into the Pacific, landing in Guam in February of the following year. By March 1521, when he reached the Philippines, he had 150 men left. A month later, Magellan got embroiled in local politics and offered to help in a battle, hoping to make a future trading partner for his own deals. When the warring natives recognized Magellan as the commander, they ganged up and impaled him with at least twenty thrusts from bamboo spears. He was forty-one. Only seventeen of the original crew made it back to Spain, yet Magellan is credited as the first to circumnavigate the globe. In reality, some historians claim it was a slave Magellan had acquired in Africa years before, one Henry the Black, who was the first to accomplish the feat.

ROCKY MARCIANO

Rocky Marciano is considered by many as the greatest fighter of all time, sporting a perfect record of 49 wins and 0 losses. As a kid, he knew from an early age that he wanted to box and practiced by punching at mailbags stuffed with rags that he'd hung behind his tenement. He grew up in poverty, son of Italian immigrant factory workers, in Brockton, Massachusetts. At first he thought that, instead of boxing, he could escape to a better life by means of baseball. When he didn't make the cut with the Chicago Cubs (he couldn't throw from home plate to second with accuracy), he fell back on Plan B and became a boxing pro a year later. No one thought this twenty-five-year-old, 190-pound, 5-foot–10-inch boxer had a chance. But he proved unbeatable, thanks to his unwillingness to quit and the ability to pack every ounce of his energy into every punch. He held the world title for three years and then retired, using his earnings to open restaurants. In 1969, as he was heading to a surprise party for his forty-sixth birthday, the private plane he flew in ran out of gas. It crashed two miles short of the runway, killing him.

MORE RINGMEN TKO'D BY ACCIDENTS

October 3, 1933: Heavyweight boxer W. L. Stribling (twenty-eight), who recorded the second most knockouts of all time with 126, was killed in a motorcycle accident. The man didn't smoke or drink and read the Bible; his career spanned 225 fights, more than 58 during one year alone. He was rushing to the hospital to see his newborn son when he had a head-on collision with a truck.

April 9, 1998: Big John Tate (forty-three), onetime WBA heavyweight boxing champion, died in an auto accident. He won a bronze medal in the 1976 Olympics and went on to hold the world title for less than six months in 1980. Shortly after, he turned to cocaine and was arrested numerous times for panhandling before his death.

September 3, 1999: Heavyweight boxer Cleveland "Big Cat" Williams (sixty-six), was killed in a hit-and-run accident in Houston, Texas. Williams fought Muhammad Ali at the

Astrodome in 1966 in a famous fight; he was knocked out in the third round. Two years before that fight, Big Cat was shot by a state trooper when the two got into an argument over a traffic ticket. This resulted in the loss of a kidney.

BOB MARLEY

Reggae king Bob Marley, credited with bringing Jamaican music to America, died of cancer that spread from his liver, lungs, and stomach to his brain at age thirty-six in 1981. Originally diagnosed with a melanoma cancer of the toe he refused treatment, based on Rastafarian beliefs: "Rasta no abide amputation. I don't allow a mon ta be dismantled." His last words before he died at Cedars Hospital in Miami were told to his son, Ziggy: "Money can't buy life." In his crypt was placed his guitar, the Bible, a soccer ball, and a marijuana joint.

"Trailer for sale or rent, Rooms to let . . . fifty cents, No phone, no pool, no pets . . . I ain't got no cigarettes," were the lyrics for Roger Miller's 1960s hit "King of the Road." Although with eleven Grammys he did eventually find a better hotel, he couldn't leave the cigarettes alone and died of throat and lung cancer at age fifty-six in 1992.

MUSICIANS' CANCER

In 1986 **Howard Greenfield,** who wrote "Breaking Up Is Hard To Do" and "Calendar Girl" with Neil Sedaka, got a brain tumor and died at age forty-nine. That same year **Linda Creed,** composer of "Greatest Love of All," ended by way of cancer at thirty-seven. In 1990 cancer got **Sarah Vaughan,** jazz singer, at sixty-six, and "That Old Black Magic" singer **Sammy Davis, Jr.,** at sixty-four.

In 1993 **Frank Zappa,** who made over sixty albums and composed songs about the weirdest stuff, such as the hit "Don't Eat the Yellow Snow," succumbed to prostate cancer at fifty-two. In 1994, **Telly Savalas,** most noted as the detective in the TV series *Kojak,* had a number-one hit "If" (1975). He died of prostate cancer the day after his seventy-second birthday party. That same year, bandleader and composer **Henry Mancini,** who wrote the theme music for *The Pink Panther,* died of liver cancer at seventy. In 1999 "Wishin' and Hopin'" was the **Dusty Springfield** (Mary Isabel Catherine Bernadette O'Brien) song that her fans were singing in earnest, but she died anyway of breast cancer at fifty-nine. In 2001 the singer called The Leatherman of the Village People, **Glenn Hughes,** known for "Macho Man," died of lung cancer at fifty. The king of punk, **Joey Ramone**

(Jeffrey Hyman), known for the song "I Wanna Be Sedated," had that right, when in the end he died of lymphoma at forty-nine. That same year, "My Sweet Lord" Beatle **George Harrison** was done from lung cancer at fifty-eight.

Fred Rogers sang many children songs, most noted "Won't You Be My Neighbor" for his long-running Mr. Rogers' Neighborhood *(1968 to 2001), featuring a low-tech puppet ensemble. Soon after he left his friendly neighborhood, he put on his famous cardigan sweater one last time before he died shortly after retirement of stomach cancer at seventy-four in 2003.*

In 2006 **Lou Rawls**, with the song "You'll Never Find Another Love Like Mine," died of brain cancer at seventy-two and **June Pointer** of the Pointer Sisters, with the hit "Jump (for My Love)," was taken by brain cancer at age fifty-two.

THERE ARE MORE THAN 50,000 NEW CASES OF LETHAL MELANOMA SKIN CANCER IN THE UNITED STATES EACH YEAR. DESPITE THE ALERTS AND SUNSCREENS AVAILABLE, THESE NUMBERS ARE RISING; SOME NOW BELIEVE THE INGREDIENTS IN SUN-BLOCKING LOTIONS ACTUALLY CAUSE CANCER. NEVERTHELESS, IT'S A DISEASE THAT IS ACQUIRED BY "LIFESTYLE," AND FOR VARIOUS REASONS, MEN ARE TWICE AS LIKELY AS WOMEN TO GET IT. IT AFFECTS PEOPLE OF ALL SKIN COLORS AND ETHNICITY. SKIN CANCER CAUSED MORE THAN 7,000 DEATHS IN 2006.

MARTIANS

My Favorite Martian (1963–1966) was a cool show about a curmudgeonly though intelligent and human-looking Martian, played by **Ray Walston**, who crashes his ship in Los Angeles. The plot centered on his relationship with a hip reporter, Tim O'Hara, played by **Bill Bixby**, who tries to keep his outerworld guest under wraps. The special effects were pretty cheap, but everyone loved to see the antennae rise out of the martian's head and see him pointing his finger to levitate things. Of the cast who went out of this world: Tim O'Hara's nosey landlady, Mrs. Brown, played by **Pamela Britton**, left by way of a brain tumor at age fifty-one in 1974. Tim's newspaper boss, Mr. Burns, played by **J. Pat O'Malley**, died in 1985 of congestive heart failure at age eighty. Detective Bill Brennan, played by **Alan Hewitt**, went by way of cancer in 1986 at age seventy-one. Bill Bixby (who later played Dr. David Banner of the *Incredible Hulk*) died in 1993 at age fifty-nine of prostate cancer. Uncle Martin was the last to leave, with the final disembarkation on New Year's Day, 2001, at the age of eighty-six of respiratory failure caused by Lupus.

*As Bill Bixby was ending his stint as Incredible Hulk, his ex-wife **Brenda Benet**, who played Lee DuMonde in* Days of Our Lives, *became distraught when their six-year-old son died of a throat infection. In 1982 Brenda put a .38 caliber pistol in her mouth to end a sorrow she could not bear, dying at age thirty-six.*

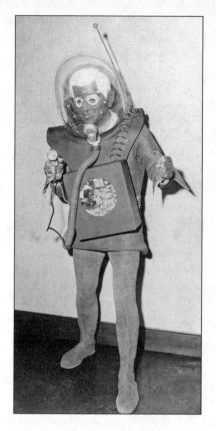

During the sixties another space show landed on the small screen: *Lost in Space* aired from 1965 to 1968 and was basically a Swiss Family Robinson re-do set in outer space. The plots were hard to believe and came across extremely fake, even for the limited special effects of the time. The dramatic tension was supposed to stem from Dr. Zachary Smith, played by **Jonathan Harris**, sent as a plant to sabotage the mission. In one episode, for example, Dr. Smith uses the last potable water to take a long shower, which doesn't get more than a kind-worded reprimand from the good-natured mom and dad, Professors Robinson, played by Guy Williams (formerly Zorro) and June Lockhart. Even kids watching the show couldn't believe Smith wouldn't be vaporized by the gamma-ray gun from the getgo. Of the cast who were lost in space for good, besides Zorro's Guy Williams, was Jonathan Harris, who died in 2002 when an embolism sabotaged his heart at age eighty-seven.

BILLY MARTIN

Baseball has always had its share of colorful rebels. Ball player and Yankee manager Billy Martin was loved and hated by an equal share of fans during his heyday. He knew how to win despite being fired and rehired as a Yankee manager a few times. On the field he was known for arguing with umpires and kicking up a cloud of dirt in their faces when a call came he didn't like. Off the field he was a confirmed heavy drinker. On Christmas Eve in 1989 at age sixty-one Martin was out drinking with a buddy when their car went off the road. Some say he died doing what he loved best—drinking and driving. The team retired the number he wore on his Yankee uniform, number one.

LEE MARVIN

Lee Marvin won best actor for his role as the drunken hired gun in the 1965 western comedy *Cat Ballou*. Offscreen Marvin drank with both hands, one for whiskey and the other for a beer chaser. Consequently he dealt with both alcohol problems and tumultuous relationships most of his life. He died of a heart attack in 1987 at age sixty-three.

GROUCHO MARX

In 1974 at age eighty-three, Groucho Marx was the oldest male actor to receive an Academy Award. He starred with his brothers in many successful films, including *Duck Soup* and *Monkey Business*. Groucho went on to become a star on TV, hosting the game show *You Bet Your Life* for eleven years, using his fast-talking wise-guy routine to maximum effect. Toward the end of his life he made news when he was seen frail, senile, and wheelchair-bound cared for by his young and beautiful companion Erin Fleming. When he died in 1977 at age eighty-six of pneumonia, Fleming was sued by Groucho's heirs and subsequently had to repay nearly half a million dollars she had been left by the Oscar-winning comedian.

Chico Marx died in 1961 at age seventy-four of a heart attack. Harpo Marx died on the operating table in 1964 at age seventy-five, and Zeppo Marx was seventy-eight when he passed away from cancer in 1979.

Thereafter, she was in and out of psychiatric institutions until, in 2003, at age sixty-one Fleming committed suicide.

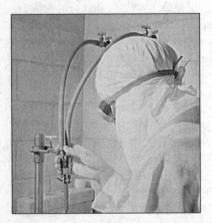

BETTY MacDONALD

Betty MacDonald put her heart and soul into her humorous memoir *The Egg and I*, which became an unexpected 1947 bestseller. The film rights to this story about a young woman on a chicken farm in Washington state were purchased for a downpayment of $100,000, a large sum at the time, with a percentage of movie profits to follow. However, soon after this financial windfall, MacDonald was sued for libel for $975,000 by the people of the small town, which was the basis of her book, on the grounds that they felt their portrayal was a humiliation. Defending herself caused the author to spend considerable money and grief, though MacDonald finally won the case when she proved that the characters in the book were composites. MacDonald eventually moved from the Washington area she loved to California, but the whole episode had put a crack in her joy and she died of cancer at the age of forty-nine in 1958.

FRANK McNAMARA

In 1950 Frank McNamara went out to dinner and was presented the bill as usual when the meal was through. He checked his wallet pocket, patted his suit jacket, and pulled out the insides of his pants' pockets. He then remembered he had left his cash in a different suit, and he paid with an IOU and a promise to be back. Later that night  McNamara came up with an economic epiphany: "Why should people be limited to spending what they are carrying in cash, instead of being able to spend what they can afford?" With the help of attorney **Ralph E. Schneider,** he established the first credit card, called Diners Club, which could be used in twenty-seven New York City restaurants, to be paid at the end of each month. On February 28, 1950, the first plastic was swiped for a meal back at the same restaurant, Major's Cabin Grill on West Thirty-third Street, to pay for a pair of charcoal-broiled thick steaks. Now, a million credit cards have been swiped in the time it took to read this sentence. Oddly, both founders died young: McNamara died in 1957 at age forty; Schneider died in 1964 at age fifty-five of what appeared to be heart failure. Soon after, long-time editor of *Diners Club Magazine*, **Sam Boal,** also died mysteriously in a fire while alone in his apartment at 403 East Fifty-seventh Street, New York City, when he was fifty-one. The company was then acquired by a conglomerate.

JOHNNY MERCER

With the lyrics "Things are never as bad as they seem … so dream," Johnny Mercer's "Dream" became the popular hit in 1945 for soldiers returning home from war. Mercer is considered one of the most prolific songwriters of all time, with a repertoire including "Moon River," "That Old Black Magic," and "Fools Rush In." Songs just flowed from him. He penned "One for My Baby (and One More for the Road)" on a napkin while sitting at P. J. Clarke's Midtown Manhattan bar in 1943. Although his brain may have been naturally wired for melody and lyrics, in 1976 at age sixty-six he died of surgical complications during an operation to remove brain cancer.

GLENN MILLER

In 1940 "Fools Rush In" was the top jukebox favorite performed by (Alton) Glenn Miller. Soon after, Miller became a cultural icon, representing the all-American, clean-cut bandleader of the time. When the war started, Miller joined the Air Corps and was promoted to major. He served by performing live for the troops and on military radio. According to official U.S. papers, Miller was in an English warplane that simply vanished as it crossed the English Channel to take him to a performance in Paris on December 15, 1944, at age thirty-nine. But no RAF flight-plan documents were found to cor-

roborate the official U.S. release. Glenn's brother, Herb Miller, stated in 1983 that Glenn died of lung cancer in a hospital in Paris and had been depressed, irritable, and exhausted during the last months of his life. In 1997 a German journalist, Udo Ulfkotte, claimed to have discovered documents that Miller was shot. Miller was allegedly having an affair with a French widow. She turned out not to be a widow after all, and when her husband returned from a German POW camp, he found Miller and his wife in bed and shot the bandleader. Another report indicated that Miller had a heart attack in a Parisian brothel, and because the government wanted to keep troop morale up, they instead decided to say Miller was missing in action as cause of death. Some say he remained in France and lived out a quiet life with his mistress until his actual death in 1981. Ultimately, Miller has four causes of death: missing, heart attack, cancer, and gun wound. No body has ever been found.

SAL MINEO

For some actors the crime portrayed on the tube followed them into real life, or vice versa. Sal Mineo is most famous for his portrayal of homosexual Plato in *Rebel Without a Cause*, though he acted in more than sixty TV programs from *Mission: Impossible*, *My Three Sons*, to *The Avengers*. He was known as the Switchblade Kid for his juvenile, wild-boy persona on and off the screen. Son of a Bronx casket maker, Sal first lived the roles on the streets that he would later play on TV and in films. In 1976 at age thirty-seven he was stabbed to death with a pearl-handled switchblade in a dark alley behind a West Hollywood apartment. Some say it was over a drug deal, while others say it was over a homosexual tryst. Prosecutors said it was a mugging gone bad and convicted career criminal Lionel Williams of murder, sentenced him in 1979 to fifty-one years to life, though he was paroled in 1990. He continues to profess his innocence.

*Another actor unable to leave a harsh real-life behind was **Tara Correa-McMullen**. In the TV drama Judging Amy (1998–2005) Tara was cast as a teen gang member, playing the role of Graciela Reyes. Her acting success didn't go to her head; she remained loyal to her neighborhood street gang. In 2005 she was killed in a gang-related shooting outside an apartment complex in Inglewood, California, at age sixteen.*

MARGARET MITCHELL

Gone With the Wind, the first and only novel written by Margaret Mitchell, was a runaway success from the moment it was published in 1936. The book won the Pulitzer Prize and is still considered the most purchased book, other than the Bible, selling over two hundred thousand copies a year. Mitchell learned of the stories she used in her epic while sitting on the laps of old Confederate veterans when she was a young girl growing up in Georgia. In fact, she wasn't told the South lost the war until she was ten. She wrote her book while laid up with a broken ankle and told no one other than her husband of her literary aspirations. At the time she was employed by the *Atlanta Journal* and had an assignment to take publisher Howard Latham from Macmillan Publishing Company around town supposedly in search of new southern writers. Margaret brought the partially completed and heaping *Gone With the Wind* manuscript to Latham's hotel later that night after a friend of hers laughed at the possibility that she possessed any talent. She sent a telegram the next day, asking Latham to send the manuscript back. He refused, convinced her of its worth, and sent Margaret Mitchell an advance to finish the book. Supposedly, Margaret wrote another book, which was recently found in notebooks among her letters, but she never pursued publication of anything else. In 1949 she was heading to see a movie and stepped into the street without looking and was hit by a taxi. She died five days later of internal injuries at age forty-eight. The twenty-five-year-old taxi driver Hugh D. Gravitt was convicted of involuntary manslaughter and sentenced to one year to eighteen months in jail. He's currently alive, living in Georgia, and unwilling to talk about the accident.

THELONIOUS MONK

Thelonious Monk was a self-taught pianist and composer. Although he performed with many of the great jazz musicians, his recordings generally sold poorly; he remained long overlooked and unpopular with all except other musicians who were formatively influenced by his playing style and his compositions. His life was punctuated by odd bursts of behavior, such as spontaneously leaping from the piano bench to run around in circles: He even became reclusive while touring, not speaking to other members of his group for months at a time. He finally communicated only through his wife until he abruptly retired and went into seclusion. Monk spent the last years of his life under the care of the Baroness Nica de Koenigswarter, a well-known patron of the arts, in her Weehawken, New Jersey, mansion. During his life Monk was sent to the psyche ward many times and was formally diagnosed as bipolar. Records indicate that he may also have been suffering from schizophrenia or a form of Tourette's syndrome, all of which manifested under symptoms classified as pathological introversion disorder. This life of autismlike mental disabilities made it more difficult for Monk to achieve the greatness he strove to attain. He died of a stroke at sixty-four in 1982.

MARILYN MONROE

Marilyn Monroe, born Norma Jean Mortenson to a mother who worked as a film cutter for RKO, was fathered by one of possibly three different men her mother was seeing at the time. She was placed in foster homes and orphanages until she was married at age sixteen. In 1945 an army photographer looking to do a spread about women behind the war effort met Marilyn working in a parachute factory and spotted her modeling potential. He had an affair with the teen and signed her to a modeling agency. Her success in modeling led to a screen test and a contract with Twentieth Century for a salary of $125 a week in 1946. She acted in a number of smaller roles until 1953 when she was given a more substantial part, the same year Hugh Hefner bought a nude layout of Marilyn taken during her struggling years and featured her in his new magazine *Playboy*. From then on she was a sensation and became an icon of sexy American beauty. She went on to marry baseball legend Joe DiMaggio and playwright Arthur Miller, in addition to having numerous affairs with leading men in both film and politics. Ultimately, seeking the unattainable love she never had as a child, she found solace in pills and booze, becoming unreliable when cast in movies, and unable to have a relationship with the few men who did try tremendously hard to love her. She was found dead, deemed a probable suicide, in her apartment at age thirty-six in 1962 from a drug overdose of Nembutal and chloral hydrate, prescription barbiturates. Due to Marilyn's affiliation with both JFK and Robert Kennedy, as well as missing telephone records and inconsistencies in the crime scene, many floated theories that Marilyn was murdered. The title of her last unfinished film, *Something's Got to Give*, prophetically summed up her last days, making the only conspiracy theory to hold weight the effort made after her death not to take the names and reputations of others down with her.

When Marilyn Monroe sang an embarrassingly sexy version of "Happy Birthday to You" for President Kennedy, she probably didn't know, among other things, that the song was written by **Patty Hill,** *a kindergarten teacher, in 1893. Whenever the song is played, Time Warner, who bought the copyright from Ms. Hill's estate after she died in 1946 at age seventy-eight, receives royalties, to the happy tune of $2 million each year. Restaurants, not wishing to pay a license fee, have since come up with goofy versions to sing to their customers. Attempts to collect from those who sing the song in private, estimated at more than one hundred million times a year, has been daunting and unsuccessful to date, although an honor system has been suggested.*

Marilyn Monroe lookalike **Anna Nicole Smith** *loved the original blond bombshell so much she even rented Marilyn's former house to live in. Although Anna Nicole had nearly as much success from her* Playboy *spread, parlaying it into a lucrative modeling career, she never matched Monroe's acting roles or the caliber of men she chose to be at her side. However, in the most contemporary example of how death is often subconsciously predetermined, she too died as Marilyn did, relying on drugs to fix it all, at age thirty-nine in 2007.*

MARIA MONTESSORI

Maria Montessori was the first modern-era woman to become a physician in Italy and yet was assigned the task, thought impossible, of educating what was considered "mentally retarded" and "uneducable" children in Rome. Her book, *The Montessori Method*, published in 1912, explained the method she used in her school, which she opened in 1907. Her technique provided a method of education that treated each child differently, and allowed her students to pass the same test as "normal" children. Before her death of pneumonia at age eighty-one in 1952 she was nominated three times for the Nobel Peace Prize but never won.

ELIZABETH MONTGOMERY

Jack Cassidy, an actor seen in numerous TV series from Bewitched *to* Columbo, *was in the end consumed by stress and alcoholism: He had fallen asleep smoking in bed and burned himself to death in 1976 at age forty-nine. David Cassidy of the* Partridge Family *was his son.*

Witches twitched their noses into American homes with the release of *Bewitched* in 1964 and aired until 1972. The sitcom portrayed a safe "mixed-marriage" for the time about a witch, Samantha Stephens (Elizabeth Montgomery), who married a mortal, Darin (**Dick York and Dick Sargent**), to the disapproval of her mother, Endora (**Agnes Moorehead**). The special effects were new to TV, though they must have had the actors exposed to some unknown carcinogenic, considering the death of its stars: **Alice Pearce**, who played the first Gladys Kravitz, died in 1966 of cancer at age forty-eight during the second season. Agnes Moorehead died of uterine cancer at age seventy-three in 1974, though she believed she was exposed to radiation during the filming of *The Conqueror* in 1956, which used a Utah nuclear testing site as a film location. Dick York, the original "Durwood," resigned from the show to enter drug rehabilitation and later gained one hundred fifty pounds and lost all his teeth. When he died in 1992 of lung cancer and emphysema, he was attempting to come out of financial ruin and destitution after a failed stint at cleaning houses. He became an advocate for the homeless. Darin number two, Dick Sargent, who later served as grand marshal at the Los Angeles Gay Pride day, died of prostate cancer at age sixty-four in 1994. Montgomery, who had affairs with both the director and producer of *Bewitched* while filming the show, died of colorectal cancer in 1995 at age sixty-two. The absent-minded Aunt Clara, played by **Marion Lorne**, couldn't keep track of all the medications required to treat her cancer and died of a heart attack before the disease could take her at age eighty-two in 1968. The only player not to succumb to this disease was Larry Tate, Darin's boss, played by **David White**. He died in 1990 at age seventy-four of a heart attack, never the same after his thirty-three-year-old son was aboard the terrorist-bombed Pan Am Flight 103 in 1988.

MOOSEKETEER

The MTV of the fifties was *The Mickey Mouse Club*, a popular TV series produced by the Disney Company. This musical and variety show included skits moralizing on how teens facing the typical obstacles of growing up could turn to trusted elders for advice. One such wise oldster was the potbellied **Roy Williams,** whom the kids called "The Big Mooseketeer." Insiders said he hid bottles all over the set and allegedly guzzled from his whiskey-filled flask whenever his back was to the camera. He was on the show supposedly as the "girls' protector," yet whenever the kid actors' guardians weren't looking, he would pull the youngsters aside and tell them raunchy jokes. When Roy died at age sixty-nine in 1976 of a heart attack, he was buried wearing his Mickey Mouse Club hat.

JIM MORRISON

Jim Morrison, a devotee of William Blake and Jean-Paul Sartre, named his group the Doors for Aldous Huxley's *The Doors of Perception*, of which he liberally oiled the hinges with alcohol, LSD, and any drug he could get hold of, except heroin. It is said he died in a bathtub in Paris of a heroin overdose, though no autopsy report or open-casket funeral followed, and the death certificate was signed illegibly by a doctor no one can find. The only person to see him dead was his girlfriend, Pamela Courson, who committed suicide a few years later. Officially, he died of an overdose at age twenty-seven in 1971; unofficially, his grave in Le Père-Lachaise Cemetery in Paris is visited frequently by an aged hippie eerily similar to Morrison.

OVERDOSE ROSTER

In 1968 **Frankie Lymon** known for "Why Do Fools Fall in Love?" and "I'm Not a Juvenile Delinquent," nevertheless must have taken some wrong turn, because

he died of a heroin overdose at age twenty-five. In 1971 **Mary Ann Ganser,** with the hit "Leader of the Pack," while with the Shangri-Las, was permanently left behind after dying of a drug overdose at age twenty-four, even if her band members insist it was an infected mosquito bite that did her in.

Janis Joplin went to superstar status with "Me and Bobby McGee," among other gravelly voice folksy-rock numbers, especially after her performance at the legendary Woodstock music festival in the summer of 1969. Caught up in the image of feminist blues singer and Beat poet, Janis downed the syrupy liquor Southern Comfort by the gallons and had a liking for speed, with a little heroin to bring her down. It's hardly a wonder she died of an overdose at age twenty-seven in 1970.

In 1972 **Brian Cole** had the hit song "Windy" while with the Association, but gasped for air and died of a heroin overdose at age twenty-nine. The next year, always the cut-up, **Rick Dey** of the Wilde Knights and the Merry-Go-Round, with the hit "Just Like Me," died of laughing gas (nitrous oxide) when he was twenty-five. In 1974, **Robbie McIntosh** of the Average White Band only enjoyed snorting large amounts of cocaine but mistakenly inhaled a lethal dose of white powder heroin instead; he died a below-average rockers' death at age twenty-four. In 1975 **Tim Buckley**, with the song "Once I Was," was no more after a heroin overdose took him at age twenty-eight.

In 1978 Blood, Sweat, and Tears sax player **Gregory Herbert** got all of that and some, when he died of a heroin overdose at age thirty-one. That same year a popular band had a double dose of bad news: Manager of the Who, **Pete Meaden** at age thirty-six, and a month later, the Who drummer Keith Moon both died of an overdose. Moon chose the same apartment Mama Cass had expired in as his final exit place at age thirty-one. In 1979, **Sid Vicious** (John Simon Ritchie) lived up to the punk stage name he used as lead man for his band Sex Pistols; while out on bail for stabbing his girlfriend, he overdosed on heroin at age twenty-one. In 1980, the wishful thinking of **Tim Hardin** when he wrote "If I Were a Carpenter" wasn't enough to save him from the music biz and his death from heroin at age thirty-nine.

The most famous rock concert ever held occurred near Woodstock, New York, on Max Yasgur's 600-acre farm on August 15–18, 1969. It exemplified the counterculture or hippie era as no other event since. More than 500,000 people attended, when only 50,000 were supposed to show. Two people officially died: one from a heroin overdose and another run over by a tractor. But in the yin and yang of it all, two births supposedly occurred as well. Max Yasgur, owner of the dairy farm where Woodstock Festival took place, died, in the longest-delayed reaction on record, of a heart attack at age fifty-three in 1973.

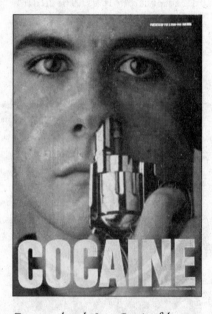

Everyone thought Jerry Garcia of the Grateful Dead was sure to die of a drug overdose, but for him it was just the opposite. After a career as the classic stoner, Garcia tried to clean up and get off drugs, but the shock of such a radical change gave him a fatal heart attack at age fifty-three in 1995.

In 1982 **James Honeyman-Scott** of the Pretenders with "Back on the Chain Gang" fame did the heroin OD at twenty-five. In 1991 front man for the Temptations, David Ruffin, went the way of a cocaine overdose when he was way too old for the stuff at age fifty. In 1998 punk rocker Will Clay of the Vomit Pigs kept the heroin overdosing going strong at age forty-three.

Another candidate who had odds in favor of death by overdose was the original *Super Freak* Rick James (James Johnson, Jr.), an outlandish funk performer, once accused of keeping women hostage and burning them with crack pipes. Although he was acquitted on that charge, he did do time in prison for cocaine possession. When released, he suffered a stroke and died of a heart attack at age fifty-six in 2004. That same year, Ol' Dirty Bastard (Russell Tyrone Jones), a rapper, noted for his kung fu dance moves, proved he was *the man* to many after he escaped from prison, only to be captured signing autographs in a McDonald's parking lot. He died of an overdose while in the recording studio two days before his thirty-sixth birthday.

Milli Vanilli was the pop duo of Frankie Farian and Rob Pilatus that won a Grammy but had to give it back when it was discovered that neither of them actually sang on their records. Lip-synching had always been common for artists to mouth their own songs previously recorded when performing, but these two went overboard and left the public feeling duped. Although the duo tried to release a comeback album featuring their actual voices, Pilatus returned to his previous life of crime and drug use, spent time in jail, and once out died of a cocaine overdose at age thirty-two in 1998.

JELLY ROLL MORTON

Jelly Roll Morton (Ferdinand Joseph Morton) was born in New Orleans in 1890. By twelve years old he was working in bordellos, banging out ragtime rhythms on the piano. He became a traveling musician, doing gigs from New York to Los Angeles, all the while supplementing his music income through gambling and shooting pool. As a result of his travels, he began to incorporate a variety of musical styles, thereby creating a sound that would come to be known as jazz. He made a few recordings of his music in 1926, but by the 1930s he had faded into obscurity and later managed a jazz club in Washington, D.C. He believed his career slide and subsequent ill health was due to a voodoo curse. Jelly was raised by his godmother, a voodoo priestess in the Creole culture of New Orleans, and believed all his successes and mishaps were attributed to voodoo. After he was seriously stabbed during a fight in Washington, D.C., it affected him both mentally and physically. He attempted a comeback in Los Angeles, but he fell sick, stayed eleven days in the hospital before dying in 1941 at the age of fifty of sepsis, an infection of the blood.

SEPSIS KILLS 210,000 AMERICANS EACH YEAR AND WORLDWIDE TAKES MORE THAN 1,400 PEOPLE EVERY DAY. IT KILLED MUPPETS CREATOR JIM HENSON AND WAS THE ULTIMATE DEMISE OF ACTOR CHRISTOPHER REEVE. ACCORDING TO DR. ALMOUJAHED, M.D., INFECTIOUS DISEASE SPECIALIST AT THE MEDICAL COLLEGE OF WISCONSIN: "SEPSIS IS CAUSED WHEN SEVERE INFECTION OVERACTIVATES THE BODY'S IMMUNE SYSTEM, SETTING OFF A CASCADE OF SYSTEMIC INFLAMMATORY RESPONSES THAT COULD POTENTIALLY LEAD TO A SEVERE DROP IN BLOOD PRESSURE AND CARDIOVASCULAR COLLAPSE."

WOLFGANG AMADEUS MOZART

Nearly everything Wolfgang Amadeus Mozart composed is now considered a classic, whether it be for symphony, chamber, piano, opera, or chorus. He was born to a father who was the most admired teacher in Europe, and he received excellent training from the best. By the age of three little Wolfgang's skills were evident, and as he grew older, he developed a gift to recall the slightest phrasing of music heard years before. He was a financially successful composer and performer during his lifetime, ranked among the top 5 percent of earners in Europe, yet he was always broke. With scant money left, he was subsequently buried in an unmarked grave after his

death at age thirty-five in 1791. Officially, he died of "military fever," a term that described an unknown condition, possibly from an exotic locale (as many soldiers acquired abroad) resulting in high fevers. The most standard cure for this disease was bloodletting, draining an unspecified amount of blood from a vein to try to get the body's systems back in balance. Symptoms Mozart experienced are also similar to rheumatic fever, which was common during this period. In addition, there were signs that he had mercury poisoning, the main ingredient used in drugs to treat syphilis. The evening before his death he was subjected to another bloodletting and died by 1:00 A.M. He was too weak to rise, saying his last words: "The taste of death is upon my lips . . . I feel something not of this earth."

> "Mozart is the greatest composer of all. Beethoven created his music, but the music of Mozart is of such purity and beauty that one feels he merely found it—that it has always existed as part of the inner beauty of the universe waiting to be revealed."
> —ALBERT EINSTEIN

On December 8, 1980, Beatle John Lennon (John Ono Lennon) at age forty was shot by a deranged fan, who claimed that the book Catcher in the Rye *instructed him to do so. Lennon had signed an album cover the night before for his killer, Mark David Chapman, who had waited in front of the Dakota building for the superstar—the last autograph Lennon would give. Lennon's desire to stay grounded, living among ordinary people, imagining, so to speak, that everyone was basically good at heart—this very character trait that made him admired and unique was the thing that killed him.*

MUSICIAN MURDERS

Chimpanzees and other primates murder frequently over territorial rights and the quest for power and lust. Certain experts say that this same genetic blueprint as a means of resolving conflict is part of man's makeup, and for musicians it seems no different. Currently, one person is murdered every sixty seconds.

In 1957 Country & Western singer **Lonnie Baron**, with the hit "You're Not the First Girl," was murdered over a lover's quarrel at age twenty-six. In 1958 "Big" **John Dolphin** of Don Julian and the Meadowlarks was done in by infighting, as he was shot and killed by a songwriter for the group at age twenty-seven.

Sam Cooke, with the hits "You Send Me" and "Bring It on Home," was shot by a motel manager after Cooke burst into the motel office in a rage with nothing on but his shoes and a trench coat after a hooker stole his clothes. Considered the father of soul, Cooke died from gunshot trauma at age thirty-three in 1964. Coroner reports indicate Cooke was inebriated at the time and deemed the incident as justifiable homicide; the Cooke estate trustees insist it was a conspiracy.

Blues singer **Bill Gillum** with the song "Got to Reap What You Sow," apparently did just that when he died after being shot in an argument at age sixty-one in 1966. In that same year **Bobby Fuller**, with the hit "I Fought The Law," was murdered by asphyxiation owing to having gasoline poured down his throat; he was quite dead at age twenty-three. In 1970 **James "Shep" Sheppard**, of the Limelites, known for "A Thousand Miles Away," surely wished he was anywhere other than where he was when he was found shot to death in his car on the Long Island

Expressway at age thirty-three. In 1971 **King Curtis** (Curtis Ousley), who did "Charlie Brown" and "Yakety Yak," was stabbed to death in a fight at age thirty-seven. In 1972 **Bobby Ramirez** of Edgar Winter's White Trash demanded service at a Chicago bar and was subsequently beaten to death at age twenty-three, supposedly because he looked disheveled and had long hair. In 1975 the Nutmegs' front man **Leroy McNeil**, singer of "Ship of Love," was stabbed in a mutinous fight and died at thirty-six. In 1980 **Nathaniel "Buster" Wilson,** the baritone of the Coasters,

"The Ballad of the Green Berets," with the practically spoken lyrics: "Fighting soldiers from the sky, Fearless men who jump and die, Men who mean just what they say . . ." was the number-one single in 1966, sung by **Staff Sergeant Barry Sadler.** *However, it was never ascertained if he was a victim of a robbery or of an assassination attempt. He was shot in the head while traveling in a cab near Guatemala City after a day of drinking. Sadler never said, though he lived for eighteen months in a coma until he died at age forty-eight in 1989.*

known for "Charlie Brown" and "Yakety Yak," was killed. These songs contained lyrics that apparently got someone really peeved (found out to be his former manager); Buster was shot, dismembered, and left in a ravine near Hoover Dam.

In 1982 "Cool Jerk" singer for the Capitols, **Samuel George** died from a stab wound at age forty. No drive-by shooting for Reggae singer **Michael Smith**— instead he was stoned (as with rocks and bricks) before he was shot for good measure in Kingston, Jamaica, at age thirty-four in 1982. In 1984 **Marvin Gaye** of "Can't We All Just Get Along?" fame was shot by his father a day before Marvin's forty-fifth birthday. In 1987 **Peter Tosh** of Bob Marley and the Wailers was shot dead during a home invasion at age forty-two. In that same year Drummer **Gary Driscoll** for the Electric Elves, a blues-rock band, was killed in an occult sacrifice in his Ithaca, New York, home by still unidentified assailants at age forty-one. Jumping the velvet ropes at a club, singer for Weather Report, thirty-five-year-old **Jaco Pastorius** (John Francis Pastorius III), was not recognized in his disheveled appearance and was beaten to death by a bouncer in 1987.

Another Coaster, this time **Cornell Gunter** (fifty-four) was shot by an unknown assailant while sitting in his car in Las Vegas in 1990. Doo-Wop singer **Pete Barin** (Peter Falciglia) of the Belmonts, known in music for his impeccable timing, walked into a grocery store at the wrong time in the Bronx, during a robbery, and was shot dead at fifty-two in 1995. That same year, **Selena Quintanilla-Pérez**, "Queen of Tejano Music," was gunned down by the president of her fan club at age twenty-three. The rapper known as **2 Pac** (Tupac Amaru Shakur) was twenty-five years old in 1996 when he was on the wrong side of a drive-by shooting. In 1997 **Christopher Burmeister** (twenty-nine) and member of the Bushpilots was sightseeing on the Empire State Building's observation deck when a lunatic opened fire, killing the musician and six others. That same year rapper **Notorious B.I.G.** (Christopher Wallace) was supposedly paid back for other drive-by shootings and killed at age twenty-four. Another Reggae musician, this time **Junior Braithwaite** of Bob Marley and the Wailers, was shot dead at age fifty in 1999. **Neal Newman** of the Blue Rhythm Band learned that cigarette smoking kills in other ways, when he stepped outside for a smoke at intermission, was stabbed in the alley, and died at forty-one in 2001.

NEFERTITI

Ancient Egyptian Nefertiti has remained remembered throughout history primarily for her legendary beauty. Nefertiti was the royal wife of two pharaohs, Amenhotep IV and Akhenaten, and later the mother-in-law of King Tut. Her name means "perfect woman," and there is no doubt she used this anatomy to gain and hold immense power in her own right. Her massive image on the side of one temple was equal to that of the king. Powerful priests disliked her, and as soon as Tut died, she vanished.

The royal house suggested she died from a plague and attempts were made to erase the memory of her existence. When her tomb was recently discovered, they found that she was indeed feared even after death. Her mummified feet were mutilated by contemporaries to make certain she didn't get up and cause more trouble in the afterlife. Other wounds found on her body indicate that she did not, in fact, die from a bad flu but was instead murdered.

RICKY NELSON

Eric Hilliard Nelson was a well known teen idol, thanks to the family radio and television show *The Adventures of Ozzie and Harriet*. His song "Poor Little Fool" ranked number eighty-three of all-time most popular songs of the twentieth century. In 1985 at age forty-five Rick died in a plane crash while heading to a New Year's Eve concert, attempting to stage a revival of his career. The last year of his life he earned nearly $700,000 from his music, but because of heavy alimony payments and, some say, an even heavier cocaine habit, he had only $40,000 left. He knew the forty-year-old charter plane the band owned needed service, though he felt that making it to the gig was more important. The plane burst into flames, with reports blaming it on the band's free-basing (using a torch to heat cocaine) as a reason for the massive fire that left Nelson and six of the band members identifiable only by dental records.

OTHER MUSICIANS DOWNED

Buddy Holly (Charles Hardin Holley), riding high on the popularity of his national rock 'n' roll hit "Peggy Sue," was killed in a charter plane crash en route to a concert, dead at age twenty-three in 1959. Also aboard was **Ritchie Valens** (Richard Steven Valenzuela), age seventeen, with the hits "Donna" and "La Bamba," and the **Big Bopper** (Jiles Perry Richardson, Jr.), age twenty-eight, just as his hit "Chantilly Lace" topped the charts. Ever since the accident a rumor persisted that the pilot was shot in midflight, causing the crash. A gun had been found next to Buddy Holly's body, and it was believed an argument among the rockers had turned deadly. In 2007 Big Bopper's son, Jay Richardson, who was born shortly after his father died, hired a forensic anthropologist to exhume the coffin of his forty-eight-year-since-dead-dad and come face to face with the father he had never met. The body was surprisingly well preserved and showed no signs of a gun battle, confirming the original report that all aboard had died instantly of massive trauma that cold and snowy day "the music died" in Iowa.

In 1963 **Patsy Cline**, known for "I Fall to Pieces," did just that after her fatal plane crash at age thirty. **David Box** was a singer for Buddy Holly and the Crickets, and although he missed the plane that crashed in 1959, he got on another fatal flight, some say part of the Holly Curse that killed him at age twenty-one in 1964. **Otis Redding**, with the hit "(Sittin' on) The Dock of the Bay," surely wished he would have been doing just that instead of dying in a charter plane that crashed into a lake near Madison, Wisconsin, killing

Ronnie Van Zant, member of the southern rock band Lynyrd Skynyrd, who was noted for "Free Bird," was in an old charter plane that crashed because it ran out of fuel. The crash killed the rocker at age twenty-nine in 1977. Three days after the band's album Street Survivors *was released, three band members, a road manager, pilot, and copilot didn't survive the ditching of the forty-seat, two-propeller plane into a remote Mississippi swamp. Van Zant could possibly have survived and actually died when his skull was crushed from the impact of flying musical equipment while he sat in the aisle, a way he often flew, being too constrained by a seat with a seatbelt. The plane had previously been rejected by the manager of the band Aerosmith because pilot and copilot were known to keep a bottle of Jack Daniels next to the throttle. Van Zant had predicted many times that he would die before he was thirty, with "his boots on." As it is so often, he somehow attracted what he visualized and died only three months shy of his thirtieth birthday.*

him at age twenty-six in 1967. "Time in a Bottle" singer **Jim Croce** didn't know how prophetic his hit song would be when he was killed in a plane crash at age thirty in 1973.

In 1982 **Randy Rhoads**, with the hit "Last Call for Rock & Roll," told the pilot of his charter plane to buzz Ozzy Osbourn's tour bus, spotted below. The wing tapped the tour-bus roof and sent the aircraft into a tailspin, killing Rhoads at age twenty-five. Rock guitarist **Stevie Ray Vaughan**'s helicopter lost its way in thick fog and smashed into a hill on the way to

a concert, killing him at age thirty-five in 1990. **Bill Graham** (Wolfgang Grajonca), known as the promoter for electrifying rock shows at the Fillmore East and West, was in a helicopter that touched a power line. He died of electrocution at sixty in 1991. "Country Roads" was one of the many big hits for **John Denver** (John Henry Deutschendorf, Jr.), which he apparently wanted to find when he died in the crash of an experimental plane he piloted at age fifty-three in 1997, just off the coast of California, near Monterey. And in 2001 the niece of Gladys Knight and wife of R. Kelly the rapper, **Aaliyah** (Aeliyatt Dani Haughton) died in a plane crash at twenty-two shortly after takeoff in the Bahamas.

NERO

NERO SINGS WHILE ROME BURNS

Nero was a Roman emperor who came to power at age seventeen. Although he wanted his legacy to be in the arts, improving culture by building theaters and promoting athletic games, he's remembered primarily for his cruelty. To stay in power, he poisoned or killed all who got in his way, including his own mother and nearly every member of his family. Anyone suspected of eyeing his crown, as well as some he simply didn't like (such as an old aunt he killed by ordering doctors to give her a fatal dose of laxatives), were most often poisoned or met with a convenient mishap. The incident that cites "Nero fiddled while Rome burned" stems from a fire that occurred at the Circus Maximus in the summer of A.D. 64 when merchants' tents went ablaze and eventually the fire spread to destroy nearly one-third of the city. It wasn't a fiddle but a lyre that Nero strummed, as a costumed actor giving a performance in a play in a town miles from Rome. In order to quell rumors that he had orchestrated fire to build more theaters, he pointed to the Christians, rounded them up, dressed them in hides of beasts, and let ferocious dogs go at them in the arena. Many were set on fire, actually as human torches, to serve, as Nero said, as "garden lighting." Nero entered the arena driving a chariot, taunting those still alive, though even the Romans, accustomed to cruelty, believed they were witnessing a sadistic madman. Nero could have cared less; he continued to consider himself a great performer. When he acted, no one was allowed to leave the theater; once a woman gave birth beneath the benches in order not to face his wrath. After thirteen years of this, the Senate finally found an opportunity to vote him out, though Nero fled before he could be captured and ridiculed with a public execution. When his enemies closed in, he had none of his favorite poisons at hand and instead ordered his servant to slit his throat. Before he died in A.D. 68 at age thirty he said: "What an artist the world loses in me."

NIAGARA DAREDEVILS

The first daredevil in U.S. history was one Sam Patch, billed as the Yankee Leaper. He began his career as a boy jumping off a mill dam near Pawtucket, Rhode Island, for the amusement of other child laborers employed by the factory. During his twenties he started to jump off higher and higher spots. By 1827 he figured he could make some money doing this and advertised a jump off the 70-foot Passaic

waterfall in Paterson, New Jersey. The large crowd was so pleased with his feat that he kept at it, finding high factory walls, ship masts and bridges to jump from. Inevitably, the greatest natural and most dramatic of all leaping spots called to him; Sam became the first to jump off Niagara Falls. On November 6, 1829, he extended a 125-foot ladder over the falls and jumped toward the swirling torrent of water 176 feet below. A few minutes later he surfaced and was picked up by a waiting boat, thereby becoming the first person to ever jump off Niagara Falls and live. The crowd wasn't as big as Sam had hoped, so he immediately planned another jump. A week later on Friday the thirteenth there were over ten thousand people in attendance. Days prior to the event, the local taverns were booming with pre-event celebrations. At the scheduled time Sam showed up, perhaps, sipping one too many steins himself and staggered out onto the ladder. Before he got to the end, he apparently fell, not achieving his typical arrow-stiff vertical descent and landed belly-whopper fashion. The thud his body made hitting the surface caused the entire audience to let out a loud, collective "Ouch!" The crowds waited for hours, but Sam at age thirty never surfaced; his frozen body was found the following spring. It was discovered that he had broken both shoulders and had drowned because he was unable to swim to shore.

RETIREMENT PLAN

The first person and only woman to go over Niagara Falls in a barrel was sixty-three-year-old Anna Edson Taylor in 1901. As a way to make money in her old age, she thought a stunt at Niagara Falls might be noteworthy and make her famous. She set about plans to make a barrel and hired a carnival promoter to attract media attention. On October 24, 1901, she sat in her specially constructed 4½ × 3 foot diameter oak barrel, weighted down with a 200-pound anvil, strapped in with a leather harness and cushioned by pillows, to be set adrift a mile upstream of the falls. Miraculously, she survived with only a few cuts. After a short stay in the hospital, she began a lecture tour, selling memorabilia and autographs. But before long, interest in her faded and the poverty she so wanted to avoid prevailed. She often sat at a table near the falls, many days through sleet and freezing drizzle, without a souvenir seeker willing to pay even a penny for her postcards. She became destitute and practically homeless, dying in 1921 in the Niagara Charity Ward. A local newspaper raised meager funds for the burial cost and managed to acquire a gravesite in a Potters Field section of Oakland Cemetery next to other dead stunters.

SIXTEEN PEOPLE HAVE TRIED TO GO OVER NIAGARA FALLS IN A BARREL OR BARREL-TYPE CONTRAPTION, WITH A COUNT OF SIX DEAD AMONG THE DAREDEVILS. ONE WHO SURVIVED, BOBBY LEACH, BROKE EVERY BONE IN HIS BODY IN HIS 1911 BARREL GO-OVER. DURING A TOUR IN 1927 AT AGE SIXTY-SEVEN HE SLIPPED ON A FRUIT PEEL AND GASHED HIS HEAD, DYING OF GANGRENE.

SUICIDE STUNT

In 1984 **Karel Soucek** billed himself as the Last of the Niagara Daredevils. He went over the falls in a lightweight plastic-and-metal barrel at a speed of 75 mph and emerged alive, bleeding from his head after bobbing in the currents below for forty-five minutes. He, too, wanted to prolong his fame and planned another stunt in a barrel at the Astrodome the following year. From the top of the dome he planned to drop 180 feet into a 10-foot-wide tank of water. Before a crowd of 45,000 the barrel launched prematurely, bounced off a rail, and missed the small waiting tank completely. He died of internal injuries and trauma at age thirty-eight.

HAING NGOR

Dr. Haing S. Ngor was one of only two nonprofessionals to ever win an Academy Award for acting. He agreed to relive for Hollywood his days of horror during his internment in a concentration camp, stemming from Cambodia's Pol Pot and the Khmer Rouge purges in the 1970s. Ten years after winning the Oscar, Ngor was accosted in front of his Los Angeles apartment by gang members. He gave over his wallet but refused to surrender a locket that held a picture of his late wife, who had died in the camps. Ngor survived the rigors of Cambodia's tortures only to be shot to death in 1996 at age fifty-five in America.

ALFRED NOBEL

The Nobel Prize was instituted by the will of Alfred Nobel, the inventor of dynamite, after he read a prematurely released copy of his obituary before he died. The notice of his death chided the destructive nature of his invention, insinuating that its use in warfare would greatly harm humanity. He subsequently decided to leave a more positive legacy and bequeathed a portion of his future royalties to prize recipients. When Nobel died in 1896 of a stroke at age sixty-three, it took five years before the first award was given on December 10, 1901. The prize is still awarded each year on December 10, the anniversary of his death.

NOBEL PEACE PRIZE

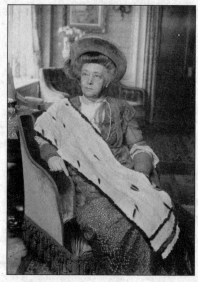

Unlike other Nobel categories, the Peace Prize has instigated the most controversy. For example, while Mahatma Gandhi was deemed unsuitable, other past winners were of dubious distinction (in regard to peace): Theodore Roosevelt, Yasser Arafat, Lê Đúc Tho, and Henry Kissinger. Adolf Hitler was nominated in 1939, as well as Joseph Stalin and Benito Mussolini.

Bertha Von Suttner was the first woman and the first recipient of the Nobel Peace Prize in 1905. Ironically, she had once answered an advertisement placed by Alfred Nobel and became his secretary-housekeeper in 1876. Although she lasted only a week on the job, she maintained correspondence with Nobel until his death. Suttner became a name in the peace movement because of a novel she wrote, *Die Waffen nieder!* (*Lay Down Your Arms*) published in 1889. Soon after, she edited a magazine urging the formation of a pacifist movement. When she was awarded the prize in 1905, Suttner was settling into a financially restricted retirement and showing the first signs of cancer. The award gave her a new burst of energy and enthusiasm despite her illness, and she traveled the world to lecture for peace. However, two months before World War I broke out in 1914, she died, at age seventy-one, from cancer. The war that followed used Nobel's invention of dynamite to kill millions.

On the other hand, **Mother Teresa** (Agnes Gonxhe Bojaxhiu), the Peace Prize winner in 1979, perhaps embodies the intended scope of the award. Mother Teresa was born in Albania and became a Catholic nun at age eighteen. She went on to start her own order, the Missionaries of Charity in 1950 with twelve other nuns who worked with the unwanted in the poorest sections of Calcutta, India. Their philosophy was "If you can't feed a hundred people, then feed just one." Today, more than one million workers are employed by the Missionaries of Charity in over one hundred different countries. Mother Teresa died in 1997 at age eighty-seven of heart failure and malaria. According to the Gallup poll, Mother Teresa was ranked as one of the most admired of the twentieth century. In October 2003 she was canonized a saint.

Joseph Rotblat received the Nobel Peace Prize in 1995. He was the only scientist to resign from the Manhattan Project, and he thereafter campaigned to eliminate atomic weapons throughout the world. He died of respiratory failure at age ninety-six.

EUGENE O'NEILL

Eugene O'Neill was a playwright known for brutally realistic though heart-wrenching portraits of human despair and disillusionment. He won the Nobel Prize in 1936 for his successful plays, including *Desire Under the Elms* and *Strange Interlude*. He would later go on to write the classics *Long Day's Journey into Night* and *The Iceman Cometh*. Although his father and brother both died of alcoholism in their forties, and his mother was a heroin addict, O'Neill's accolades allowed him to persist. He did battle with depression and alcoholism as well, and suffered from Parkinson's  disease, to such an extent that during the last ten years of his life he was unable to compose. Although newspapers at the time stated he died of alcoholism, his autopsy revealed he actually died of neurodegenerative disease called cerebellar cortical atrophy (CCA), not related to alcohol or Parkinson's, in 1953 at the age of sixty-five.

DEAD OSCARS

Receiving an award posthumously, obviously, does little to increase longevity; but some believed that dying, in fact, helped sway the judges in considering the following for honors. The first posthumous Oscar winner was screenwriter **Sidney Howard** for *Gone With the Wind*. At age forty-eight he was run over by a tractor on his Massachusetts farm in 1939, months before the film debuted. The Academy win also made him the first playwright to receive both a Pulitzer Prize (1925) and an Oscar, though his love of rural life, perhaps, and not the accolades of his peers caused his early demise. **Peter Finch** won a best actor Oscar for *Network* (1976) but couldn't accept the award because he was dead. While on a promotional tour for the film, he suffered a heart attack at age sixty-four. In 1983 **Ralph Richardson** was up for best supporting actor for *Greystoke: The Legend of Tarzan, Lord of the Apes*, but left an empty seat at the award ceremony due to his death of a stroke at age eighty. And **Massimo Troisi** had no clue he was nominated for best actor for *The Postman* (1995). He had postponed heart surgery to finish the filming of the movie and died less than twelve hours after the last scene was finished of a heart attack at age forty-one.

P

CHARLIE PARKER

Charlie Parker, known as Bird, or Yardbird, never made it to the big time during his life, yet after his death he was recognized as one of the greatest saxophone players of all time. As a result of a car accident as a teen, he became addicted to morphine, which later matured into a hardcore addiction to heroin. When his supply of dope dried up, he turned to alcohol and consumed it to a point where he needed support to stand upright onstage. He played his music with virtuosity yet took care of his physical self with abandon. In 1955 he died from complications of obesity, liver disorder, though primarily of a bleeding ulcer at age thirty-four. He was watching Tom Dorsey's *Stage*

Show on television when he died. After his death, Beat writers canonized Parker and gave the impression that narcotics were related to his musical genius, causing many musicians, for decades to follow, to use drugs to imitate their idol.

> "Dope never helped anybody sing better or play music better or do anything better. All dope can do for you is kill you—and kill you the long, slow, hard way."
> —BILLIE HOLIDAY

BORIS PASTERNAK

Boris Pasternak, a poet and novelist, best known for the epic novel *Doctor Zhivago*, declined the Nobel Prize in Literature in 1958, though it seems he wished to accept it. When news first arrived, he sent a telegram expressing his gratitude only to follow it with a regret four days later: "Considering the meaning this award has been given in the society to which I belong, I must reject this undeserved prize which has been presented to me." Pasternak feared he would lose his Soviet citizenship if he accepted a capitalist prize and could not consider his banishment from the country he loved—regardless of its politics—for he would die of heartbreak. In a letter to Khrushchev in 1958, Pasternak wrote, "Departure beyond the borders of my country is for me equivalent to death." He died two years later at the age of seventy in 1960 of lung cancer.

GEORGE PATTON, JR.

General George Patton, Jr., nicknamed Blood and Guts, was born to be a soldier. Raised by an affluent family of military veterans and surrounded by stories of war, he decided at an early age to become a hero. Since he had learning disabilities, namely dyslexia, it took him five years to get through West Point. After graduation he entered the Olympics in 1912, representing the United States in the pentathlon event. He came in fifth due to a marksmanship technicality: All but two of his bulletholes went through the exact same place in the target with such accuracy that the judges erroneously deemed these as misses. He served in World War I, went in as a captain, and came out as a colonel. In World War II he insisted that soldiers shave daily and instilled a strict sense of discipline. Although he wasn't popular with the men at first, his victories swayed opinion in his favor. He helped push the Germans out of northern Africa and then took his fight to Italy. He couldn't tolerate cowards and once slapped two hospitalized soldiers he believed showed no spine. It was later found they were suffering from post-traumatic stress syndrome and malaria. The incident nearly got Patton fired, and he was temporarily relieved of command. He finished the war liberating Czech Republic cities, with his famous pearl-handled revolvers at his side. In 1945 he was riding as a passenger in a car in Germany, after returning from a pheasant shoot, when the vehicle went off the road. The crash left him paralyzed from the neck down. Three weeks later he died of an embolism at age sixty. Twenty thousand soldiers volunteered to be his pallbearers.

JOHN PEMBERTON

The secret soda syrup used in Coca-Cola was developed by pharmacist John Pemberton in 1886. He was wounded while serving in the Civil War in the Confederate army and became addicted to morphine and cocaine. Before Coke, another chemist invented Vin Mariani, a cocaine-laced Bordeaux wine that flopped as a popular beverage but gave Pemberton the idea to add cocaine to drinks. For $1,750 Pemberton sold the cola formula to his bookkeeper Frank Robinson who came up with the current soda name and whose fine script became the current logo. Robinson, in turn, sold it to Asa Candler for $2,300, yet the exact transfer of rights to the formula remains clouded in suspected forgery and other questionable business practices. Pemberton died in 1888 from the complications of morphine and cocaine addiction, practically destitute at age fifty-seven. Today, Coca-Cola is worth more than $58 billion.

COCAINE IS USED BY MORE THAN 1.5 MILLION AMERICANS ON A REGULAR BASIS. THE DRUG SETS OFF CHAOTIC HEART RHYTHMS, INCREASES BLOOD PRESSURE, AND SHOOTS UP THE BODY TEMPERATURE TO DANGEROUS LEVELS. WHEN MIXED WITH ALCOHOL, THE COKE TURNS INTO COCAETHYLENE, AN EVEN DEADLIER TOXIN. BETWEEN 2000 AND 2005 THERE WERE 3,000 DEATH CERTIFICATES IN THE UNITED STATES THAT CITED COCAINE OVERDOSE AS THE PRIMARY CAUSE, ALTHOUGH THIS IS ONLY A FRACTION OF THE COCAINE FATALITIES, SINCE MOST ARE LISTED AS DEATH DUE TO CARDIAC ARREST.

PERICLES

Pericles was a Greek politician and military commander who ruled Athens and many of the small neighboring city-states under one allegiance with a new concept, as he said, "It is called a democracy, because not the few but the many govern." Without him, Athens and Greek culture would not have had the reputation as a center for arts and literature that it did. Many structures still standing, including the Parthenon, were built by Pericles. His years of leadership were not without scandal. Before elections the tradition of mudslinging was born, oftentimes with his associates and even himself accused of misappropriation of funds. Throughout his leadership, the warrior city to the south of Athens, Sparta, remained his nemesis. His strategy not to meet their superior army on the battlefield was probably a militarily smart move; however, in order to steal victory from Athens' enemy, he ordered evacuation of cities in their path. A swell of population came to live within the walls of Athens. After years of this overcrowding, disease spread, and typhus, a bacteria transmitted by rats and body lice, became epidemic. Not the sword but microbes laid Pericles low. After he lost two sons to the disease, his resolve weakened and he, too, died from the ravages of typhus at age sixty-six in 429 B.C.

EDWIN PERKINS

Before Nebraska chemist Edwin Perkins hit upon the invention of Kool-Aid, he did well selling his Nix-O-Tine Tobacco Remedy, an herbal mixture to kick smoking. In 1927 he devised a way to make an easily shipped soft drink powder that didn't need bottles, modeling his product on Jell-O. He sold the first Kool-Aid packets for a dime. Six flavors included: raspberry, cherry, grape, lemon, orange, and root beer. Perkins liked raspberry the best and drank it most of his life. He died in 1962 at age seventy-three of liver disease and complications from diabetes. Surely no backward country boy, this savvy sugar-drink inventor left to his heirs a $45-million fortune.

THE U.S. DEPARTMENT OF AGRICULTURE (USDA) SAYS SUGAR IN SMALL AMOUNTS IS OKAY—35 GRAMS, OR 8 TEASPOONS OF SUGAR PER DAY. ACCORDING TO USDA DATA, SUGAR CONSUMPTION IN 2006 WAS 154 POUNDS PER PERSON. THIS IS EQUIVALENT TO ABOUT 237 GRAMS, OR 50 TEASPOONS OF SUGAR PER DAY, 30 PERCENT HIGHER THAN IN 1992. EACH YEAR 24,000 PEOPLE BECOME BLIND BECAUSE OF DIABETIC EYE DISEASE; 38,000 PEOPLE WITH DIABETES UNDERGO TREATMENT FOR KIDNEY FAILURE; AND 86,000 WILL NEED DIABETES-RELATED LOWER-EXTREMITY AMPUTATIONS. MORE THAN 60,000 DIED IN 2005 OF DIABETES-RELATED COMPLICATIONS.

FRANCISCO PIZARRO

In 1532 Pizarro conquered the Inca Empire of Peru, defended by an army of 80,000, with only 180 men and 27 horses. His march into Peru was not a one-two affair. It was nearly a dozen years in planning and trial runs. When at first the Incas called the Spanish "children of the sun" because of their light complexions and shining armor, word of their cruel actions preceded them. When Pizarro encountered the Inca ruler Atahualpa, his plan for victory involved striking at the core of power, ambushing Atahualpa before the Incas could attack. He held the Inca ruler for ransom. Despite a room filled with gold for Atahualpa's release, the Inca ruler was garroted and strangled with iron chains. Owing to an ongoing civil war in the region, this effectively ended the Inca Empire. In 1541 at age sixty-two Pizarro was assassinated by the son of a rival conquistador that Pizarro had executed. He was shot in the abdomen with a pistol at close range. Before Pizarro died, he painted a cross with his own blood on his chest.

PLATO

Plato descended from a line of Greek kings and was well respected in his lifetime. After witnessing Socrates' execution, Plato began to see the truth to his old teacher's logic and complaint about a certain aspect of democracy: Because someone learned how to manipulate elections and rise to power did not make that person wise or just. Plato left Athens shortly thereafter and traveled through Italy before returning at age forty to open an academy of philosophy, the earliest-known organized school in Western civilization. He wrote furiously and left behind numerous manuscripts of his thoughts, offering a new perspective, which suggested that there is another truth than what is seen and represented in form. Never marrying or producing heirs, Plato died at age eighty in 347 B.C. of a heart attack while attending a wedding feast.

ULCERS AND KNOWLEDGE

After Plato's death, his most famous student, Aristotle, did not take over the academy, as was expected, although he would become the most influential philosopher of classical Greece. Aristotle was a polymath, later termed a Renaissance Man, excelling in multiple fields, including arts and science. He was sought out by Alexander the Great and became an adviser on ethics, politics, philosophy, and even zoology. At that time, philosophy meant the study of all things. Aristotle's method of looking for logic and the use of deductive

reasoning were the precursors for much of Western scientific thought. When Alexander the Great died, Aristotle's popularity waned. Officials in Athens tried to drum up charges of atheism against him, as they did against Socrates. But Aristotle chose to flee, saying he preferred that Athens not be remembered for sinning against philosophy twice. He died of abdominal tumors and stomach ulcers in 322 B.C. at age sixty-three.

POCAHONTAS

Pocahontas, a nickname meaning "little spoiled one," was born **Amonute**, daughter of Chief Powhatan in 1595. She was an extrovert from a young age, inquisitive and naturally good-natured. At eleven years old she played a minor role in securing John Smith's survival. Later she was the go-between for trade among the settlers and Indians bartering at Jamestown. The fictionalized version of her love affair with Smith may, in fact, bear some truth, but in a much more disturbing way for our modern sensibility. Today, a thirty-year-old having sex with a preteen is pedophilia and a crime. But, in that era, intercourse with non-Christian pagans of any age was not considered wrong. Pocahontas was known to have "long, private conversations" with Smith during her frequent visits to the Jamestown complex, yet the true dimensions of these encounters are a matter of conjecture. A few years later she was betrothed to the older Englishman John Rolfe, only after she agreed to be baptized in

John Rolfe returned to Virginia and established tobacco as the main export crop of the New World before he died at age thirty-seven during the Indian Massacre of 1622. John Smith died in 1631 at fifty-one of the thrush, a yeast infection of the mouth and throat. At the time thrush was believed to be acquired by people who embellished the truth but was actually a result of unsanitary conditions and the lack of basic hygiene.

1614. Two years later Rolfe took her to London, where she was received as a celebrity, billed as a real live Indian princess by high society, and held an audience with King James. In 1617 she believed the smoky air of London was the cause of her coughs and bouts of weakness and wished to return to the forests she had known. Along with Rolfe she boarded a ship to return to Virginia, but the vessel only made it to the end of the Thames River before it turned back. Pocahontas died in London at age twenty-two of a disease called the king's evil, a form of tuberculosis characterized by swelling of the lymph glands.

POLAR EXPLORERS

Vitus Bering, the explorer who discovered the body of water between Russia and North America, died of scurvy in 1741, at age sixty, while sailing near the Aleutian Islands off Alaska. The next Polar explorer to die was **George Washington DeLong**, when he attempted to reach the North Pole via wooden ship in 1881 by sailing up the Bering Strait. Within no time, the ship's hull was crushed by forming ice. DeLong and thirty-two crew members escaped in rowboats and struggled to survive the winter on a small, frozen, barren island. DeLong, age thirty-seven, and nineteen of his crew, died of starvation.

At the turn of the twentieth century, the race to be the first man to reach the North Pole—to stand on top of the world—was a very captivating idea. It was so appealing that 756 men had died trying to get there.

Robert Edwin Peary in 1909, and five other men, Matthew Henson and four Eskimos, planted the American flag on the North Pole. He thought he was the first, but upon his return he learned that Frederick Albert Cook claimed discovery a year before. Until his death in 1920 at age sixty-three of anemia, Peary spent the next twelve years trying to debunk Cook's claim, an effort that sapped the life out of him and his chance for untarnished glory.

In 1897 during one of Peary's Nordic expeditions, he encountered a group of Eskimos and persuaded six of them to come back with him to New York City. The group—consisting of a six-year-old boy, **Minik Wallace**, the boy's father, and four men—were installed as a living human zoo of sorts at the American Museum of Natural History. However, since Peary failed to plan for their care, soon all adults died of tuberculosis. The boy pleaded with Peary to allow traditional burial procedures, but the bodies were secretly whisked away and de-fleshed. Unbeknownst to the boy, his father was reinstalled in the museum, exhibited as a species of an Eskimo skeleton. Minik was eventually released and worked as a laborer at odd jobs until he died at age twenty-eight during the Spanish flu epidemic of 1918.

Frederick Cook claimed to be the first to reach the North Pole in 1908, but he was discredited and never believed, especially after he became involved with a scheme seeking investors to buy Arctic oil rights and was sent to prison for mail fraud in 1922. Twelve years later, finally paroled, he wrote his memoirs. But he failed to entice a publisher before he died in 1940 at age seventy-five from a cerebral hemorrhage. (His book, *Return from the Pole*, was published posthumously in 1951.) Experts at the National Geographic Society say Peary was probably no more than five miles from the North Pole and never actually made it to the top. Cook, in all probability, did get nearly as close, but to date, his reputation has never recovered from Peary's smear campaign of one hundred years ago.

BOLDLY GO ANYWHERE THERE'S NO SPIDERS
Henry Robertson Bowers, known as Birdie of the Antarctic, was a fearless explorer. The only thing that scared

him was spiders. He was offered a place in an Amazon River expedition but instead signed on with **Captain Robert Scott** on his quest to be the first to reach the South Pole. In 1912 Bowers, Scott, and three others died of starvation and frostbite inside their tent, trapped on the spiderless tundra in a blizzard.

*In 1929 **Richard Evelyn Byrd** became the first person to fly over the South Pole, documented on newsreels, making it the first media-covered exploration. On a subsequent Antarctic excursion he nearly died of carbon monoxide poisoning from barbecuing inside his tent. During another near-fatal incident at the Antarctic base camp called Little America, he refused to signal an SOS call for help, knowing that others would die trying to rescue him. After years of exposure to barbecue fumes, he developed cancer and died in 1957 at age sixty-nine.*

LEW POLLACK

Before cigarettes were linked to cancer, the entertainment world had many a celebrity and sex symbol puffing away onscreen and in promotional advertisements. The 1934 song "Two Cigarettes in the Dark" used smoking as a metaphor for sex and allowed all the listening public who had a dime for a pack of smokes to feel like movie stars. The song was recorded by Bing Crosby and written by Lew Pollack, who died, of what else, but lung cancer and, ultimately, of a heart attack in 1946 at age fifty.

MARCO POLO

The Venetian uncle and guardian of Marco Polo saw trouble brewing in Constantinople where they lived and decided to move farther east. Good thing, because shortly after, all in the Venetian Quarter were blinded by branding irons, and Marco Polo's destiny to see and tell the world of the wonders of the Orient was spared. At age twelve he became the first Westerner to make it along the dangerous Silk Route all the way to Beijing, China, where Kubla Khan held court. The Mongol ruler was so fascinated by young Marco he kept him close for seventeen years, as an honored prisoner of sorts. Once home in Venice, Marco dictated his story *The Travels of Marco Polo*, which was published in French and became an instant bestseller. People remained skeptical of his stories, although they adopted many of the things he learned in the East, such as how to make ice cream and how to make lo mein noodles, which the Italians quickly relished, calling it spaghetti. Polo died of fever at age sixty-nine in 1324 a wealthy merchant and a well known literary superstar of the first travel book. On his deathbed he was asked to confess his lies concerning his account of the Far East. He replied, giving the perfect blurb that still accompanies his book: "I have not told half of what I saw, the rest is too impossible to believe."

Ponce de Leon.

JUAN PONCE DE LEÓN

Ponce de León had sailed with Columbus on his second voyage. He was eventually named governor of Puerto Rico. In his later years he sailed north to Florida to claim it for Spain. When he set off to explore the Florida peninsula, he was not looking for the mythical Fountain of Youth, as the story goes, but rather a return to the glory of *his* youth, which only honors and gold could buy. In the end, the only immortality he found was in history books because he was shot in the stomach with poisonous arrows and died at age sixty-one in 1521.

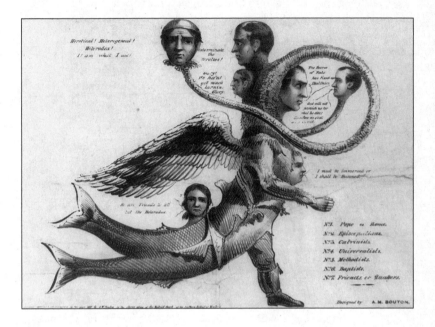

POPES

From Jesus' apostle—right-hand man, Peter—to Pope Benedict XVI, there have been 265 popes, some great, some not so. Records indicate there may have been one additional pope, a woman, **Pope Joan,** who disguised herself as a man for more than three years. Official sources have expunged documents of her existence, yet for the next thousand years, and even to this day, the papal procession makes an inconvenient detour to avoid the street where she was murdered. It appears that Pope Joan was en route to a function when she unexpectedly gave birth while riding in her carriage. Her papal robes were ripped off and she was stabbed repeatedly on the spot in A.D. 858. But the real wild times of papal history fall between the years 882 to 1042, when thirty-seven popes came and went, some wearing the big hat for no more than a month. At least forty popes bribed or bought their way in and continued their noble lifestyle, replete with entourages of mistresses, despite the vows they took to acquire the job. **Leo V** was the pope for only thirty days in 903 before he was imprisoned and tortured. When he wouldn't die, he was personally strangled by **Christophorus,** who then declared himself pope and infallible, in his judgment, of committing his recent popeicide. But his tenure likewise lasted less than a few months before he was beheaded by a Roman nobleman, who became **Pope Sergius III.** This pope established a seven-year rule and is noted for governing via "pornocracy," that is, giving power to his extended group of mistresses until A.D. 911 when he died of symptoms reminiscent of old Roman poisoning techniques. One woman, a famous escort, Theodora, passed most of the rules and laws during Sergius's reign and made sure her daughter, one of Sergius's lovers, bore a son who was later made into Pope John XI in 931. **Theodora** died of cancer before she was able to see her grandson—John's son, Pope John XII—take over at age nineteen in 955, although he, too, got into trouble for sleeping with his father's mistress and castrating deacons.

ELVIS PRESLEY

When Elvis Presley died at age forty-two, his family agreed to an autopsy. It was concluded that Elvis had been sitting on the toilet, nude, and reading. He then staggered a few feet to the dressing room and collapsed facedown into a plush shag rug. He had been given drugs for a blocked colon and had serious trouble moving his bowels. The initial autopsy report stated his death was "natural," with probable cause cited as HCVD, a code for hypertensive cardiovascular disease. It was determined heart arrhythmia was the cause, even though his heart was not in such a state that a heart attack under normal circumstances would occur. The cause of his heart's malfunction—if the combination of drugs found in his system can be momentarily disregarded—was his continued frustration at not being able to have a normal evacuation. As it is with many who experience this discomfort, Elvis attempted to forcibly push out the contents of his bowels while keeping his mouth and nose closed by pinching his nostrils. Called the Valsalva maneuver, this increases pressure within the thoracic cavity and stops the return of blood to the heart. Usually it results only in dizziness for healthy individuals. However, because of his compromised health, in addition to at least ten different traces of drugs in his bloodstream, the findings of the autopsy report make this the most probable and true cause of the king's death. Subsequent analysis of his organs (his brain and heart are still in storage at Memphis Baptist Hospital) preferred to call his death a result of "polypharmacy," that is, the mixing of many prescribed drugs. However, the man who lived by the motto "Taking Care of Business," died when he tried to finish one of life's necessities a bit too fast.

ERNIE PYLE

Ernie Pyle's nonfiction book *Brave Men* was the big hit in 1945, not only because he was a good writer and told stories, devoid of political opinion, of soldiers in the battlefield, but, more important, because he died. In April of that year the rambunctious 110-pound 5-foot-7 reporter decided to go back to covering the war in the Pacific. He felt it unpatriotic not to, even though the fighting was effectively over in Europe, where he had earned his reputation as the best correspondent of the era. He had landed with troops on the island of Ie Shima, off the coast of Okinawa, and was sprayed by enemy machinegun fire while riding in a Jeep. All jumped to the dirt unhurt, but when Pyle raised his head to see if everyone was all right, he was hit between the eyes by a bullet. He died instantly at age forty-four. The year before, Pyle had earned a Pulitzer Prize for his reporting on the unglamorous death of a U.S. Army captain and had a book, *Here Is Your War*, on the bestseller list.

RAMSES II

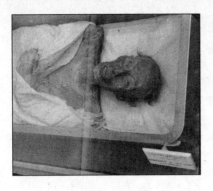

Egyptian pharaoh Ramses II is honored today as a brand name on condoms, even if the pharaoh was believed to have fathered over one hundred sixty children. He was the one who built the most stunning pyramids that still fascinate and mystify. He became pharaoh at age sixteen and retained power for nearly sixty-seven years, ending his reign in 1213 B.C. His mummy revealed that he was a tall Egyptian, standing five-feet-seven, and had a strong jaw and a hooked nose. He suffered from arthritis and poor circulation. It seems he died from infections caused by tooth decay.

REALITY TV

Contemporary daytime talk and variety shows have become the Circus Maximus and the Roman Forum format rolled into one, ranging from the current queen Oprah to the class clown Jerry Springer, proving for now that life's foibles, especially those of others rather than our own, offer the greatest variety and entertainment.

In 1999 *The Jenny Jones Show* thought it would be fun for a man to "come out of the closet" in front of a live audience. The segment featured thirty-two-year-old Scott Amedure revealing he was gay and had a crush on twenty-four-year-old Jon Schmitz. Scott told the ooing and giggling audiences that he wanted "to tie Jon up in [a] hammock and spray whipped cream and champagne on his body." The show flew the pair back home together to a suburb north of Detroit, not known as a gay-friendly area. Later that night, Schmitz showed up at Scott's trailer park home and fired two shotgun blasts into his chest.

In 2000 *The Jerry Springer Show* featured the segment "Secret Mistresses Confronted." Ralf Jurgen Panitz showed up with his new wife and accused his ex-wife, Nancy, of stalking the couple. When Nancy said she wasn't stalking because Ralf was still coming over for regular sex, the audience chanted and applauded with approval. Hours after the show aired, Ralf killed Nancy during an argument in her home.

Reality shows take the threat of death up a notch. It started with *America's Funniest Home Videos*, which seemed to particularly delight in home footage of hopeful contestants featuring their dumb stunts and personal injuries. Recently, reality shows sent contestants to exotic locales and made them participate in dangerous stunts to win a prize.

In 2003 a contestant Todd S., who was a claustrophobic, died of a heart attack after being padlocked inside a wooden box with air holes for three days as part of a "Face Your Fear" challenge. (The show's producers donated $10,000 to claustrophobia research.) In 2004 a show submerged people to see who could hold his breath longer. A twenty-six-year-old physical trainer was retrieved unconscious and spitting up blood. However, his death two days later was deemed from other, preexisting causes.

In 2005 a seventeen-year-old girl died after filming a show that placed participants in the Australian outback to see how they would survive with primitive tools. In that same year *Extreme Makeover* was sued for $1 million. They found hopeful Deleese W. and promised to change her looks through plastic surgery. The show filmed family members saying how Deleese is "considered ugly," countered by a doctor who promised by the time the show was over to give the woman "a Hollywood smile like Cindy Crawford." Although she was flown to Los Angeles, the segment was canceled hours before surgery was to begin. Once sent home, unchanged, Deleese committed suicide.

What caused more outrage than these deaths was the French show *Celebrity Farm*, which had fifteen minor celebrities tending to animals. During production fifteen chickens and a duck died after pecking at phony sand that turned out to be poisonous, a rooster was crushed by a carelessly tossed bale of hay, a hen was electrocuted by cables, and a pony was injured and put down after being forced to walk up an escalator.

In 2006 Thailand TV raised the reality show to the max. It features the 1,000 death row inmates, via "death row cam," scheduled to die for drug trafficking. Many Westerners housed in the Bangkok prison—known as the Bangkwang Hilton, a facility built for 90,000 that holds 250,000 and where inmates take turns sleeping on available floor space—are shown as they are taken from their cells, marched down the corridor, and executed. The show's producers say the program is a public service to discourage drug dealers.

ERICH MARIA REMARQUE

All Quiet on the Western Front by Erich Maria Remarque (pseudonym of German author **Erich Paul Remark**) was a bestseller in 1929, a novel depicting the horror and hopelessness of World War I, stemming from the author's experience as a trench soldier in the German army. When the book was published, he went from being a man of marginal finances to being a wealthy playboy, driving fast cars and involved with a messy divorce. In 1933 the Nazis publicly burned and banned his works. By then, living in his château in Switzerland, he was unperturbed by Hitler's taunts and remained a staunch pacifist. He became a U.S. citizen in 1939, spent some time in Hollywood and New York, but moved back to Switzerland a decade later, where he stayed, rarely giving interviews, until he died of an aortic aneurysm in 1970 at age seventy-two.

> "A hospital alone shows what war is."
> —ERICH MARIA REMARQUE

IRA REMSEN

Ira Remsen, the father of artificial sweeteners, came upon the discovery of saccharin by accident. After working in the lab one day, experimenting with coal tar, he rushed home to have dinner with his wife. While buttering a roll, he licked his fingers and tasted something sweet that left a bitter aftertaste. Puzzled, he quickly went back to the lab to taste and sample all the chemicals he had been handling that day. He isolated the oxidation of a thing called toluenesulfonamide and dubbed it saccharin, the first sugar substitute. Long before the Food and Drug Administration required warning labels on artificial sweeteners, Remsen died in 1927 from a cerebral hemorrhage.

Saccharin used to have a warning label as a known human carcinogen, though it was removed from the danger list by the FDA in 2000. Overall incidence of brain and central nervous system cancers began to rise since the use of all artificial sweeteners, an industry that rakes in over $2 billion in U.S. sales each year.

RICHARD THE LIONHEARTED

RichardtheLionhearted,inhisownday, was oddly referred to as Richard Òc-e-Non, meaning Richard of the Yes and No. As son of King Henry II he was second in line for the throne after his older brother. In royal court Richard stood out and was said to be handsome, taller than most, with blond hair and light eyes. Before long, King Henry's sons tried to take the father's throne but failed. Richard then went to France where he made sure his father heard that he and King Philippe "ate from the same dish and at night slept in one bed." On July 4, 1189, Richard returned with the help of Philippe's army and made Henry declare Richard the next rightful heir. Two days later Richard bludgeoned his father and reportedly held the dying king's head, with "blood running out of his nose" in his hands. Richard had no love for England and said that if he could find a buyer for London, he'd sell it. Within a year he emptied dead Henry's treasury and then formed the Third Crusade with Philippe in the hope of raising more money. When Richard returned to England to regain power, he heard that a Roman treasure was found on the land of one of his subjects and quickly led a small army to seize the much-needed loot. While pacing the secured castle walls one night, he saw a figure in the darkness holding a crossbow and a frying pan as a shield. At first Richard laughed and applauded the bold one's audacity after an arrow struck the stone wall at his feet. Seconds later, a second arrow pierced Richard's shoulder. He tried to pull it out in private but eventually asked for a doctor's help. The removal so mangled his shoulder that it quickly became infected with gangrene. Before Richard died, he asked that the shooter be brought to him. When his assassin was found to be a young boy that said he shot the king for revenge for Richard's part in killing his father, those in attendance waited to hear if Richard would say yes or no to the boy's execution. Richard brought the boy close to him and spent time in private, eventually setting him free with 100 shillings. Richard died shortly after, supposedly content, at age forty-one in 1199.

SINCE A.D. 871 WHEN ALFRED THE GREAT BECAME KING OF ENGLAND, THE ENGLISH PEOPLE HAVE HAD 60 MONARCHS AND 2 LORD PROTECTORS. THE AVERAGE AGE OF DEATH OF A RULING KING OR QUEEN WAS 48.6 YEARS.

DAR ROBINSON

The greatest stunt made for film was performed by Dar Robinson during the 1979 production of *Highpoint,* when he jumped off the 1170-foot CN Tower in Toronto. He attached himself to an eighth-of-an-inch-thick cable to stop him just inches from the ground. He broke nine world records and entered the statistic books with twenty-one "world's first" feats. His nineteen-year career as a professional Hollywood stuntman was unblemished, with not a single broken bone. However, during the filming of the *Million Dollar Mystery* in 1986, while riding a motorcycle, he was accidentally run off a cliff by another stuntman and died at age thirty-nine. He can be seen doing most of Mel Gibson's more outlandish stunts in *Lethal Weapon,* a film dedicated to his memory.

GENE RODDENBERRY

Gene Roddenberry, the creator of *Star Trek*, died in 1991 at age seventy of a blood clot that caused a heart attack. Although he was married to the actress who played Nurse Chapel (Majel Barrett-Roddenberry) and the voice of the computer, he supposedly had an affair with communication's officer Uhura (Nichelle Nichols) while filming the series. But Roddenberry didn't reveal the truth before his death, at which time his ashes were placed in a lipstick-sized capsule, the first to be sent into orbit around Earth.

Star Trek debuted in 1966 and went on to become a success unheard of in TV history: The show spawned 6 separate Star Trek TV series, with 726 episodes and 10 motion pictures. What fans of the show liked was the underlying theme that there is a hopeful future for humanity, with all the possibility of cool gadgets it might bring. Of the original cast, DeForest Kelly (Dr. McCoy) died in 1999 at the age of seventy-nine of stomach cancer. Engineer Scotty, James Doohan, was beamed up in 2005 at age eighty-five of pneumonia.

RICHARD RODGERS

By 1935 the worst of the Depression was over. The big band sound with full orchestra and all the razzle and dazzle it presented, became the most popular on radio and in film. This is the year when a nationally broadcast radio program first began, *Your Hit Parade*, which reached American homes with the weekly top-ten hits. Top honors that year belonged to "The Most Beautiful Girl in the World," a waltz written by Richard Charles Rodgers. He wrote more than nine hundred songs and the scores for forty Broadway musicals. If ever a life depicted the motto "the show must go on" it was his. Rodgers, in his later years, battled back from cancer of the jaw, a heart attack, and a laryngectomy until the finale, when his heart gave out and he died at age seventy-seven in 1979.

JOHN AND WASHINGTON ROEBLING

John Augustus Roebling, designer of the Brooklyn Bridge, died at age sixty-three in 1869 of a tetanus infection after his leg was crushed by a ferryboat while he was inspecting pilings near Fulton Street on the Brooklyn side of the East River. His son, Washington A. Roebling, whom the senior Roebling considered marginally competent—despite a distinguished career in the Union Army, where he reached the rank of colonel—actually finished the bridge his father had planned, nearly dying himself a number of times during the seventeen years it took to complete. Washington, dogged by the "you're not good enough" specter of his father, proved his dead father wrong. Once the bridge was completed,

he retreated to New Jersey and put societal demands behind him. He died, caring little of what others thought of him, at the age of eighty-nine of a heart attack while doing what he loved to do—collecting rocks.

JOE ROSENTHAL

The most famous photo of World War II is the hoisting of the flag at Iwo Jima in 1945. One quarter of all medals of honor given out during World War II were awarded to marines for their actions during this battle, in which more than seven thousand U.S. forces died. The photo of raising the flag is the most produced photo of any war, shot by photographer Joe Rosenthal. It won a Pulitzer Prize, the only one to do so in the same year as its first publication. Of the six men featured, three died shortly after: **Franklin Sousley,** age nineteen, was killed by a Japanese sniper; **Harlon Block** (twenty) was killed by mortar shrapnel; **Michael Strank** (twenty-six) was the leader of the group, ordered to climb the hill to lay a telegraph wire. When he was told to replace the small flag already there with a bigger one, he thought that idea not too bright and only made them a better target for the Japanese. He was later killed by friendly fire from U.S. artillery shells. The three who initially

survived were **John Bradley,** who died of a stroke in 1994 at age seventy and whose son, James Bradley, wrote the bestseller, *Flags of Our Fathers*; **Ira Hayes,** a Native American, returned to the reservation and suffered from post-traumatic stress syndrome and alcoholism. He was found dead in a pool of his own blood and vomit at age thirty-two in 1955. **Rene Gagnon** was the only survivor who had tried to cash in on his celebrity, appearing in a few movies, but eventually became bitter and alcoholic, working as a janitor. When he was fired from this job on Memorial Day, no less, he died a few months later in 1979 at fifty-four of a heart attack. Rosenthal, the photographer, died in his sleep in a nursing home at age ninety-four in 2006.

BABE RUTH

George Herman Ruth, the Sultan of Swat, remains baseball's greatest legend and its home run king, hitting 60 in one year, 714 in total, without carrying the stigma of suspected steroid and amphetamine use or asterisks after his name. He was born in Baltimore to saloon keepers, raised on the streets, and was in enough trouble by the age of seven that his father signed away custody to St. Mary's Industrial School for Boys, a reform school. There, an athletic priest used baseball as a way to teach rules to the incorrigibles and to channel learning or behavioral disabilities into the love of a sport. According to tests conducted by psychologists at Columbia University in 1921, Ruth had been born with an above-average eye, ear, and muscle coordination due to hyperactive brain function, primarily in the posterior parietal cortex, the middle to rear section of the brain most often associated with spatial interpretations. Biologically, he might have been an equally good safe-cracker if never introduced to the game. Ruth's ultimate death from throat cancer at the age of fifty-three in 1948 was due most probably to his penchant for smoking cigars, chewing tobacco, and dipping snuff. However, studies have now shown that his fatal carcinoma, located in the nasopharynx, or the upper part of the throat behind the nose, are more often linked to other risk factors. The enhanced gamma-band activity (electrical signals) of his posterior parietal cortex, something he was born with, enabled him to pack the sensory stimuli of three lifetimes into one and might explain his well known womanizing, love of food, drink, and his excellence at baseball. The high-functioning spatial portion of his brain (think of a Pac-Man gobbling up dots) triggered his odd case of malignant cancer. What made him great—the anatomy of his brain—is what killed the Babe at a young age.

SACAGAWEA

Sacagawea was the young Shoshone Indian woman who served as Lewis and Clark's translator on their 1803 expedition to explore the uncharted western regions of America. She made the entire journey to the Pacific, and the return trip, with a newborn baby on her back; many believe that without her aid, the journey, commissioned by President Thomas Jefferson, would have ended in failure. Some accounts say she died in 1812 at age twenty-five of putrid fever, while others believe she died in 1884 on an Indian Reservation in Wyoming. The child she carried in a papoose was **Jean-Baptiste Charbonneau**, nicknamed Pompy, meaning first-born, who eventually attended St. Louis Academy with tuition paid by Clark. Pompy later met Prince Wilhelm of Germany while on a natural history expedition and traveled back to Europe with him, where Pompy learned to speak four different languages. But by the time he was twenty-four Pompy was back in North America living as a mountain man. When the Gold Rush of '49 started, he got caught up in the fever and died from too much time wading through cold rivers panning for gold. His cause of death was bronchitis at age sixty-one, and his portrait is the only one of a child on any U.S. coin.

*When **Meriwether Lewis** returned from the four-year expedition, he asked the new administration in Washington to pay his out-of-pocket expenses but was refused and left with a burdensome debt. He became an alcoholic and committed suicide at age thirty-five in 1809.*

***William Clark** became superintendent of Indian Affairs, assigned to place all the Indians he had met along his journey onto reservations, until his death at age sixty-eight in 1838 of pneumonia.*

JONAS SALK

Jonas Salk was the most celebrated medical scientist of the twentieth century. While researching a cure for the common cold, he developed an effective vaccine against polio. Before this, 57,600 would be crippled by polio each year. He died at age of eighty in 1995 of congestive heart failure. As an inventor without a shred of profit motive, he was one of the last of a rare breed. He once said, "Who owns my polio vaccine? The people! Could you patent the sun? It would be like selling air or water."

GEORGE SANDERS

George Sanders won an Oscar for a supporting role in *All About Eve*, but by the late sixties he was playing Mr. Freeze on the *Batman* TV series. In 1972 at age sixty-five he decided he had had enough and overdosed on barbiturates. His farewell message summed it up: "Dear World: I am leaving because I am bored. I feel I have lived long enough. I am leaving you with your worries in this sweet cesspool. Good luck."

EARL OF SANDWICH

The sandwich was named after **John Montagu,** the fourth Earl of Sandwich, a busy man of England seen always at his desk attending to the affairs of the navy and collecting art. To save time, he combined all the portions served on his plate inside a sliced small loaf of bread. Records indicate he began this custom in 1762. Although he lived a prosperous life, he had ill luck in marriage, sandwiched, some say, between two tragedies. His first wife went insane, and his second wife was murdered on his doorstep. He subsequently died of "grief" at age seventy-three in 1792.

Heartbreak Syndrome is now a condition recognized by medical science and capable of causing fatalities. The traumatic effect on victims of a crime, or persons who hear the news of a loved one's death or of some other equally personal tragedy, can actually trigger the heart to stop. A release of adrenaline and a massive amount of proteins produced by the nervous system acts as toxins to the body's system and overwhelms the heart, actually stunning it, causing sudden cardiac inactivity. For centuries, people knew this was possible, and heartbreak or sometimes "grief" and "nostalgia" were regularly cited as causes of death. Between 1766 and 1910, reportedly 31,987 people died from hearing that a loved one had died, or from missing their home, or from a prolonged overwhelming melancholy.

JEAN-PAUL SARTRE

Jean-Paul Sartre was awarded the Nobel Prize in Literature in 1964 but outspokenly declined to accept it, not wishing to be aligned with an institution or associated with official honors of any kind. Sartre was an existential philosopher, playwright, and novelist. He believed that man was entirely isolated in an indifferent universe and could be made to have a temporary semblance of worth only by his own experiences and self-interpretation of those actions. By 1964, the year of the award, Sartre officially denounced all literature as a preoccupation of the bourgeois mind and an absurd substitute for involvement in real life. He did live an ascetic existence with little material comforts and often indulged in drugs, such as LSD, when he deemed it necessary to augment his work, which he labored over at a merciless pace. At the end, he was blind and taking amphetamines to finish another volume of his long piece on ethics *L'idiot*, which was never fully completed. He died of edema of the lung in 1980 at age seventy-four and bequeathed his literary rights to his mistress, Arlette Elkaïm, one of the "family" of women he kept in flats throughout Paris and whom he legally adopted fifteen years before.

> "One is still what one is going to cease to be and already what one is going to become. One lives one's death, one dies one's life."
> —JEAN-PAUL SARTRE

THOMAS SAVERY

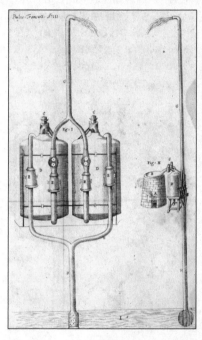

Thomas Savery is credited with building the first steam engine in the late 1600s. His machine was originally developed to pump water from flooded English mineshafts, saving many miners' lives and allowing greater productivity. He then took his invention to market and advertised its use for many other applications, such as running mills and pumping water into dry land or gardens. This use of machines, ones that used heat to move things, signaled the start of the very beginning of the Industrial Revolution. Savery died in 1715 at the age of sixty-five from dropsy, a condition often associated with living in poorly heated living quarters. Steam engines were used to evenly circulate heat, making cold English months bearable, though not in widespread use soon enough to save the life of its inventor.

DROPSY WAS THE SEVENTH LEADING CAUSE OF DEATH IN THE 1700S AND OFTEN MANIFESTED AS SWOLLEN FEET AND LEGS AND FAINTING SPELLS. THAT THE PERSON FELL DOWN OR DROPPED TO THE FLOOR WITHOUT WARNING, ONCE AFFLICTED WITH THE AILMENT, LED TO THE ORIGIN OF THE DISEASE'S NAME.

REBECCA SCHAEFFER

She co-starred in the TV sitcom *My Sister Sam* (1986–1988) playing the teenage sister of Pam Dawber. While on the show, Rebecca began to receive hundreds of letters from the same fan. The fan then began to stalk her. A year after the show was canceled, he obtained Rebecca's home address from the Department of Motor Vehicles. He confronted her outside her apartment in 1989 and stabbed her to death when she was twenty-one. The murderer, Robert Brado, had previously stalked Madonna and Tiffany before turning his fatal attention toward Rebecca. He is currently serving a life sentence without the possibility of parole.

Margaret Mary Ray was the dangerously persistent celebrity stalker of cerebral funnyman and Late Show *host David Letterman. Ray believed she and Dave were soulmates. She stole his Porsche in 1988, spied on his Connecticut home through binoculars, and was arrested more than half a dozen times for stalking. In 1998, at age forty-six, she committed suicide by kneeling in front of an oncoming train.*

IT IS ESTIMATED THAT 8 PERCENT OF AMERICAN WOMEN AND 2 PERCENT OF AMERICAN MEN WILL BE STALKED IN THEIR LIFETIMES— THAT'S 1.4 MILLION AMERICAN STALKING VICTIMS EVERY YEAR. THE MAJORITY OF STALKERS HAVE BEEN IN RELATIONSHIPS WITH THEIR VICTIMS, BUT HIGH PERCENTAGES WERE JUST ACQUAINTANCES, NEIGHBORS, FRIENDS, CO-WORKERS, OR DERANGED FANS.

FRANZ SCHUBERT

The term "Mad Hatter" described a person seen talking to himself, mumbling incoherently, and acting in bizarre and unpredictable ways. Hatmakers in the nineteenth century used mercury to preserve cloth and to give it a shapeable form. An inordinate amount of hatters subsequently went mad.

Franz Schubert's musical output is incredible, considering his humble origins—born to a peasant schoolteacher—and his short life. Over six hundred of his songs, sonatas, symphonies, and operas remain. Although he never achieved the fame or financial rewards of his contemporary composers, he did manage to see at least one hundred pieces of his work in print before his death. By age twenty-five Schubert was already showing signs of syphilis, and he began taking mercury in large quantities. He also began praying fervently to the Virgin Mary, and he wrote the famous "Ave Maria" in hopes of a cure for his illness. Apparently neither method worked. No one knew at the time that mercury affects the nervous system, causing nervousness, trembling, and dementia. Reportedly, his last years were punctuated by periods of apparent normalcy and times of being as mad as a hatter. It seems that Schubert also contracted thyroid fever in his last year, though most likely he died of the mercury at age thirty-one in 1828.

SEINFELD CURSE

The *Seinfeld* curse was a phenomenon attributed to the main cast members of that popular sitcom when it ceased producing new episodes and related to the inability of its stars to establish hits on their own (up until Julia-Louis Dreyfus's new sitcom *New Adventures of Old Christine* somehow managed to get picked up for its second season). Luckily, it didn't apply to real-life longevity. The only regular member deceased in 2006 was Jerry's TV father Morty Seinfeld, played by **Barney Martin**. A former New York City police officer and Irish Catholic, he played the quintessential Jewish father to a tee. Although Martin died of cancer at age eighty-two in 2005, he did live longer than Jack Klompus, his TV nemesis, played by **Sandy Baron** (Sanford Beresofsky), who died at age sixty-three of emphysema in 2001. **John Randolph**, who played George Costanza's father for the first season, died in 2004 at age eighty-eight of respiratory failure.

SEINFELD SYNCOPE

Certain individuals watching reruns of *Seinfeld* experienced fainting spells, and one man passed out facedown into his plate of food while the program aired. The condition was dubbed Seinfeld Syncope but actually has nothing to do with Jerry and the gang. It is related to narrowing of the arteries and the sudden drop of blood pressure caused by laughter.

ROD SERLING

Shows about spaceships and aliens were popular for viewers of TV in the fifties, and they were more on the mind after Americans began the race to the moon.

From 1959 to 1964 *The Twilight Zone*, created and written by Rod Serling, introduced America to the fifth dimension of the imagination and the supernatural. With stories of fantasy and science fiction, Serling perfected the ironic twist-ending as in the classic episode, "Time Enough at Last." Here, a bespectacled bookworm, played by Burgess Meredith, is dogged by the disturbances of modern life, always unsettling the quiet he needs to read. At the end, he alone survives a nuclear holocaust and stands on the steps of the New York Public Library with a big smile. That is, until his thick glasses fall off and he crushes them beyond repair, thus being unable to read a word of print in this desolate world of books. Serling wrote this and nearly all of the one hundred fifty-six episodes. He also wrote for the cinema, including *Planet of the Apes*. But like many of the characters he wrote about, his own struggle for success would be the very thing that undid him. After years of chain-smoking and Hollywood's ups and downs, his heart couldn't handle it by age fifty. In 1975, while finally acquiescing to go under the knife for bypass surgery, assured it was the only way to improve his heart, Serling died the next day of heart failure. As for Burgess Meredith—unable to recall the bookworm episode or much of anything else, he died of the *Twilight Zone* twist-ending of the age, Alzheimer's disease, in 1997 at age eighty-nine.

ANNE SEXTON

Autopsy reports present the best clues to determine facts no one could possibly be privy to, regardless of how much was known about a person's life. For example, when poet Anne Sexton (forty-five), who wrote notoriously about death (winner of the Pulitzer Prize for *Live or Die*), finally committed suicide, we know she did so in a red 1969 Cougar within the garage of her home in Boston on October 4, 1974. In her stomach there was ten ounces of vodka. She had stripped her hands of all jewelry and put on her mother's fur coat before she climbed into the driver's seat, turned on the ignition, and then the radio. Here the science of the autopsy report must be augmented with a mechanic's handbook: That type of car engine did not have a catalytic converter that removes lead from burning gasoline, thereby increasing the amount of carbon monoxide it would emit. Since the car in which she sat idled in a closed environment, it would produce enough carbon monoxide to be fatal, poisoning and ultimately killing Sexton of asphyxiation, within twenty-five to thirty-five minutes. Owing to factors such as the alcohol in her bloodstream and her body weight, Anne Sexton began to experience asthmatic gasping, that is, breathing only through her mouth, within approximately twenty minutes. No more than five minutes later Anne Sexton, who wrote, "Put your ear down close to your soul and listen hard," was dead. How hard she was listening at the end is unknown, but it is certain what she heard. The radio in her car was tuned to a rock station, WZBC, 90.3 on the dial. Derived from the coroner's time of death and WZBC's archived play list, the last song Anne Sexton heard was Steve Miller's "Fly Like an Eagle." Anne liked rock and roll, and singing along with the upbeat song most probably distracted her from imminent danger, making it uncertain if this was another trial run or the way she really wanted to die.

Sylvia Plath was an American poet, known for The Bell Jar *and* Ariel, *who was equally fixated on death and suicide. In 1963 at age thirty Plath killed herself with gas by putting her head inside her kitchen oven.*

WILLIAM SHAKESPEARE

Considered the greatest writer of the English language, Shakespeare wrote 38 plays and 154 sonnets, becoming modestly wealthy and celebrated for his genius during his life, though tremendously more so after death. Although he was married and fathered three, some say the bulk of his poems, written to a "Fair Lord," an anonymous young man, indicated bisexual tendencies he kept hidden. Others also claimed that he stopped writing in 1604 and that Thomas Marlowe or Francis Bacon wrote many of his works, though this remains a foolish proposition for most scholars and reflects the mystery how a man of such ordinary origins was able to capture so many epiphanies of humanity that remain true to this day. Shakespeare died on his fifty-second birthday in 1616. According to the vicar of the local church, a position responsible for noting death records, "[Shakespear] drank too hard . . . and died of a feavour there contracted." The fever actually had nothing do with drinking to excess, though may have weakened Shakespeare's immune system, and he succumbed to typhus, of which an outbreak occurred in London during that year.

Laurence Olivier was the only performer to win an Oscar for a Shakespearean role, playing Hamlet in 1948. "To be, or not to be: that is the question," and for Olivier his "not to be" happened in 1989 from cancer at the age of eighty-two.

GEORGE BERNARD SHAW

George Bernard Shaw was the first person to win a Nobel Prize for Literature in 1925 and an Oscar in 1938 for the screenplay *Pygmalion*. If nothing else, Shaw was a man of opinion and used his writing prowess to make his views known. As a socialist, he believed that land and capital should be divided equally, and for a period he even spouted approvingly on the virtues of the Stalin regime in Russia. He was also a dedicated vegetarian and an advocate of some bizarre health-related issues, such as his belief that wearing wool suits stimulated longer life. Whether from wool suits, winning, or stating his cause (or all of the above), he lived long and died in 1950 at age ninety-four of pneumonia.

WILLIAM L. SHIRER

In 1941 William L. Shirer made it to the top of the nonfiction bestseller list with *Berlin Dairies*, an inside look at the rise of Nazi Germany and World War II up to that date. Shirer had been a broadcast journalist stationed in Berlin, and he had attended most of Hitler's rallies and knew the leading players of the Third Reich firsthand. Despite his nasal-voice presentation, there wasn't an American unfamiliar with him and his partner **Edward R. Murrow,** who delivered real news from around the world in a style that CNN and all future journalists would later copy. Shirer bravely stayed inside Germany even as English bombs dropped on the city, but he got out shortly before the Gestapo tried to set up a case against him to arrest him as a spy. He thought at first to flush the papers that would become the *Berlin Diaries* because if he was caught, the material would get him executed. He bluffed his way through customs, hiding his journals under official Gestapo-stamped propaganda material. Thus he was able to provide a true view of Hitler's Germany, to the horror of millions. Despite his efforts during the war, Shirer was ultimately abandoned by Murrow and fired from a news show in 1950 after his name appeared in a pamphlet written by a former FBI agent, *Red Channels: The Report of Communist Influence in Radio and Television*. Shirer's name was among 151 others. For the remainder of the decade Shirer managed to earn a meager living on the lecture circuit and faced near ruin until his 1960 book *The Rise and Fall of the Third Reich*, a thousand-page tome that went through twenty-five printings the first year, again made him a bestselling author. Murrow's betrayal could not be forgotten by either man and the two never mended their friendship. Murrow died of cancer in 1965 two days after his fifty-seventh birthday. Winning bestseller status two times kept Shirer alive much longer; he died in 1993 at age eighty-nine of heart disease.

DINAH SHORE

"Shoefly Pie and Apple Pan Dowdie" became a hit for Dinah Shore (Frances Rose Shore) and the **Guy Lombardo** band in 1946 and apparently appealed to the public for the urge to get back to old-fashioned, pre-war American home-style living. (There are over one thousand American songs with food in the title from "A Chicken Ain't Nothin' but a Bird" to "You're the Cream in My Coffee.") Nevertheless, Dinah became the première southern belle of manners and class. She had eighty singles on the charts and hosted one of the longest-running television talk shows, *The Dinah Shore Show*, from 1951 to 1963 and again from 1970 through 1980. Although she overcame polio she contracted while young, and other hardships, she eventually succumbed to ovarian cancer in 1994 at age seventy-seven. Guy Lombardo is best remembered for his New Year's Eve television special broadcast from the

Waldorf Astoria Hotel from 1959 through 1976. He died of heart failure in 1977 at age seventy-five while rehearsing for that year's New Year's Eve show.

BERNARD SILVER

As grocery stores grew bigger, carrying more and more items, all in the food industry hoped for a day when they could keep track of the ever-changing inventory. In 1948, electrical engineering graduate student Bernard Silver, then attending Drexel Institute of Technology, overheard the CEO of Philly's *Food Fair* grocery chain ask the dean of the college to research and develop an inventory system. The dean refused, but Silver, along with his friend, mechanical engineer Norman J. Woodland, became fascinated. They subsequently developed the first bar code (also called Universal Product Codes, or UPCs) by looking at morse code, as Woodland said, "I just extended the dots and dashes downward and made narrow lines and wide lines out of them." When the vision of how to create bar codes came to Woodland, he was sitting in Miami Beach on a lounge

chair and began to draw lines in the sand. The pair patented the idea in 1952 but never made much commercial success of their invention, since the scanning technology that was required to make it valuable would not be perfected for another twenty years. The bar code wasn't used in a grocery store until the 1970s, first printed on a package of Wrigley's gum. Silver and Woodland sold the patent and all royalties to Philco in 1962 for $15,000. Philco in turn sold it to RCA. Today, the bar code is a $6-billion industry. Silver, the technical wizard behind the invention, died in 1963 at age thirty-eight of a blood disorder, apparently due to exposure to chemicals.

FRANK SINATRA

Frank Sinatra (Francis Albert) won an amateur showcase in 1937 and was soon singing with big bands, moving up quickly as the vocalist for the Tommy Dorsey band, which got Sinatra's name on the weekly hit parade. In 1942 he decided to go solo and recorded "Night and Day." Soon after, a new phenomenon was born— screaming fanatics, eventually dubbed "fans." Ten thousand youths gathered to get tickets to his next performance and in the rush a stampede ensued in which girls fainted and people were trampled before the ticket booth was destroyed.

From then on the icon status of a musical performer became an aspect of American culture. If nothing else, Sinatra had a gift of reinventing himself and never lost popularity during his sixty-five long years of performing, despite rumors of Mafia ties, or his womanizing and boozing. Eventually, his swaggering "My Way" attitude earned him the moniker Chairman of the Board, and he became regarded by many as one of the most influential musical performers of the twentieth century. The man who had been a heartthrob, making millions of girls' hearts go a-flutter, had his own heart throb and flutter one last time. He died on May 14, 1998 at age eighty-two of cardio respiratory arrest at his home in Beverly Hills, California.

ISAAC BASHEVIS SINGER

Isaac Bashevis Singer grew up in the Yiddish-speaking poor Jewish quarter of Warsaw and came to the United States fleeing the Nazi regime in 1935. Singer won the Nobel Prize for Literature in 1979 for publishing eighteen novels, fourteen children's books, and numerous short story collections which thematically explored the clash between new and old cultures. He died of a stroke in 1991 at age eighty-seven.

"When I was a little boy, they called me a liar, but now that I am grown up, they call me a writer."
—ISAAC BASHEVIS SINGER

RICHARD "RED" SKELTON

Richard "Red" Skelton was a limber-legged, rubber-faced clown—with or without makeup—who starred in twenty-three movies and had his own radio and television shows. His TV show, *The Red Skelton Hour*, was on the air for twenty years from 1951 to 1971. Each show ended with the famous, "Good Night and God Bless." His well-known clown personas were Freddy the Freeloader and

Clem Kadiddlehopper. Red died at eighty-four of heart disease and, ultimately, of pneumonia in 1997. Some said in private he was a cheerless and forlorn man, embittered because he felt he had been embezzled by a number of his associates. He never forgave CBS for canceling his show, for what he believed, was his support of the Vietnam War. He did make $2 million a year in his old age from his paintings of clowns, but he died trusting no one with his money.

BESSIE SMITH

Bessie Smith began her professional singing career at the age of eighteen in 1912, earning eight dollars a week. For many years she toured on the minstrel and vaudeville show circuit until she made her first recording in 1923, "Down-Hearted Blues," which sold over 750,000 copies in the first year, thereby making her the most successful black performer of her era. Her stage performances then earned fifteen hundred dollars per session, a tremendous sum at the time, although she received no royalties from the recordings; Bessie Smith received only thirty dollars per record of the one hundred sixty she recorded. Although many would now consider that she was duped into signing such a recording contract, Bessie was a hard-drinking, swaggering woman who reportedly would get into a knockdown fight over the slightest insult. The woman known as Empress of the Blues lived hard and fast. She died at the age of forty-three in 1937 in Mississippi. The speeding car she drove in as a passenger slammed into the rear end of a truck. Her arm was nearly severed, and she died of trauma and blood loss. Her bootlegger boyfriend, Richard Morgan, the driver of the car, was unharmed. No Breathalyzer tests were available to determine the root cause of the accident. Newspaper reports suggested that Bessie Smith died because she was taken to a segregated white hospital that refused treatment. However, records confirm that she was transported directly to Clarksdale's, a black hospital, where she died six hours later.

SOCRATES

Socrates' greatest achievement is considered to be the beginning of philosophical thought, which urged man to question his existence and pursue a deeper meaning in life. However, he disagreed with the basic principles of democracy, believing most people were too deluded and unable to govern themselves. As he aged, a famous Oracle called him the wisest man in Athens. But he was often portrayed by contemporaries as a comic fool who roamed the streets, discoursing about irrelevant things, asking rhetorical questions, such as "What is piety?" and "What is wisdom?" He was frequently beaten for his persistent questioning. Nevertheless, Socrates' open-air classes of youth grew larger, and the more serious meanings of his philosophical notions were disregarded by his enemies, who instead focused on Socrates' dislike of democracy. Certain officials viewed these beliefs as a serious threat. He was brought to trial on charges of atheism (not believing in the gods of the state) and of corrupting youth. His trial took nine hours with a jury of 500 citizens chosen by lots, seated on wooden benches, hearing arguments for and against. Many of the men of Athens at the time were bisexual, yet a few in the jury still didn't like the idea of Socrates sleeping with their sons. In the end, 280 members of the jury voted guilty, more for political reasons than for sexual conduct, proposing the penalty of death. Socrates could have chosen banishment and even escaped once in jail, but he was old and preferred to die. Under Athenian law, the condemned were executed by drinking a cup of poisoned hemlock that caused a slow and agonizing paralysis of the central nervous system. Socrates died at age seventy in 399 B.C.

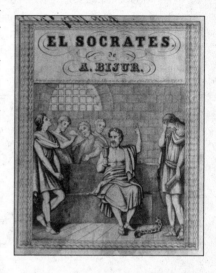

SOLOMON

When Solomon struggled for the throne of Judea in 968 B.C., he had his competition executed. This included his brother Adonijah, a rival's sympathizer Joab, and a traitor Shimein, all "struck down" to guarantee his rule. Once in power, he indentured thirty thousand men to build a massive temple, where he held court and ruled wisely. Nevertheless, he also reportedly took seven hundred princesses and three hundred concubines to bed before he died from termites. At the end of his life, he died standing on his feet. Accordingly, it was termites, which had eaten his cane, that caused him to fall down dead in 928 B.C. at the age of seventy-two.

BIBLE LONGEVITY

The people of Judea, a small country amid the forever conflicting boundaries of massive empires, left the most recorded names of ancient persons who upon investigation actually existed. The preserved scripture, or history of the Hebrews, known as the Old Testament, is the primary reason the Jewish religion and culture has existed for so long. If nothing had been written, within no more than a few generations all traces of their existence would have been impossible to find and unlikely to have passed from millennium as it has. These first Semitic people kept alive the lineage by tracing ancestry to **Abraham**, considered the founder that led his clan out of Northern Mesopotamia to settle in a land called Canaan,

now present-day Israel, in around 2000 B.C. It was not an easy feat, and it seemed that he is remembered in writings of Judaism and Islam as a man who had more of this intangible thing called faith than anything else, belief in a singular god of his imaginings called "I Am" or Yahweh. Three different texts say he lived to the age of one hundred seventy-five and fathered his son Isaac when he was one hundred. Abraham's wife **Sarah** died at the age of one hundred twenty-seven.

Moses, who lived a blockbuster life, died a "delightful death" when God figured he had had enough. Moses handed off his famous staff and walked alone into the mountains, even though he wasn't sick or particularly wanted to die. He obeyed the command for what reads like a cosmic euthanasia. At least, we're told, the angels were on hand to perform the burial service when he died at age one hundred twenty in 1405 B.C. According to the Bible, other figures lived to incredibly old ages as well: **Adam,** the first man, lived nine hundred thirty years, **Methuselah** lived to age nine hundred sixty-nine. **Noah** lived nine hundred fifty years, three hundred fifty years after the Great Flood. For all, besides Noah, it seems after this event man's longevity took a serious plunge, where fifty years old was ancient. Scientists looking for clues to these seemingly impossible life spans say the earth's atmosphere during this period was less radioactive and didn't cause aging as rapidly as it did afterward. Natural radiation now places 60 mrems (the measurement for radiation) per year into the organs of everything alive, which will cause the growth of cancerous cells and irreparable aging of human cells when the accumulative mrem count reaches 10,000. Back then, theoretically, there was no radiation or much less. Others say the Bible's longevity is an error in translation and that the cycles of the moon were counted as years. Nevertheless, those fanatical about longevity are blocking the killer environmental radiation by constructing houses with lead-lined walls and wear woven lead apparel for ventures outdoors.

HERNANDO DE SOTO

Beginning in 1539, Hernando de Soto explored the mainland of North America and spread a minor cold—previously unexperienced in the region—that eventually killed 75 percent of the native population. His was a three-year odyssey in search of gold and an open passage to the Pacific Ocean, which led him to hike from Florida up to Lake Michigan, discovering the Mississippi River and venturing down into Texas. The route he took later became U.S. roads; where he camped became the first cities; and the places where he crossed rivers are the sites where bridges still stand. During the third year, while trying to build ships to take him back to Cuba, he died of exhaustion and a runny nose he couldn't shake at age forty-five in 1542. His men tied rocks around his feet and sunk his body in the Mississippi.

SPARTACUS

In 73 B.C. Spartacus led an escape of seventy gladiator-slaves armed with only utensils and considerable stealth from their chambers below the Roman Coliseum. Because slaves outnumbered the ruling class in Rome, this rebellion was seen as a serious threat. Three thousand soldiers were dispatched to recapture Spartacus' entourage, though they were humiliated and repelled by the gladiators who used only vines, sticks, and a handful of weapons. Eventually, more than 120,000, including old slaves, women, and children, were inspired by

Spartacus to run away. He welcomed them and employed them to make weapons for their defense. His rag-tag army managed to defeat whatever Rome sent against him for two full years, until he was cornered in the boot of Italy as he sought ships to take his people back to their homelands. There, eight Roman Legions separated and defeated Spartacus' force piecemeal. Although Spartacus left captured Roman soldiers unharmed, the Romans, once victorious, showed no mercy. More than 6,600 of his men were crucified. Their bodies, rotting corpses, and then skeletons remained for decades on the main road to Rome, serving as gruesome billboards for slaves contemplating escape. Some say Spartacus died in the last battle, but there were too many dead for his body to be retrieved or recognized. Others say his men were so loyal that none would give up his identity and that he, too, was crucified in 70 B.C. at age forty-nine.

JOHN STEINBECK

John Steinbeck won the Nobel Prize for Literature in 1962 for his novels depicting the underdog and the rural American life of the migrant worker. His classic *Of Mice and Men* is still read by a multitude of school-children every year. Steinbeck was a socially accepted writer, more so than Faulkner or Hemingway, and was friend to Presidents John F. Kennedy and Lyndon B. Johnson. Other than his masterpiece *Grapes of Wrath*, which won the Pulitzer Prize in 1939, his works are currently considered by

many as less literary and too preachy. He died of heart failure in 1968 at age sixty-six.

> "It seems to me that if you or I must choose between two courses of thought or action, we should remember our dying and try so to live that our death brings no pleasure on the world."
> —JOHN STEINBECK

DAVID STRICKLAND

David Strickland played the rock music reporter Todd Stites in the sit-com *Suddenly Susan* (1996–2000). Two years into the show Strickland was busted for cocaine possession, put on probation, and sent to rehab. In 1999, three days before he was due in court, he went on a seventy-two-hour drug and alcohol binge. As the judge's gavel pounded, ordering a warrant for his no-show, Strickland was dead at age twenty-nine, hanging from bed-sheets he tied to a ceiling beam.

ED SULLIVAN

The debut of the *Ed Sullivan Show* in 1948, originally called the *Toast of the Town*, set the tone for TV variety and entertainment shows for years to come. Ed Sullivan, a former jour-nalist, despite his stiff and awkward stone-faced persona made his "really big shew" a Sunday TV night standard for over two decades until 1971. His introductions of guests were no less fluid: "This is José Feliciano. He's blind. And he's Puerto Rican." Nev-ertheless, the show was indeed big and introduced more than a few who became cultural icons, from Elvis (shot only from the waist up), to the unknown Barbra Streisand, to the Beatles. The cross section of talent on the program reached out to every demographic by presenting the eclec-tic mix that was becoming American culture, from Pearl Bailey (died at age seventy-two in 1990 of heart failure) to opera great Maria Callas (died in 1977 at age fifty-three of heart failure). Ed Sullivan signed off permanently in 1974 at age seventy-three of the worst form of stiff neck possible, cancer of the esophagus.

Another candidate for rehab, **Robert Pastorelli** played the housepainter in Murphy Brown *(1988–98)* and gave a chilling performance as a killer in the film Striking Distance *in 1993. In 2001 his girlfriend, Charemon Jonovich, was found dead in his apartment, and he told police he had tried to stop her from committing suicide when the gun went off. In 2004, after word was out that the authorities had decided to change the cause of the girlfriend's death from accidental gunshot to murder, Pastorelli was found dead the next day of a heroin overdose at age fifty.*

"Television is going to be the test of the modern world . . . we shall discover a new and unbearable disturbance of a general peace or a saving radiance in the sky. We shall stand or fall by television—of that I am quite sure," E. B. White *wrote in 1938.* **Elwyn Brooks White,** *the author of* Charlotte's Web *and* The Elements of Style, *among other books, noted for his precision in grammar, unfortunately, succumbed to Alzheimer's at age eighty-six in 1985 when the most popular show on TV was* Growing Pains.

The first televised sports extravaganza featured the Joe Louis–Billy Conn heavyweight fight at Yankee Stadium in June 1946. The program shocked advertisers with the reach this new medium had to audiences. It was estimated that 150,000 people saw the fight on 5,000 sets. More than 30 people crowded around in homes with this new invention, many seeing a sporting event on TV for the first time. The television picture screen was ten inches wide, set in a cabinet that weighed ninety-five pounds, and cost $352 at a time when the average annual salary was $2,992 and the cost of a loaf of bread was fourteen cents. **Billy Conn** *had lost his championship bout to Joe Louis in 1941, and this '46 rematch was a long-awaited event. Conn was knocked out in the eighth round, which effectively put an end to his career. He died in 1993 at age seventy-five of pneumonia.* **Joe Louis** *died of a heart attack in 1981 at age sixty-six.*

JOHN L. SULLIVAN

America's first nationally recognized sport celebrity was Irishman John L. Sullivan, billed as The Boston Strongboy. He stood 5-foot-10-inches and weighed, at his heaviest, 229 pounds. His official record, between 1878 and 1905, states he fought 35 fights and won 31, with over half of them by knockout. This doesn't include his cross-country tour when he staged 195 boxing presentations in 136 different cities, charging $250 to anyone dumb enough to get in the ring with him. John grew up in the Roxbury part of Boston, then overcrowded and teeming with Irish immigrants. He was arrested many times as a teenager for fighting at neighborhood makeshift rings set up for taking bets. By the time John turned pro, bare-knuckle fights were typically replaced by the use of padded gloves, and most of his matches followed these rules. He does go down as the last fighter to participate in a bare-knuckle match in 1889, and one that incidentally lasted for an unbelievable 75 rounds. Sullivan rallied after he puked all over the canvas during the forty-fourth round and remained toe-to-toe until the opponent finally threw in the towel hours later. Big John's endurance was incredible by any standards, especially since he rarely trained and was often dragged off a barstool and brought directly to the ring. Eyewitnesses said his handshake could bring tears to your eyes. In 1905, while still sporting his signature broom-handled mustache and slight Irish brogue, John publicly renounced alcohol and joined the temperance movement. Still, the American champion and first sports celebrity died from complications of liver disease and, ultimately, cardiac arrest at age fifty-nine in 1918. He reportedly made $1 million from his fighting career but spent most of his fortune on drink, before he swore off it, for himself and his friends.

SUPERMAN

Superman, the Man of Steel, originally a comic book character, was adapted for a television series in 1952. **George Reeves** (George Keefer Brewer) starred in 104 episodes of the program that stayed in syndication for decades. Along with *The Lone Ranger,* Clayton Moore, Reeves was one of the biggest stars loved by kids of the 1950s and early sixties. This popularity backfired for Reeves, who considered himself a movie actor primarily, first seen in the 1939 film *Gone With the Wind.* When *The Adventures of Superman* was canceled, he found he was typecast thereafter as Clark Kent disguised. Saddened more than his friends knew, especially his fiancée **Lenore Lemmon,** Reeves supposedly shot himself at age forty-five three days before his wedding. Officially, Reeves's death was listed as suicide, but many believed it was a hired killing. Six months prior, Reeves had dumped his girlfriend, a married woman, **Toni Mannix,** eight years his senior, who had been publicly distraught and harassed Reeves after the breakup. (When Mannix's husband, an MGM executive with alleged mob ties, died in 1963, the once-jilted lover transformed her mansion into a shrine for Reeves, with his pictures and memorabilia covering every inch of wall space.) Others say Lenore Lemmon was the shooter and that after a night of partying they had a quarrel, in which Reeves had called off the wedding, and that his will, which proved correct, had bequeathed his entire estate to Toni Mannix. She died at age seventy-seven in 1983 from complications with Alzheimer's disease. Lemmon, a one-time lounge singer, banned from clubs for brawling and supposedly setting a waitress

on fire, died in 1990 age sixty-six of cancer. Before Mannix or Lemmon had died the actors who played Jimmy Olsen and Lois Lane had opened an investigation to find out the true cause of foul play but came up with no conclusive answers.

REAL LIFE KRYPTONITE

The actor **Christopher Reeve,** who played in the *Superman* movies, starting in 1978 through 1987, was not related to George Reeves, though this seemed to some an eerie coincidence. In 1995, after suffering an equestrian accident where his head was totally detached from his spine and held together by neck muscles, he subsequently, after successful surgery, was bound to a wheelchair and ventilator, paralyzed from the neck down. Although Reeve admitted to considering suicide, he instead showed real-life Superman heroics and eventually started spinal injury research foundations and continued to act. An infection in the bone marrow entered his blood and killed him of a heart attack at age fifty-two in 2004. Two years later, Christopher's wife, Dana, succumbed to lung cancer at age forty-four.

WILLIAM TAFT

William Taft, the twenty-seventh president (1909–1913), is usually remembered for his distinction as the largest president, weighing at times over 350 pounds. Early medical records indicate Taft suffered an accident from a horse at age eleven, which possibly disturbed his pituitary gland and caused his unregulated weight gain. By the time he was eighteen years old Taft was 5 feet 11 inches and weighed 240 pounds. Today, Taft would be considered an emotional eater; his large weight gains correlated to stress. Although he was immensely obese, when calculated by body mass standards, his surprising longevity—he died at age seventy-two—may be attributed to his abstinence from all alcohol, for which he was ridiculed and dismissively called a teetotaler. Before the age of microphones, to keep up his loud and booming voice, medicines mixed with cocaine were regularly prescribed. This exacerbated his heartburn, acid reflux, gout, and what he called internal inflammation, or severe indigestion, which kept him bedbound for weeks at a time.

William Taft went on periodic diets and fluctuated 100 (plus or minus) pounds in weight. He was diagnosed with chronic cystitis, a condition resulting in recurring discomfort or pain in the bladder, hardening of the arteries, angina, and oxygen deprivation or breathlessness. Today, he might be diagnosed, as well, with Alzheimer's disease, but most likely his memory loss and confusion were results of a lifetime of obesity. When he said, before he died—according to

Taft's bid for a second term scored the worst incumbent defeat in presidential election history. During the reelection campaign Taft was often immobilized by indigestion. A bad stomachache, it may be said, allowed Woodrow Wilson to become president, which altered the course of U.S. involvement in World War I.

*At a Fourth of July celebration in 1850 at the Washington Monument, President **Zachary Taylor** sampled many of the covered dishes donated by citizens. He became very ill, possibly from food poisoning of the Listeria variety, and died three days later. Many historians had their doubts and exhumed his body in 1991. When arsenic was found during the autopsy, it was believed he was murdered, although the original death certificate stated "Acute Indigestion."*

the death certificate, of "debility"—"I don't ever remember being president," there is a very good possibility that he really meant it.

NIKOLA TESLA

If ever there was a candidate to prove that time travelers from the future have made appearances throughout history, Nikola Tesla would surely be one modern inventor eligible for consideration. From the details of his birth, arriving on Earth at midnight, during a strange and curiously fierce electrical storm, to his peculiar and lonely death, his life manifested an extraordinary talent. As an adult, Tesla had the persona of a magician, mysterious and aloof, who unveiled his creations with the fanfare of a performer. Many of his inventions, even to this day, remain futuristic in design and concept, from teleportation, death rays, and anti-gravity warships to alternating current, the spark plug, and the radio. Nevertheless, Tesla made a powerful enemy when he beat Thomas Edison, proving how Edison's direct current electricity was not safe and that his alternating current, with the backing of George Westinghouse, was better. In addition, Tesla was bizarre and spoke of things too far-out for investors not to shy away from, especially after his obsessive-compulsive disorder made him always circle a block three times, fold things three times, and do everything in threes. Without marketing prowess, he lost his patents for many inventions, including the radio to Guglielmo Marconi. (The credit as the inventor of the radio was eventually given back to Tesla, following his death in 1943.)

According to a recent Gallup poll, 100 million Americans think aliens have visited Earth. Devotees believe that one-third of the missing-person cases in America are unsolvable because the individuals have been abducted by aliens—not aliens across the border but those from outer space. Data compiled by the FBI lists over 800,000 missing-person reports in 2006. More than half will remain forever missing or, as some believe, living with aliens and more than 13,000 will be found deceased.

Tesla spent much of his later years living in a New York hotel trying to use his radio waves to signal deep into the solar system, convinced transmissions were being sent from outer space. Destitute, weakened by coronary disease, he died alone in his hotel room at age eighty-six. When his body was found,

Edwin Armstrong went on to perfect the radio but was baffled when his invention of the FM radio-band signal was not embraced as the best sound to deliver music over the airwaves. He subsequently jumped out of his apartment window and died when he hit the ground thirteen stories below at age sixty-four in 1954.

it seemed to some similar to a sack of skin, the way a snake would shed its casing. There are those who believe his preoccupation with listening to space and what to many seemed a squandering of his genius, was perhaps his quest to get back to the time from which he arrived. Nevertheless, the FBI seized most of his writings and has yet to release them; they're still classified as top secret.

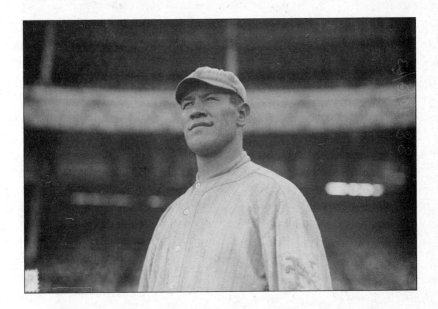

JIM THORPE

The first nationally recognized football star was Jim Thorpe, a two-time Olympic gold-medal winner who began playing pro football in 1913. Thorpe was a Native American and considered by many as the greatest all-round athlete of the twentieth century, eventually holding records in college and pro football, track and field, and baseball. In 1920 he was elected the first president of the American Professional Football Association, which later became the NFL. By age forty-one he retired from sports and struggled at odd jobs to feed his family. He played cameo roles as an Indian chief for a few Hollywood movies, but mostly he struggled with poverty and his Achilles' heel, alcoholism. He died of complications from this disease, and ultimately, cardiac arrest while eating dinner in his Lomita, California, trailer home in 1953 at age sixty-four.

THE STRAIN OF SCREAMING

The man most influential in transforming football into the modern sport was legendary coach **Glenn "Pop" Warner.** He taught players to use formations and cross-body blocks. He put numbers on jerseys and encouraged the use of shoulder pads and thigh pads. A lawyer at first, he gravitated to coaching soon after graduating from Cornell in 1894 and remained one of the most winning coaches for forty-four years. In 1929 he started the Pop Warner Youth Football League, which still exists, to teach youth "the strain of struggle and the joy of victory." He died in 1954 at age eighty-three of cancer of the throat.

TIGHTROPE WALKERS

The funambulist, or tightrope walker, has long been the visually stunning symbol of a risk taker, often associated with circuses and by definition regularly performing death-defying acts. Although walking on a wire at any height requires skill, it only becomes of value when the wire is strung high above the ground, making no margin of error the thrill.

The Wallenda Family are the best-known modern-day high wire stunt and circus performers. The patriarch, German-born Karl Wallenda, began learning the trade at age six in 1905 and, along with his brother, joined the Barnum Circus, making their sensational American debut at Madison Square Garden in 1928 without a net. More and more family members joined the troupe until they had enough to perfect the famous seven-person pyramid on the wire. In 1962 the pyramid collapsed and son-in-law Richard Faughnan and nephew Dieter Schepp died from injuries sustained in a 38-foot fall. In 1972 another son-in-law was electrocuted while climbing a pole to perform his part of the act. Eventually, Karl went solo and walked above football stadiums and made a 1,200-foot daredevil tiptoe across the Tallulah Falls Gorge in Georgia when he was sixty-five years old. In 1978 at age seventy-three he died when he fell from a cable 750-feet-long strung between beachfront hotels in Puerto Rico. A strong gust of wind blew him off 100 feet to the ground, where he landed on a taxi cab before bouncing to the sidewalk, dying of multiple fractures and trauma.

Harold Davis, billed as *The Great Alzana*, performed the wildest acts on the high wire, back-flipping, cycling, and jumping rope. He refused to use a net. "If ye have it," he said, "ye fall into it." He broke his back on three separate occasions: in Miami, Boston, and New York. After his last accident, New York State passed a law requiring trapeze artists to use a net. When he retired, he sat in the backyard of his Sarasota, Florida, house, perched on a ladder and walked on a low wire he had strung in his garden, performing for an audience of ants and crickets. He eventually gave himself a heart attack and died at age eighty-two in 2001.

SPENCER TRACY

Spencer Tracy won two Oscars, one for *Captains Courageous* (1937) and then the following year best actor for *Boys Town* (1938). He shared the record of most nominations, totaling nine, with Laurence Olivier. Tracy, from hard-drinking Irish American stock, once said, "Hell, I used to take two-week lunch hours!" He died of a heart attack at age sixty-seven in 1967.

SOJOURNER TRUTH

Sojourner Truth (1797–1883) was born a slave in New York but gained her freedom in 1827, after most of her thirteen children had been sold. In 1836 Truth became the first black to win a slander tort against the press. In 1851 at a Women's Convention in Akron, Ohio, she delivered a famous speech called, "Ain't I a Woman," which overwhelmed even detractors. She had remarkable intelligence despite her illiteracy, and became a tireless speaker and the "world's oldest lecturer" at eighty-six. During the Civil War she collected food and clothing to give to black regiments, and once she had a meeting with Abraham Lincoln at the White House and asked if one day he could outlaw segregation in public places, such as on streetcars and at restaurants. In 1883 she became ill with an ulcer on her leg. Dr. Kellogg of the Battle Creek Sanitarium, later noted for cornflakes, grafted some of his own skin onto Sojourner's leg in a failed attempt to save her.

TUTANKHAMEN

Ancient Egypt was ruled by pharaohs who were considered divine, yet most rulers ended their lives in very earthly ways, usually through murder, mayhem, or mysterious disappearances. Tutankhamen, or King Tut, is the most famous pharaoh, known as "the Boy King." His mummy has traveled the world since his tomb was discovered in 1922 and has been viewed by millions. X-rays of his remains reveal his cause of death to be a blow to the back of the head he most likely received while he slept. However, a few less realistic experts say he died of natural causes, perhaps a brain tumor or lung disease. He began his pharaohship at age nine in 1334 B.C. and died ten years later at age nineteen.

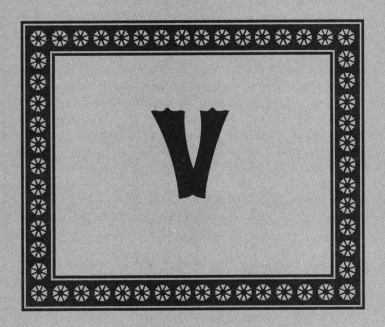

RUDOLPH VALENTINO

Rudolph Valentino, half French and half Italian, with androgynous good looks, was the first male to be a cinema sex symbol. Although a professional tango dancer and recording artist, he made a name for himself in silent pictures, in particular *The Sheik* (1925), in which an endless harem of women swooned into his arms. He died before the Academy Awards started, but he was no doubt the box office winner of the silent movie era from 1914 to 1926, when he officially passed away from complications of ulcer surgery at age thirty-one. Unofficially, it's believed the hole in his stomach was from a gunshot wound he received when a jealous husband caught him in one of his many trysts. More than one hundred thousand people came to Valentino's funeral. Newspapers across the country reported that women were committing suicide, and stories circulated of at least two dozen fans supposedly dying of a heart attack when they heard the news. In fact, Valentino's beloved guard dog, Kahar, waited by the door for two weeks for his master to return, and then died suddenly and for no apparent reason.

RUDY VALLÉE

"As Time Goes By" was a popular Rudy Vallée (Hubert Prior) number in 1931, championing romantic love with the sentiment that no matter what happens "love will last, as time goes by." (The song was later used in the movie *Casablanca*.) Before there was Sinatra or Elvis, girls swooned at the voice of Rudy Vallée, aka the Vagabond Lover, singing through a megaphone. By the end of World War II, Vallée's singing career fizzled but not his drive to stay active. He acted in more than fifty films and television productions until his death in 1986 of throat cancer a few weeks before his eighty-fifth birthday. He died while watching a television program showing the unveiling of the improved Statue of Liberty, took a deep breath, and expired. His death certificate reported that he died of a heart attack.

CORNELIUS VANDERBILT

In the early 1800s, at age sixteen, Cornelius Vanderbilt started his first ferry service, transporting farmers from Staten Island to sell their produce at Whitehall Street in Manhattan. He worked around the clock, fearing neither the weather nor the competition, often resorting to slug matches to make a place for himself on the rough waterfront. In no time he dominated the waterways by lowering fares to cripple the competition until the competition was forced to buy him out at tremendous profit. When the Gold Rush hit in '49, Vanderbilt saw the opportunity to get people west faster than by covered wagon via steamships. He built a canal attached to a series of lakes straight across Nicaragua. When partners tried to double-cross him, Vanderbilt sent this note, infamous in the annals of American business: "Gentlemen: You have undertaken to cheat me. I won't sue you, for the law is too slow. I'll ruin you."

When a Tennessee preacher, **William Walker,** declared himself dictator of Nicaragua and interfered with Vanderbilt, the tycoon barricaded Walker's supplies until he was driven from power, fleeing to Honduras where he was executed by a firing squad (at age thirty-six in 1860). Again, Vanderbilt was paid to leave Central America, this time for a fee of $56,000 per month. After the Civil War he put his same bullying business tactics into the railroads by buying and manipulating stocks. Vanderbilt was not generous (philanthropy was left to his descendants) dying in 1877 of what the *New York Times* cited as "exhaustion" at age eighty-two as the richest man in the world, valued at $100 million, equivalent to $8 billion in today's money.

The cause of death cited as "exhaustion" on a male's death certificate was quite common in the 1800s. It indicated that the deceased was admired, displaying society's value in the work ethic of the time. Lower-class individuals never had this term mentioned; to the contrary, the cited cause of death was "lacking fortitude." Women would equally never see "exhaustion" cited as a cause at the end of their lives, although it was frequently cited when death occurred during childbirth.

GIOVANNI DA VERRAZANO

In 1524 an Italian sailing under French colors, Giovanni da Verrazano, explored the North American coast from Newfoundland to the Carolinas and was the first to discover New York Harbor. He described the inhabitants of New York City at the time: "The people are almost like unto the others, and clad with feather of fowls of diverse colors. They came towards us very cheerfully, making great shouts of admiration." But Verrazano didn't get the same welcome when he sailed south to the Caribbean and anchored off Guadeloupe. There, in 1528 at the age of forty-three, he was placed in a boiling cauldron and eaten while still fresh.

AMERIGO VESPUCCI

Amerigo Vespucci was an Italian cartographer who supposedly made two voyages under the Spanish flag to the New World, although questions arise whether he actually did. He was the first, for certain, to make Europeans realize what Columbus had discovered were two entirely new continents and not part of Asia, as even Columbus believed until the day he died. He was a well-educated merchant, widely read, and had some art tutelage lessons by Michelangelo on his résumé. His renderings and map published in 1507 used Amerigo's first name so prominently that the landmasses were eventually referred to as America. The map publisher had tried to rename it on the second printing, but America sounded exotic enough that the tag stuck. Vespucci was given a job in Seville as chief of navigation to train sailors until his death in 1512 at age fifty-eight of intermittent fever (either typhus or malaria). He caught the fever from a sailor returning from the continents that bore his name.

VIKINGS

The Vikings had their heyday from the eighth to the eleventh century, when Norsemen from the Scandinavian regions used long ships, powered by sails and oars to invade most of Europe, even down to Baghdad, and into Russia. Vikings

were rightly feared because they attacked in stealth, not interested in taking too many prisoners. One leader, **Erik Bloodaxe,** had a name that summed up his career. At first he was admired for his ability to wield the unique Viking weapon, a heavy iron ax blade capable of halving a head like a walnut. Bloodaxe was made king for a while, but he was dispelled by popular demand, some say he had an image problem with a name like his, particularly during peacetime. He was lured into the moors of North England's Teesdale by the agent of a rival king and murdered by an even bloodier ax in 954.

Erik the Red (no relation to the Bloodaxe family) was named for his flaming red hair and beard, although it could have been for his temper as well. When he was young, his father was expelled from Norway owing to "some killings." He moved with his family to Iceland. There, just like his father, Erik was eventually banished for "some killings" and murder of his neighbors that forced him to venture five hundred miles west, where he settled in Greenland. If he had been less of a hothead, America would never have been discovered. From Greenland he encouraged trips farther west, until his son **Leif Eriksson** stumbled upon Newfoundland, which he called Vinland, for the wild grapes they found growing in the woods. From 1000 to 1003, along with his sister and brothers, Leif tried to establish a North American colony, sending excursions down as far as Maryland. After Erik died of influenza in the winter 1003 at age fifty-three, Leif never made another voyage back to Vinland and stayed to lead the settlement at Greenland. He did send his brother, Thorwald, who was killed by Native Americans, as well as his other brother, Thorstein, who went to retrieve the body but was blown out to sea. Leif died in 1020 at age fifty-eight of pneumonia. His last words: "If two men think alike, then one of them is not thinking."

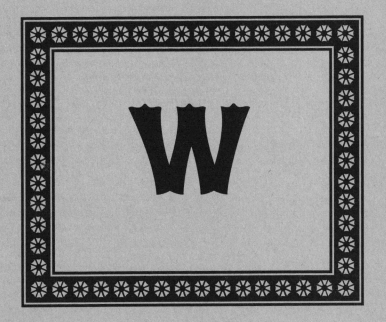

FATS WALLER

Fats Waller (Thomas Wright Waller), born in 1904, had his first music job as an organist in movie theaters when he was sixteen, but by the mid–1920s he was recording and composing songs. His most famous, "Ain't Misbehavin'," was

written for the Broadway production of *Hot Chocolates* and performed by Louis Armstrong in 1929. Fats (weighing over 300 pounds) had an insatiable appetite for life, infatuated not only by his music but by women, alcohol, and food as well. Due to the stress of palimony and alimony suits, his weight and alcohol abuse increased, and he struggled in his last years with ill health (diagnosed once as walking pneumonia) to keep up with a grueling touring schedule. In 1943 he died unexpectedly of a heart attack, resulting from pneumonia, at age thirty-nine on board a train heading to the next performance near Kansas City, Missouri.

Nowadays, when a doctor gives a person a diagnosis of walking pneumonia, he is usually referring to an infection from an organism called Mycoplasma pneumoniae, *a bacteria that affects the respiratory system which is unlikely to do as much damage as full-blown pneumonia. Back in Fats' day, it meant he was suffering from immune system deficiencies, brought on by stress and an improper lifestyle that allowed microorganisms, viruses, chemical irritants, or foreign bodies to affect his heart and kill him.*

GEORGE WASHINGTON

George Washington became the first president of the United States in 1789. He was offered a salary of $25,000 (exorbitant at the time), which he at first turned down, not wishing to ruin his reputation as a selfless public servant. He was convinced to accept it, not to set a precedent that would have future presidents come only from a pool of the wealthiest citizens. After he left office in 1797, he retired to his Mount Vernon estate. There he helped a neighbor whose carriage ran into a ditch during a storm. He came down with a sore throat and summoned his personal physicians when it grew worse. Back then, even the most respected doctors believed that illness resulted from an imbalance in the body's four life-sustaining fluids, called humors, and that draining significant quantities of blood from a patient would return the body to a healthy, balanced state. Washington's doctors drained a pint of his blood and made him drink a concoction of molasses, vinegar, and melted butter.

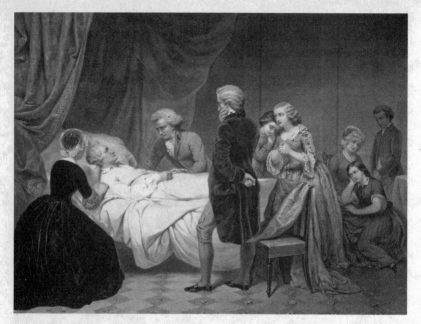

Heedless of Washington's protests, they repeated this three times, until he died soon after, at age sixty-seven in 1799. Pneumonia was the official cause listed on Washington's death certificate—not malpractice. Moments before his death Washington pulled his doctor close to his lips and whispered that he was not to be buried promptly; his fear of being buried alive was so great. The church bells tolled for four days without stopping before his casket was placed in the ground.

For the fiftieth anniversary of the Declaration of Independence, the government declared 1826 a "year of national jubilee." While across the country people celebrated the Fourth of July with real cannons and live bullets, two authors of the historic document, both former presidents, died hours apart: Thomas Jefferson succumbed to chronic digestive and urinary problems and diarrhea at age eighty-three. John Adams died of pneumonia at age ninety.

There have been only thirty-nine dead presidents so far, with an average age at death of sixty-nine years.

THOSE NOT LISTED ELSEWHERE

At age fifty-three **James Polk** in 1849 got cholera and died from diarrhea.

At age fifty-seven **Chester Arthur** in 1886 died of chronic renal failure.

At age fifty-eight **William McKinley** was shot in Buffalo, New York, on September 6, 1901, and died September 14. He died of internal bleeding before the procedures of blood transfusion were known.

At age sixty **Theodore Roosevelt** died in 1919 of a heart attack.

In 1912 Roosevelt was shot in the chest, and with the bullet lodged in his ribs, he continued to deliver a ninety-minute speech.

At age sixty **Calvin Coolidge** died of a heart attack in 1933.

At age sixty-three **Franklin D. Roosevelt** died of a stroke in 1945.

At age sixty-three **Ulysses S. Grant** died of throat cancer in 1885. *When Grant was on his deathbed a minister in attendance exclaimed: "It is Providence. It is Providence." Grant asked for a piece of paper and wrote, "No, it was the brandy and cigars."*

At age sixty-four **Lyndon B. Johnson** died in 1973 unexpectedly of a heart attack and was found on his bed with a hand reaching for the telephone.

At age sixty-four **Franklin Pierce**, no teetotaler, died of cirrhosis of the liver in 1869.

At age sixty-six **Andrew Johnson** died of a stroke in 1875.

At age sixty-seven **Woodrow Wilson** died in 1924 of multiple diseases. The cause of death was cited as apoplexy, which was defined back then as a sudden termination of all the senses.

At sixty-seven **Benjamin Harrison** died of pneumonia in 1901.

At age seventy **Rutherford B. Hayes** died of a heart attack in 1903.

At age seventy-one **Grover Cleveland** had a fatal heart attack in 1908.

At age seventy-one **John Tyler** died in 1862. His death certificate reads, "biliousness," which is jaundice associated with liver disease. Sick or not, he treated himself for years with mustard plasters, brandy, and a morphine cough medicine.

At age seventy-three **James Monroe** died of tuberculosis in 1831. *It is believed that Monroe, who was seriously infirm, suffered his final seizure after drinking a cup of tea he made of poisoned mushrooms.*

At age seventy-four **Millard Fillmore** died of a stroke in 1874.

At age seventy-seven **James Buchanan** died of pneumonia in 1868.

At age seventy-eight **Andrew Jackson** died in 1845 of "consumption and dropsy from old wounds." Dropsy is swelling, and consumption—in Jackson's case—meant tuberculosis. Looking at himself propped up in bed before he died, he said, "I am a blubber of water."

At age seventy-eight **Dwight D. Eisenhower** died of congestive heart failure in 1969. *After President Eisenhower died, surgeons removed from his body gallstones and an upper molar. These souvenirs are currently on display at the National Museum of Health and Medicine.*

At age seventy-nine **Martin Van Buren** died of pneumonia in 1862.

At age eighty **John Quincy Adams** wobbled out onto the floor of the House, waited for the applause to end, and then collapsed from a stroke and died in 1848.

At age eighty-one **Richard Nixon** died of a stroke in 1994.

At age eighty-five **James Madison** died in 1836 of "debility," which at that time meant old age and being wornout.

At age eighty-eight **Harry S. Truman** died in 1972 of collapsed arteries and heart failure.

At age ninety **Herbert Hoover** died in 1964 of internal bleeding.

At age ninety-three **Ronald Reagan** died of complications from Alzheimer's disease in 2004.

At age ninety-three **Gerald Ford**, the longest-lived president, died in 2006 from pneumonia.

JOHN WAYNE

After acting as either a cowboy or a soldier in nearly one hundred films, John Wayne finally won a best actor Oscar for *True Grit* (1969). The quintessential macho man was himself exempt from service during World War II owing to an inner-ear problem. Winning the Oscar, some say, added another ten years to his life. Although he was a longtime smoker, averaging four packs a day, Wayne nevertheless died of gastric cancer at age seventy-two in 1979.

In 1955 John Wayne was among two hundred twenty cast and crew members who worked on the film The Conqueror. *It was shot on a location in Utah, which was* contaminated by radioactive fallout from atomic bomb tests. Much of the soil was transported back to Hollywood for studio scenes. By 1980 more than ninety of those who had worked on the movie contracted cancer; forty-six died. Even though Wayne knew of the danger, often carrying a Geiger counter onto the set, he believed the risk insignificant.

JACK WEBB

The TV program *Dragnet* was a police show of the procedural variety much like the later *Hill Street Blues* and *NYPD Blue*. It probably ranks as the most famous of all cop shows. "Just the facts, ma'am," is likely the best one-liner a hard-boiled TV cop has ever uttered. The show appeared from 1951 to 1959 and again from 1967 to 1970. The never-excitable Sergeant Joe Friday was played by Jack Webb. Although remembered as the tough cop, Webb was all over the place as director, producer, and writer (under the pseudonym John Randolph) in dozens of TV, radio, and film productions. At work, he was a stickler for detail and worried about the small stuff, believing it necessary to get the realism he was after. This trait and his smoking habit caused his death by heart attack in 1982 at age sixty-two. Cops everywhere loved Webb's portrayal of Sergeant Joe Friday, so much so that when he died, the LAPD gave him a full-police burial and retired his imaginary badge number 714, even though Webb had never been a cop in real life.

The first show to feature the lawyer angle of crime melodramas was Perry Mason, *a character who appeared in eighty novels, written by Erle Stanley Gardner, before it debuted on TV in 1957 and ended in 1966. Tough as nails,* **Ray Collins,** *who played Lieutenant Tragg, was finally taken down in 1965 at age seventy-five of emphysema.* **William Hopper** *played Detective Paul Drake, whose job it was to dig up evidence to acquit Mason's wrongly accused clients. He died mysteriously in 1970 of pneumonia at age fifty-five. Defense attorney Perry Mason was played by* **Raymond Burr** *(who later played the chief of detectives in* Ironside*). Burr received the ultimate subpoena from cancer of the kidney in 1993 at age seventy-six.*

GEORGE WELCH

The Japanese surprise attack on Pearl Harbor gave no time for U.S. forces to get planes into the air, and only twenty managed takeoff under fire. One pilot, heir to a huge grape juice fortune, George Welch, and his buddy **Ken Taylor** were finishing an all-night poker game when they emerged and saw the dawn sky filled with Japanese planes. The pair of brash pilots flew headstrong into the battle, guns blazing. Welch knocked four bombers from the sky before his P-40 Tomahawk was hit and forced to land. Welch went on to have another twelve kills in the

Pacific theater. His actions were depicted in the movie *Tora! Tora! Tora!* He was denied the Medal of Honor since, it was cited, he took off without official flight orders. Welch later went on to be the first to break the sound barrier, but he was not credited with the feat because of the use of supposedly unofficial speed-recording devices. He died in 1954 at age thirty-six when dur-

ing another experimental test flight he was forced to eject. His body was still strapped to the ejection seat; he died from trauma and internal injuries. Ken Taylor went on to become a brigadier general and died in 2006 at age eighty-six.

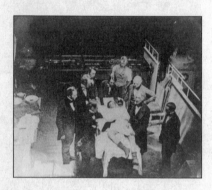

HORACE WELLS

When Connecticut dentist Horace Wells witnessed the effects of nitrous oxide during a carnival show that displayed how a person under the influence seemed conscious though deliriously unperturbed by pain, he knew he was on to something. He experimented on himself and soon used the gas on patients. He tried to promote its application among members of his profession but was met with disdain. Contemporary experts referred to it as a "humbug affair." Wells then sought to find another anesthesia and settled on chloroform, to which he became seriously addicted, subsequently becoming his best customer. After he was accused of taking advantage of female patients under the influence, he found two prostitutes passing by on the street and dumped sulfuric acid over them. In 1848 three days before his thirty-third birthday he ended his own life by slitting the femoral artery on his leg and inhaling a stiff dose of chloroform.

OCCUPATIONAL HAZARD

Higher-than-normal addiction rates from painkillers, such as meperidine hydrochloride (Demerol) and other narcotics, are attributed to physicians. The availability, coupled with the mistaken notion that physicians can process the knowledge of how to control their use, is partly the reason. Some in the medical field combine pharmaceuticals with alcohol and frequently use drugs for speedier hangover recoveries. Many who imbibe also display mild to severe narcissistic-type personalities, similar to that of Horace Wells. Today, the highest suicide rate by means of drugs among all professions belongs to the white male doctor, aged twenty-four to thirty-five.

EDITH WHARTON

Edith Wharton won a Pulitzer Prize in 1921 for *Age of Innocence* and again in 1927 with *Twilight Sleep*. Born into wealth as Edith Newbold Jones, she was married at age twenty-three to Teddy Wharton. After nearly twenty-five years, she divorced in 1913 and then went on to have a number of highly publicized affairs. She was strongly drawn to all things European and made cross-Atlantic trips sixty-six times, no slight undertaking in those days. She was friends with all the big names of the age, including Henry James, F. Scott Fitzgerald, and Ernest Hemingway, as well as Theodore Roosevelt. Wharton continued writing until her death at age seventy-five in 1937 of an apoplectic stroke.

CHARLES WHILDEN

During the Civil War, flag bearers were important for morale, toting the colors of the regiment and national allegiance aloft at the front of the charge. However, this position was usually the one most enemy marksmen put first in their

sights, and the soldiers clutching the flag often became human magnets for flying lead. For example, the Battle of Fair Oaks in 1862, with one thousand killed, had twelve flag bearers killed on the southern side alone. It could be assumed that those looking for a fair chance of survival stayed clear of the flag-carrying duty whenever possible. Nonetheless, it was just the opposite for Confederate private Charles Whilden. This forty-year-old soldier insisted on bearing the colors, even though he could barely walk and was obviously beaten into old age by the war. According to one eyewitness, Whilden was "feeble in health and totally unfitted for active service. . . . In fact, he was stumbling at every step." When the flagpole was shredded to splinters by gunfire, he wrapped the flag around his body and led the assault. He was eventually hit in the shoulder with a bullet and carried to the medics, still clinging to the flag. When discharged, he was given the flag, though scant else, and died two years later during an epileptic seizure. He survived the war but drowned in a two-inch puddle of rainwater. The flag Whilden bore is currently on display in the Capitol building in Columbia, South Carolina.

THORNTON WILDER

Thornton Wilder won the Pulitzer Prize and had the bestselling novel, *The Bridge of San Luis Rey* in 1928, a story about a bridge in Peru that collapsed and killed five people. He was also a playwright, best known for *Our Town*, which won another Pulitzer in 1938. A third play, *The Skin of Our Teeth*, also won in 1943. Although he never publicly acknowledged his homosexuality, his lifestyle was admired by the gay community: His close friend, the writer Samuel M. Steward (*Understanding the Male Hustler*) was allegedly his lover. Wilder died in 1975 at age seventy-eight of a heart attack.

WILLIAM I

William of Normandy—known as William the Conqueror or as William the Bastard to many—invaded England in 1066 and established an ironfisted rule that lasted for twenty-one years. At age fifty-nine in 1087 he had returned to France to war against his former ally, King Philip. However, during the attack, the same fancy saddle that he used to win England killed him. The pommel, the front part of the saddle that curved upward, jammed into his abdomen so violently that he died slowly from internal bleeding. As he lay dying, he said, "I treated the native inhabitants of the kingdom with unreasonable severity . . . and caused the death of thousands by starvation and war." He wanted to donate his wealth, which he admitted he had acquired "with evil deeds," to the poor and to the churches of the city of France he had just burned to the ground. The moment he expired, those in atten-

dance stole his robes and left his body nearly naked on the ground. No one wanted to deal with the corpse until a low-ranking and reluctant knight was assigned the dead-king duty, sailing the body down the Seine and handing it over to monks in the city of Caen. Once the funeral began, some of the assembled nobility began shouting and protesting that the very land he was to be buried in was robbed by William. In addition, the stone sarcophagus they prepared wasn't measured properly, and the tall body of the king didn't fit. They tried to cram it in, but while doing so, the body exploded, causing such a foul odor that many fainted and many more vomited right and left. They lit all the incense they could find to finish the ceremony as quickly as possible.

BILL WILSON

Bill Wilson, the co-founder of Alcoholics Anonymous, died in Miami in 1971 at the age of seventy-five. He developed a program that helped millions escape the ravages of a disease once considered irreversible, without demonizing alcohol or calling for a prohibition for those who could drink. During his life he made the idea of self-help through a twelve-step program the most accepted form of mental health useful for everything, including alcohol, overeating, gambling, and even battling cancer. Aldous Huxley, a well-known thinker and writer, called Wilson "the greatest

THE 'BUM' DRINKS THE ALCOHOL FROM THE CIGAR LIGHTER.

social architect of the twentieth century." When Wilson died, the *Washington Post*'s obituary notice indicated that he had pneumonia, but this was actually a secondary ailment caused by his fatal emphysema. Bill W. had smoked two packs of cigarettes a day for over fifty years. Days before his death, he pleaded with those at his bedside to bring him a bottle of whiskey. His last wish was not fulfilled. William Griffith Wilson's thirty-five years of sobriety and his status as an icon for recovery remained intact. Dr. Bob (**Dr. Robert H. Smith**), who together with Bill started this movement in 1935, was the perfect restraint for Bill's tendency toward grandiosity. Bill had at one time tried to take the recovery concept to Rockefeller for financial backing. Dr. Bob quietly sponsored (a term the organization refers to as a personal mentor) more than five thousand men and women and ultimately helped save a vast number of the hopeless from themselves. He died sober in 1950 at age seventy-one of cancer. His last words to Bill: "Don't screw it up. Keep it simple."

IT'S ESTIMATED THAT THERE ARE 12 MILLION ALCOHOLICS IN THE UNITED STATES. IN 2006 THERE WERE OVER 78,000 DEATHS DIRECTLY ATTRIBUTED TO EXCESSIVE ALCOHOL CONSUMPTION.

THOMAS WOLFE

Thomas Wolfe had a bestseller in 1935 with his novel *Of Time and the River*, the story of a man's search for fulfillment on his journey from small-town America to New York City and beyond, with strong autobiographical elements depicting his life in Chapel Hill, North Carolina, and his journey to become a writer. He wrote four novels, although only two were published while he was alive. His first novel, *Look Homeward Angel* (1929) was dedicated to a married woman twenty years his senior with whom he had had a troubled though whirlwind affair. In 1938 he contracted pneumonia, and during an operation he was discovered to have tuberculosis of the brain, which caused his death at age thirty-seven.

ALEXANDER WOOLLCOTT

Alexander Woollcott was a household name via his weekly radio show "Town Crier," a well-known theater critic for the *New York Times*, and a gossip columnist for *The New Yorker*. He wielded the power to make or break a new play or film with either acidic putdowns or flamboyantly lavish praise. Fearing his criticism, a number of Broadway theaters banned him from attending an opening. Nevertheless, in real life he was quite a character and a lifelong bachelor who referred to himself as a "fabulous monster" and greeted close friends with "Hello, Repulsive." In 1943, while on live radio, he suffered a heart attack and lingered long enough for the program to end before he died four days after his birthday at age fifty-six.

FRANK WOOLWORTH

America's original five-and-dime store was opened by Frank Woolworth in 1878 with the idea of selling all kinds of general merchandise for either a nickel or ten cents. This put many other retailers out of business, and Woolworth soon spread his concept across the country. By 1910 he had commissioned a skyscraper to be built in New York City and paid for it with cash. The Woolworth Building, which served as the company headquarters, was the tallest building in the world until 1930. The five and dime concept went out of favor by the 1970s and was replaced by large discount stores. Woolworth's five and dime competitor, S. S. Kresge Co. turned into Kmart, and Woolworth's became Foot Locker. F. W. Woolworth, the son of a farmer who had started out with a table, selling discounted items on Main Street in Watertown, New York, and then worked for free at a dry goods store to learn the trade, was worth $65 million at the time of his death with over one thousand stores across the country. However, one of the richest men in the world was afraid of going to the dentist; he died of a periodontal infection at the age of sixty-six in 1919, five days before his birthday.

In the 1800s toothache was the fifth-leading cause of death. It was often the wealthy, rather than poorer classes, who had more cavities and gum problems due to excessive sugar in their diets. Bacteria from the infected teeth enter the bloodstream and become trapped in the heart; extreme abcesses cause septicemia, or blood poisoning.

FRANK LLOYD WRIGHT

Frank Lloyd Wright was an innovative architect who redefined how buildings can interact with nature. A pacifist during World War II, he en-

couraged his students to refuse the
draft, which eventually landed Wright
on Senator McCarthy's un-American
blacklist, and explains why no government buildings in the United States
were designed by him. Ceaselessly
at work until his death in 1959 at age
ninety-one, he died from complications after surgery, during the construction of his famous Guggenheim
Museum in New York, which featured
a spiral ramp running through the
building. Asked what he could offer
those wanting sound advice, he said,
"Pepper. Don't eat it. It will kill you
before your time."

WILBUR AND ORVILLE WRIGHT

Wilbur and Orville Wright are credited with inventing the first airplane that actually flew. The Wright Brothers were certainly not the first and might have been
relegated to the column of near misses if Wilbur Wright wasn't hit in the face with
a bat while playing a game in 1886 at age nineteen. This accident forced Wilbur
to remain homebound for four years, owing, in part, to a heart ailment believed
to have been caused by the forceful blow to his head. During his convalescence

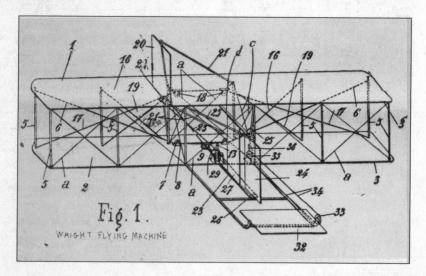

he spent time reading extensively through his father's library, searching out
everything ever written about aviation. Consequently, he became the dreamer
of the pair. When all the current published data on aviation seemed flawed, the
brothers built their own wind tunnels and test foils, made models, gliders, and
towers to send their crudely built flying equipment into the air, until their first

plane made a twelve-second flight on its own propulsion for 120 feet in 1903. The dreamer, Wilbur, died at age forty-five in 1912 of thyroid fever. Three years later, in 1915, the mechanic, Orville, lost interest in the aviation company they formed and sold it. He died at age seventy-six in 1948 of heart failure.

*In 1908 **Thomas Selfridge**, age twenty-six, became the first person killed in a powered aircraft while flying in a plane piloted by Orville Wright that crashed after engine failure. Orville was seriously hurt in the accident and never felt quite the same about flying after that.*

IN MEMORIAM BRIGHAM YOUNG.
"AND THE PLACE WHICH KNEW HIM ONCE SHALL KNOW HIM NO MORE."

BRIGHAM YOUNG

Brigham Young became an explorer and hero to many when he embarked on the best-organized westward migration in U.S. history in 1847. Motivated by a vision to find a safe haven for his religious ideas, he brought the Mormon Church to Utah and, in so doing, helped shaped the American West. When he came upon the Great Salt Lake Valley, he said, "It is enough, this is the right place." For thirty years he supervised Mormon settlements in Utah, Nevada, Idaho, Wyoming, Arizona, and California. Before Young died at the age of seventy-six in 1877 of acute appendicitis, he had more than fifty wives.

YOUNG, CLEVELAND

CY YOUNG

The pitching great Cy Young (born Denton Young, nickname Cy, short for Cyclone) emerged during baseball's Dead Ball period, an era of low scoring games that was dominated by pitchers. Cy Young played pro ball for an amazing twenty-two years and still holds the record for most wins, most innings pitched, and most complete games (749), long before the current trend of bringing in a designated closer. On and off the field, Cy was a down-home country boy at heart, never boastful and conducting himself with a much-admired reserve and integrity. After he retired from baseball in 1912, he lived on $450 per year, which he received from stock investments. Cy died of a heart attack while sitting in a chair, during a visit with a neighbor near his Ohio farm in 1955 at age eighty-eight. His longevity has been attributed to a life of few regrets and recognition from his peers.

THE BEANBALL

Since the beginning of the game, pitchers have tried to unnerve a batter by throwing a fastball close to the head. When they miss and hit the batter's head, it's called a beanball. Thousands of hitters have been "beaned," with only a few deaths, most occurring before the mandatory use of helmets: in 1906, Thomas Burke of the New England League; Charles Pinkey in 1909 of the Central League; and Ray Chapman of Cleveland in 1920 were all professional players who were beaned and died.

LESTER YOUNG

Lester Young got his musical training with his father's band, playing drums in circus tents and traveling shows when he was ten years old. He ran away from home in his late teens to become a musician in his own right and was quickly recognized for his talent on saxophone and clarinet. He soon developed a distinctive jazz style of holding the saxophone out to the side while he played it like a flute. He and Billie Holiday found a natural rapport in each other's musical technique and together recorded many of their most famous songs. It was difficult for sensitive types like Lester, who could play on stage but because of segregation couldn't get served a meal. Billie Holiday said, "I got tired of scenes in crummy roadside restaurants over getting served. I got tired of having a federal case over breakfast, lunch and dinner." Lester Young sought drinking and drugs to cope with the music business and died from it in 1959 of cirrhosis of the liver at age forty-nine.

ROBERT YOUNG

In 1960 the then-chief of the FCC, Newton Minow derided TV as a "vast wasteland," and initiated a crackdown on any suggestive or inappropriate material broadcast over the airwaves. This resulted in networks rushing to offer programs that portrayed inauthentic, sugar-coated views of reality. Two popular shows that fostered the myth of the perfect family were *Leave It to Beaver* and *Father Knows Best*. *Leave It to Beaver* was sliced-white-bread America at its best, portraying family ideals and moral lessons to be learned over the smallest things. In real life, **Stanley Fafara,** who played Beaver's pal Whitey, became a petty criminal and street junkie and died of liver and intestinal complications caused by drugs during a surgery at age fifty-three in 2003. *Father Knows Best* was so popular it was the only program to be seen on all three major networks at one time. The father, Robert Young, was anything but the dad he portrayed, sadly suffering from depression, alcoholism, and attempted suicides. He died of respiratory failure in 1998, in what seemed more like a life sentence than a life, at age ninety-one.

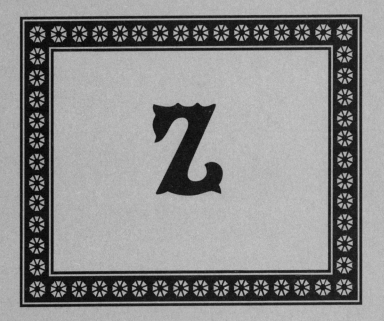

ZIP-A-DEE-DOO-DAH

"Zip-A-Dee-Doo-Dah" won the Academy Award for best song of the year in 1947. It was featured in a Disney animated movie *Song of the South*, performed by fictional character Uncle Remus, sung by **James Baskett**. In later years, anything to do with Uncle Remus (the narrative character of an African American collection of folktales published in 1881), was considered racist and panned, even though the animated movie portrayed blacks as wise and friendly surrounded by not-so-together hicks. Some blogs in recent years claimed that the song was written by a Ku Klux Klan Imperial Wizard, when in fact it was composed by Connecticut native Ray Gilbert, who died in 1976 at age sixty-three. Baskett was a radio comedian who also made a few movies, though he died at age forty-four of a heart attack in 1948. That year Baskett received a posthumous Academy Award as a beloved storyteller for children, the very first African American to win an Oscar.

ZORRO

Zorro was a huge hit during the fifties and sixties. The daring masked man in a black cape who made his signature Z with quick slashes of his rapier was imitated by millions of kids; Z's carved into the tops of wooden school desks across the country became endemic. There were many Zorros, but the one best known on the early TV series was played by **Guy Williams**, born Armando Catalano—6 feet 2 inches, handsome, athletic. He had more than a few would-be senorita-moms turning the show on for their children. Finally unmasked, Zorro died in 1989 at age sixty-five of a brain aneurysm.

LIVING A RERUN

On September 7, 1999, baby-boomer Dr. Allan Zarkin—later dubbed "Dr. Zorro"—used his scalpel to carve his initials into a mother's abdomen after he delivered her baby by Caesarean section. A three-by-one-inch Z was carved in such a manner as to be permanent.

APPENDIX

THE DEATH CODE

To truly appreciate the grandeur and inexorable nature of human resiliency, one could do no worse than to consider the surprising details found in autopsy reports. The findings of postmortem surgeries prove that the human body is a miraculously durable machine, capable of withstanding an incredible amount of self-inflicted abuse and unavoidable environmental detriment. If a person dies of an unusual circumstance, a medical and toxicological examination of the body attempts to determine a cause. In the 1950s nearly everyone who died in a hospital had an autopsy performed, whereas today less than 10 percent of hospital fatalities get one. All deaths have to be classified under one of the following subheadings: Natural, Accident, Homicide, Suicide, or Undetermined. "Natural" is interpreted as the end result of any of the more than three thousand known disease-causes of death. When someone dies, and the remaining four categories are suspected, an autopsy is usually performed, but it is not mandatory unless it's part of a criminal investigation. Although autopsy findings reveal many clues and causalities, it's a science still subjected to the artful interpretation of the attending pathologist. The problem with the quest for creating a standardized record of how humans really die, despite extensive medical code systems in place, such as ICD–9-CM International Classification of Diseases and SNOMED (Systematized Nomenclature of Medicine information), has to do with the near impossibility of achieving univocal analysis. For example, what one person may see as light brown, the other might call maroon. Even with thousands of codes for every aspect of disease and body function, accuracy relies on inputting the information into the system correctly. Whether to use natural language or coded language is an ongoing debate among professionals performing autopsies. Nevertheless, if the findings have to be presented in a criminal matter, the report must use words a layperson could read and understand.

NUTS AND BOLTS

Narrative autopsy reports follow a formula and begin by describing the corpse before them. Indicating if the corpse is cool to the touch; if the hue of the skin

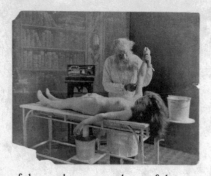

is purple-blotchy, yellow, or blue; and describing the extent of rigidity of the limbs serve to create a vivid image. The hair length, color, and style also warrants mention. How the body was discovered, the surroundings, and what the examiner knows about the circumstances set the scene for a postmortem mystery. Every part of the body—every small scar, condition of the teeth, tongue, shape of the ears, size of the penis, or width of the vagina, and wear and tear of the anus—receives a final scrutiny, to which, most likely, it was never subjected in life. Then the body gets the scalpel and receives a Y-shape incision to remove the chest plate with a crack sound that resembles the snapping of a twig. The internal organs, till now only seen by X-ray, are handled, removed, and placed dripping on a scale. A body disassembled part by part tells the story of how a life was lived from a clinical perspective. The lungs may reveal how many packs of smokes they managed to handle, for example, but there's no way to know how many times the lungs filled with air to blow out a candle on a birthday cake. The brain, likewise, removed from the skull and snipped free from the stem is a dense mass of tissue with many ridges and folds. Once resting on a stainless tray, it hardly seems like a monument to any life. Nevertheless, in order to determine the true cause of death requires the approach of a keen scientific eye not clouded by sentiment or distracted by metaphysical quagmires, pondering, for example, the meaning and mystery of life itself.

"When I'm looking inside a person's body . . . it's a wondrous thing. And it never fails to convince me that each one of us is a miracle."
—MICHAEL BADEN, M.D.

FINAL WORDS

**HERE ARE THE OFFICIAL WORDS WRITTEN ON THE
DEATH CERTIFICATES OF THE FAMOUS AND RICH.**

Bud Abbott / April 24, 1974 / 75 / Respiratory Failure DUE TO acute CVA AND cerebral metastasis

Claude Akins / January 27, 1994 / 67 / Cardiopulmonary arrest DUE TO congestive heart failure AND cancer of stomach with metastases

Jack Albertson / November 25, 1981 / 74 / Adenocarcinoma of colon DUE TO mestases to liver AND adenocarcinoma of colon

Irwin Allen / November 2, 1991 / 75 / Cardiopulmonary arrest DUE TO Acute myocardial infarction AND atherosclerotic heart disease

Morey Amsterdam / October 27, 1996 / 87 / Cardiopulmonary arrest DUE TO acute myocardial infarction AND coronary artery disease

Dame Judith Anderson / January 2, 1992 / 94 / Respiratory failure DUE TO Brain tumor—primary

Royce Applegate / January 1, 2003 / 63 / smoke inhalation

Eve Arden / November 12, 1990 / 82 / Cardiac arrest DUE TO arteriosclerotic heart disease

Mary Astor / September 25, 1987 / 81 / Respiratory failure DUE TO Pulmonary Emphysema

Eleanor Audley / November 25, 1991 / 86 / Acute Cardiorespiratory arrest DUE TO Acute myocardial infarction AND chronic hypertensive heart disease

Gene Autry / October 2, 1998 / 91 / Cardiopulmonary arrest DUE TO Respiratory failure AND Lymphoma

Hermione Baddeley / August 19, 1986 / 77 / Cardiorespiratory arrest DUE TO Cortical necrosis AND cerebral arterial occlusion

Bonny Bakley / May 4, 2001 / 44 / Multiple gunshot wounds

Red Barry / July 17, 1980 / 69 / gunshot wound perforating head and neck

Ethel Barrymore / June 18, 1959 / 79 / Pulmonary infarction DUE TO arteriosclerotic heart disease AND generalized arteriosclerosis

Billy Barty / December 23, 2000 / 76 / Cardiopulmonary arrest DUE TO atherosclerotic cardiovascular disease

Ralph Bellamy / November 29, 1991 / 87 / Cardiac insufficiency DUE TO chronic obstructive pulmonary disease

William Bendix / December 14, 1964 / 58 / Pneumonia

Jack Benny / December 26, 1974 / 80 / Carcinoma of Pancreas

Paul Bern / September 5, 1932 / 42 / gunshot wound of head

Ted Bessel / October 6, 1996 / 61 / Cardiac arrest DUE TO dissecting aortic aneurysm

Carl Betz / June 18, 1978 / 56 / Bronchogenic carcinoma

Amanda Blake / August 16, 1989 / 60 / Cardiopulmonary arrest DUE TO hepatic failure AND CMV Hepatitis

Madge Blake / February 19, 1969 / 69 / Arteriosclerotic cardiovascular disease DUE TO fracture of left ankle

Mel Blanc / July 10, 1989 / 81 / cardiopulmonary collapse DUE TO coma AND stroke

Joan Blondell / December 25, 1979 / Myeloid leukemia

Humphrey Bogart / January 14, 1957 / 57 / generalized carcinomatosis DUE TO carcinoma of esophagus

Ray Bolger / January 15, 1987 / 83 / Metastatic transitional cell cancer of bladder

Margaret Booth / October 28, 2002 / 104 / Respiratory failure DUE TO pneumonia AND cerebrovascular accident

Clara Bow / September 27, 1965 / 58 / Coronary thrombosis DUE TO Coronary atherosclerosis

William Boyd / September 12, 1972 / 77 / Bronchopneumonia and congestive heart failure DUE TO metastatic squamous cell carcinoma—primary sight unknown

Lloyd Bridges / March 10, 1998 / 85 / cardiopulmonary arrest DUE TO congestive heart failure

Charles Bronson / August 30, 2003 / 81 / Respiratory failure DUE TO metastatic lung cancer

Foster Brooks / December 20, 2001 / 89 / Cardiorespiratory arrest DUE TO arteriosclerotic heart disease

Mae Busch / April 26, 1946 / 44 / Carcinomatosis DUE TO Carcinoma of rectum

Francis X. Bushman / August 23, 1966 / 83 / Massive Hemopericardium DUE TO Myocardial infarction with rupture, recent AND Coronary Thrombosis

Spring Byington / September 7, 1971 / 84 / Carcinoma of Rectum

Rory Calhoun / April 28, 1999 / 76 / Cardiorespiratory arrest DUE TO emphysema

Eddie Cantor / October 10, 1964 / 72 / Myocardial infarction DUE TO Arteriosclerotic Heart Disease

Truman Capote / August 25, 1984 / 59 / Deferred

Macdonald Carey / March 21, 1994 / 81 / Cardiopulmonary arrest DUE TO metastatic lung cancer AND primary adenocarcinoma lung

Nell Carter / January 23, 2003 / 54 / Deferred

John Cassavetes / February 3, 1989 / 59 / Liver failure DUE TO cirrhosis of the liver

Jeff Chandler / June 17, 1961 / 42 / Shock- peripheral vascular collapse DUE TO staphylococci septicemia AND Pneumonitis

Lon Chaney / August 26, 1930 / 47 / Carcinoma of right upper bronchus

Lana Clarkson / February 3, 2003 / 40 / Gunshot wound of head and neck

Rosemary Clooney / June 29, 2002 / 74 / Respiratory arrest DUE TO end-stage lung cancer

James Coburn / November 18, 2002 / 74 / Cardiac arrest DUE TO coronary artery disease

Imogene Coca / June 2, 2001 / 92 / Cerebrovascular accident DUE TO Alzheimer's disease

Iron Eyes Cody / January 4, 1999 / 94 / Cardio respiratory arrest DUE TO congestive heart failure

Ray Collins / July 11, 1965 / 75 / Bronchopneumonia, terminal DUE TO pulmonary emphysema

Bert Convy / July 15, 1991 / 57 / Cardiac Arrest DUE TO Glioblastom, MuliformBrain

Jackie Coogan / March 1, 1984 / 69 / Cardiac arrest DUE TO arteriosclerotic heart disease AND hypertensive cardiovascular disease

Gary Cooper / May 13, 1961 / 60 / Carcinoma of colon

Ellen Corby / April 14, 1999 / 87 / Cardiopulmonary failure DUE TO ischemic enterocolitis AND Arteriosclerosis

Lou Costello / March 3, 1959 / 52 / Ventricular fibrillation

Broderick Crawford / April 26, 1986 / 74 / Respiratory arrest DUE TO pneumonia

Richard Crenna / January 17, 2003 / 76 / Carcinoma of pancreas

Hume Cronyn / June 15, 2003 / 91 / Hemoptysis DUE TO thrombocytopenia AND Metastatic prostate carcinoma

Robert Cummings / December 2, 1990 / 80 / Cardiac arrest DUE TO hypotension AND Thrombotic Thrombocytopenic Purpura

Dorothy Dandridge / September 8, 1965 / 42 / Acute drug intoxication DUE TO ingestion of tofranil

Rodney Dangerfield / October 5, 2004 / 82 / Sepsis DUE TO Ischemic colitis AND atherosclerotic vascular heart disease

Brad Davis / September 8, 1991 / 41 / Mycobacteria Avium Complex DUE TO AIDS AND intravenous drug abuse by history

Albert Dekker / May 5, 1968 / 52 / Asphyxiation DUE TO Suffocation and Constriction of Neck by Ligatures

Cecil B. DeMille / January 21, 1959 / 77 / Congestive heart failure DUE TO Coronary thrombosis and myocardial infarction

Peter Deuel / December 31, 1971 / 31 / Cerebral destruction DUE TO gunshot wound to the head

Selma Diamond / May 13, 1985 / 64 / Bronchogenic carcinoma

Troy Donahue / September 2, 2001 / 65 / Cardiac arrest DUE TO cardiogenic shock AND myocardial infarction

David Doyle / February 26, 1997 / 67 / Acute pulmonary edema DUE TO Acute myocardial infarction AND arteriosclerotic heart disease

Marie Dressler / July 28, 1934 / 62 / congestive heart failure

Dominique Dunne / November 4, 1982 / 22 / Anoxic encephalopathy DUE TO Strangulation

Irene Dunne / September 4, 1990 / 88 / Myocardial insufficiency DUE TO arteriosclerosis, general

Jimmy Durante / January 29, 1980 / 86 / Terminal pneumonitis

Wyatt Earp / January 13, 1929 / 80 / Chronic Cystitis DUE TO hypertrophied Prostate

Hope Emerson / April 24, 1960 / 62 / Carcinoma of colon with metastases to liver and lung

Harry Essex / February 6, 1997 / 86 / Cardiopulmonary arrest DUE TO arteriosclerotic heart disease

Douglas Fairbanks / December 12, 1939 / 56 / Arteriosclerosis AND Coronary sclerosis DUE TO Coronary occlusion

Norman Fell / December 14, 1998 / 74 / Cardiopulmonary failure DUE TO Pneumonia AND multiple Myeloma

Verna Felton / December 14, 1966 / 76 / Cardiac failure DUE TO CVA AND Arteriosclerotic heart disease

W.C. Fields / December 22, 1946 / 66 / Cirrhosis of the liver DUE TO chronic alcoholism

Susan Fleming / December 22, 2002 / 94 / Cardiopulmonary failure DUE TO cardiomyopathy AND Myocardial infarction AND Probable coronary artery disease

Henry Fonda / August 12, 1982 / 77 / Cardiorespiratory arrest DUE TO chronic cardiac failure AND Restrictive Cardioryopetly

James Franciscus / July 8, 1991 / 57 / Respiratory arrest DUE TO aspiration pneumonia AND anoxic encephalopathy d / t cardiomyopathy

John Frankenheimer / July 6, 2002 / 72 / Bilateral Cerebral infarct DUE TO pulmonary embolus AND metastatic lung cancer AND thoracic Spinal metastasis

William Frawley / March 3, 1966 / 79 / Myocardial insufficiency DUE TO arteriosclerosis

Allen Funt / September 5, 1999 / 84 / Congestive heart failure DUE TO cardiomyopathy

Clark Gable / November 16, 1960 / 59 / Coronary Thrombosis

Magda Gabor / June 6, 1997 / 78 / Sepsis DUE TO acute renal failure AND pyonephritis

Gretchen Gailing / June 15, 1961 / 45 / Cardiorespiratory failure DUE TO Extreme carcinoma of ovary

Janet Gaynor / September 14, 1984 / 77 / Pneumonia DUE TO suspect complication of trauma

Christopher George / November 29, 1983 / 52 / Ventricular fibrillation DUE TO coronary insufficiency AND arteriosclerotic heart disease

John Gilbert / January 9, 1936 / 38 / Acute Myocarditis (alcoholic) DUE TO Chronic alcoholism

Trevor Goddard / October 14, 1962 / 40 / Multiple drug intoxication

Alexander Godunov / Found May 18, 1995 / 45 / Chronic alcoholism

Ronald Goldman / June 13, 1994 / 25 / Multiple sharp force injuries

Samuel Goldwyn / January 31, 1974 / 91 / Cerebral vascular accident DUE TO Arteriosclerotic heart disease

Gale Gordon / June 30, 1995 / 89 / Cardio pulmonary arrest DUE TO Lung cancer

Stewart Granger / August 16, 1993 / 80 / Chronic respiratory failure DUE TO metastatic prostate cancer

Anne Gwynne / March 31, 2003 / 84 / Acute cerebral infarction DUE TO atherosclerosis

Buddy Hackett / June 30, 2003 / 78 / Acute myocardial infarction DUE TO arteriosclerotic heart disease AND diabetes mellitus

Joan Hackett / October 8, 1983 / 49 / Abdominal metastatses DUE TO clear cell carcinoma of kidney

Oliver Hardy / August 7, 1957 / 65 / Acute cerebral vascular accident (Thrombosis) superimposed DUE TO chronic right-sided hemiplegic aphasia AND atherosclerosis generalized

Jean Harlow / June 7, 1937 / 26 / Acute respiratory infection; Acute Nephritis; Uremia

William S. Hart / June 23, 1946 / 81 / Acute Pyelonephritis DUE TO chronic suppurative prostatitis with calculi

Bryan Hartman / May 28, 1998 / 40 / Gunshot wound to the head

Gabby Hayes / February 9, 1969 / 83 / Acute myocardial infarction DUE TO coronary thrombosis AND arteriosclerotic heart disease

Susan Hayward / March 14, 1975 / 57 / Cerebral seizure and Bronchopneumonia DUE TO cancer of brain

William Randolph Hearst / August 14, 1951 / 88 / Cerebral Vascular accident DUE TO Arteriosclerosis

Paul Henreid / March 29, 1992 / 84 / Cardiorespiratory arrest DUE TO progressive respiratory failure AND parkinsonism

Jon-Erik Hexum / October 18, 1984 / 27 / Gunshot wound to the head

Bob Hope / July 27, 2003 / 100 / Pneumonia

Hedda Hopper / February 1, 1966 / 75 / Acute pulmonary edema DUE TO arteriosclerotic heart disease

Curly Howard / January 18, 1952 / 48 / Cerebral hemorrhage DUE TO cerebral arteriosclerosis

Moe Howard / May 4, 1975 / 77 / Cancer of lung

Shemp Howard / November 22, 1955 / 60 / Acute coronary thrombosis DUE TO heart disease

Roy Huggins / April 3, 2002 / 87 / Respiratory failure DUE TO pulmonary fibrosis AND Pulmonary obstructive disease

Jill Ireland / May 19, 1990 / 54 / Pulmonary insufficiency DUE TO pulmonary metastases AND carcinoma of breast

Graham Jarvis / April 16, 2003 / 72 / Multiple myeloma

George Jessel / May 24, 1981 / 83 / Cardio respiratory arrest DUE TO arteriosclerosis

Al Jolson / October 23, 1950 / 64 / Myocandic infection DUE TO commay selemin

Carolyn Jones / August 3, 1983 / 53 / Metastatic carcinoma DUE TO carcinoma of colon

Danny Kaye / March 3, 1987 / 74 / Gastrointestinal hemorrhage DUE TO esophageal

Buster Keaton / February 1, 1966 / 70 / Carcinoma of lung

Ruby Keeler / February 28, 1993 / 82 / Metastatic Kidney Cancer

Gene Kelly / February 2, 1996 / 83 / Sepsis DUE TO Renal failure acute AND Cerebrovascular Accident AND Diabetes Mellitus

Robert F. Kennedy / June 6, 1968 / 42 / Gunshot wound of right mastoid penetrating brain

Percy Kilbride / December 11, 1964 / 76 / Hypostatic Pneumonia DUE TO cerebral contusion, slight

Mabel King / November 9, 1999 / 66 / End-stage renal failure

Nancy Kulp / February 3, 1991 / 69 / Metastatic Laryngeal cancer

Fernando Lamas / October 8, 1982 / 66 / Cardio respiratory DUE TO renal failure AND undifferentiated carcinoma

Dorothy Lamour / September 21, 1996 / 81 / cardiac arrest DUE TO intestinal infarction AND mesenteric thrombosis AND generalized arteriosclerosis

Burt Lancaster / October 24, 1994 / 80 / Arteriosclerotic coronary heart disease

Walter Lantz / March 22, 1994 / 94 / Cardiopulmonary arrest DUE TO congestive heart failure AND mitral regurgitation

Wesley Lau / August 30, 1984 / 63 / Cardiac arrest DUE TO Acute myocardial infarction AND atherosclerosis

Stan Laurel / February 23, 1965 / 74 / Myocardial infarction massive (posterior) DUE TO Arteriosclerotic left bundle branch block AND Atherosclerosis advanced

Gypsy Rose Lee / April 26, 1970 / 56 / Acute Congestive heart failure and shock DUE TO lung cancer

Peggy Lee / January 21, 2002 / 81 / Cardiorespiratory arrest DUE TO myocardial infarction AND atherosclerotic heart disease

Janet Leigh / October 3, 2004 / 77 / Cardiopulmonary arrest DUE TO dilated cardiomyopathy

Jack Lemmon / June 27, 2001 / 76 / Carcinomatosis DUE TO metastatic cancer of bladder to colon

Audra Lindley / October 16, 1997 / 79 / Acute myelogenous Leukemia DUE TO Myelodysplasia

Julie London / October 18, 2000 / 74 / Respiratory arrest DUE TO chronic obstructive pulmonary disease

Richard Long / December 21, 1974 / 47 / Cardiac arrest DUE TO multiple myocardial infarctions AND coronary atherosclerosis

Bela Lugosi / August 16, 1956 / 73 / Coronary Occlusion with Myocardial DUE TO fibrosis

Ida Lupino / August 3, 1995 / 77 / Bronchopneumonia DUE TO Metastatic colon cancer

Rita Lynn / January 21, 1996 / 74 / Metastatic ovarian cancer

Meredith MacRae / July 14, 2000 / 56 / Glioblastoma

Fred MacMurray / November 5, 1991 / 83 / Pulmonary edema DUE TO Sepsis syndrome AND urinary tract infection

Guy Madison / February 6, 1996 / 74 / Respiratory arrest DUE TO End-stage emphysema AND smoking history

Nancy Marchand / June 18, 2000 / 71 / Lung cancer

Helen Martin / March 25, 2000 / 88 / Cardiopulmonary arrest DUE TO atherosclerotic cardiovascular disease

Mary Martin / November 3, 1990 / 77 / Metastatic colon cancer DUE TO adenocarcinoma of colon

Walter Matthau / July 1, 2000 / 79 / Cardiac arrest DUE TO atherosclerotic heart disease

Victor Mature / August 8, 1999 / 86 / Myelodysplasia

Doug McClure / February 5, 1995 / 59 / Cardiorespiratory arrest DUE TO metastatic lung cancer

Ann Miller / January 22, 2004 / 80 / Arteriosclerotic cardiovascular disease

Carmen Miranda / August 5, 1955 / 40 / Coronary Occlusion

Robert Mitchum / July 1, 1997 / 79 / Respiratory arrest DUE TO Emphysema

Montie Montana / May 20, 1998 / 87 / Right cerebral infarction DUE TO cerebral arteriosclerosis

Vic Morrow / July 23, 1982 / 53 / Rotor blade injury to head, neck, and shoulders

Edward Mulhare / May 24, 1997 / 74 / Metastatic lung cancer

George Nader / February 4, 2002 / 80 / Cardiopulmonary failure DUE TO aspiration pneumonia AND multiple cerebral infarctions AND atherosclerosis

Alan Napier / August 8, 1988 / 85 / Respiratory failure DUE TO Pneumonia AND pulmonary emboli due to deep vein thrombosis

Harriet Nelson / October 2, 1994 / 85 / Cardio respiratory failure DUE TO ASHD AND hypertension

Ozzie Nelson / June 3, 1975 / 69 / cardiac failure DUE TO neoplastic intestinal obstruction with irritation AND metastatic adenocarcinoma (colon)

Jeanette Nolan / June 5, 1998 / 86 / Respiratory failure DUE TO cerebrovascular accident AND acute myocardial infarction AND atherosclerotic cardiovascular disease

Lloyd Nolan / September 27, 1985 / 83 / Respiratory arrest DUE TO carcinoma of lung

Ramon Novarro / October 31, 1968 / 69 / Suffocation DUE TO aspiration of blood AND multiple traumatic injuries of face, nose and mouth

Alice Nunn / July 1, 1988 / 60 / Cardiorespiratory arrest DUE TO repeated cardiovascular accident AND arteriosclerosis—generalized

Pat O'Brien / October 15, 1983 / 83 / Cardiac arrest DUE TO arteriosclerotic heart disease AND Acute coronary occlusion

Carroll O'Connor / June 21, 2001 / 76 / Cardiac arrest DUE TO acute myocardial infarction AND arteriosclerotic heart disease

Donald O'Connor / September 27, 2003 / 78 / Congestive heart failure DUE TO atherosclerotic coronary artery disease

Hugh O'Connor / March 28, 1995 / 32 / Gunshot wound to head

Heather O'Rourke / February 1, 1988 / 12 / Cardio respiratory arrest DUE TO suspected septic shock AND acute bowel obstruction

LaWanda Page / September 14, 2002 / 81 / Cardiopulmonary arrest DUE TO septic schock AND fungal sepsis AND diabetes

Bert Parks / February 2, 1992 / 77 / Interstitial pneumonia DUE TO lung cancer

Louella Parsons / December 9, 1972 / 91 / Cardio vascular accident DUE TO generalized arteriosclerosis

Gregory Peck / June 12, 2003 / 87 / Cardiorespiratory arrest DUE TO bronchopneumonia

George Peppard / May 8, 1994 / 65 / Respiratory failure DUE TO Leukemia

Anthony Perkins / September 12, 1992 / 60 / Gram Negative Bacteremia DUE TO Bilateral Pneumonitis AND AIDS

River Phoenix / October 31, 1993 / 23 / Acute multiple drug intoxication

Mary Pickford / May 29, 1979 / 85 / Cerebrovascular hemorrhage DUE TO chronic arteriosclerotic heart disease AND chronic myocarditis

Cole Porter / October 15, 1964 / 73 / Myocardial insufficiency DUE TO pyelonephritis, bilateral bronchopneumonia AND Emphysema, arteriosclerosis

Robert Preston / March 21, 1987 / 68 / Renal failure DUE TO metastatic carcinoma of liver and lung AND Primary carcinoma of tongue and floor of mouth

Vincent Price / October 25, 1993 / 82 / Emphysema DUE TO Carcinoma of Lung

Freddie Prinze / January 29, 1977 / 22 / Gunshot wound through head

George Raft / November 24, 1980 / 85 / Cardio respiratory arrest DUE TO acute bronchopneumonia AND severe pulmonary emphysema

Dirk Rambo / February 5, 1967 / 25 / Extensive thermal burns of entire body

Martha Raye / October 19, 1994 / Aspiration pneumonia DUE TO Multi cerebral infarction AND Arteriosclerosis

Donna Reed / January 14, 1986 / 64 / Metastatic carcinoma of pancreas

Robert Reed / May 12, 1992 / 59 / Colon Lymphoma

Lee Remick / July 2, 1991 / 55 / Brain metastasis

Tommy Rettig / February 15, 1996 / 54 / Deferred

John Ritter / September 11, 2003 / 54 / Cardiopulmonary arrest DUE TO thoracic ascending aortic dissecting aneurysm

Edward G. Robinson / January 26, 1973 / 79 / Metastatic carcinoma of bladder

Robert Rockwell / January 25, 2003 / 86 / cardiopulmonary arrest DUE TO metastatic prostate cancer

Roy Rogers / July 6, 1998 / 86 / Congestive heart failure DUE TO arteriosclerotic heart disease

Cesar Romero / January 1, 1994 / 86 / Cardiorespiratory arrest DUE TO pulmonary embolus AND thrombophlebitis—RT. Leg AND Bronchitis

Charlie Ruggles / December 23, 1970 / 84 / Carcinoma of colon

Gail Russell / August 27, 1961 / 35 / Fatty liver, severe DUE TO Acute and chronic alcoholism

Rosalind Russell / November 28, 1976 / 69 / Intestinal obstruction DUE TO carcinoma of the breast

Fran Ryan / January 15, 2000 / 83 / Cardiac Arrhythmia DUE TO coronary artery disease

George C. Scott / Found September 22, 1999 / 71 / Ruptured abdominal aortic aneurysm

Randolph Scott / March 2, 1987 / 89 / Cardiac decompensation DUE TO arteriosclerotic coronary cerebral disease

E. C. Segar / October 13, 1938 / 43 / Portal Cirrhosis

Ann Sheridan / January 21, 1967 / 51 / adenocarcinoma, gastric esophageal with massive liver metastases

Elizabeth Short / January 14 or 15, 1947 / 22 / hemorrhage and shock DUE TO concussion of brain AND lacerations of face

Bugsy Siegel / June 20, 1947 / 41 / Cerebral hemorrhage DUE TO Gunshot wound of the head

Phil Silvers / November 1, 1985 / 74 / Cardiac arrest DUE TO coronary arteriosclerotic heart disease

Nichole Brown Simpson / Found June 13, 1994 / 35 / multiple sharp force injuries

Hal Smith / Found January 28, 1994 / 77 / Arteriosclerotic cardiovascular disease

Barbara Stanwyck / January 20, 1990 / 82 / Pneumonia DUE TO Chronic obstructive lung disease AND Emphysema

Craig Stevens / May 10, 2000 / 81 / Malignant Lymphoma

Jimmy Stewart / July 2, 1997 / 89 / Cardiac arrest DUE TO pulmonary embolus AND right leg thrombosis

Robert Stack / May 14, 2003 / 84 / Myocardial infarction DUE TO coronary artery disease

Florence Stanley / October 3, 2003 / 79 / Cardiovascular accident

Rod Steiger / July 9, 2002 / 77 / Respiratory failure DUE TO sepsis AND renal failure AND pancreatic cancer

Inger Stevens / April 30, 1970 / 35 / Acute Barbiturate intoxication DUE TO ingestion of overdose

Jay Stewart / September 17, 1989 / 71

/ gunshot wound to head

Dorothy Stratten / Found August 14, 1980 / 20 / Gunshot wound of head

Lyle Talbot / March 3, 1996 / 94 / Congestive heart failure DUE TO coronary atherosclerosis

Natalie Talmadge / June 19, 1969 / 69 / Massive acute pulmonary edema DUE TO Arteriosclerotic cardiovascular disease

William Talman / August 30, 1968 / 53 / Bronchogenic carcinoma

Jessica Tandy / September 11, 1994 / 85 / Cardiopulmonary arrest DUE TO ovarian cancer

Sharon Tate / August 9, 1969 / 26 / Multiple stab wounds of chest and back, penetrating heart, lungs, and liver, causing massive hemorrhage

Vic Tayback / May 25, 1990 / 60 / Arteriosclerotic cardiovascular disease

Robert Taylor / June 8, 1969 / 57 / Lung cancer

Danny Thomas / February 6, 1991 / 79 / Cardio respiratory arrest DUE TO acute pulmonary edema AND acute myocardial infarction

Lawrence Tierney / February 26, 2002 / 82 / Cardiac arrest DUE TO congestive heart failure AND hypertension

Mel Tormé / June 5, 1999 / 73 / Cardio pulmonary arrest DUE TO congestive heart failure AND Coronary heart disease AND Diabetes Mellitus

Claire Trevor / April 8, 2000 / 90 / Cardiopulmonary collapse DUE TO acute respiratory failure AND pneumonia

Bobby Troup / February 7, 1999 / 80 / Cardiopulmonary arrest DUE TO pulmonary edema AND Myocardial infarction AND pneumonia

Lana Turner / June 29, 1995 / 74 / Cancer of Nasopharynx

Robert Urich / April 16, 2002 / 55 / Cardiopulmonary arrest DUE TO multisystem failure AND metastatic sarcoma

Vivian Vance / August 17, 1979 / 64 / Cardio respiratory arrest DUE TO metastatic carcinoma

Nancy Walker / March 25, 1992 / 69 / Adenocarcinoma both lungs

Lew Wasserman / June 3, 2002 / 89 / Cardiorespiratory arrest DUE TO cerebrovascular accident AND Essential hypertension

Ethel Waters / September 1, 1977 / 80 / Renal failure DUE TO metastatic endometrial carcinoma

Clifton Webb / October 13, 1966 / 76 / Acute congestive heart failure DUE TO chronic heart failure AND atherosclerotic heart disease

Lawrence Welk / May 17, 1992 / 89 / Broncho Pneumonia

Orson Welles / October 10, 1985 / 70 / cardiopulmonary collapse

Mae West / November 22, 1980 / 87 / Cerebral thrombosis

Mary Wickes / October 22, 1995 / 79 / Acute renal failure DUE TO Massive Gastrointestinal bleeding AND Severe hypertension AND ischemic cardiomyopathy

Billy Wilder / March 27, 2002 / 95 / Respiratory failure DUE TO pneumonia

Walter Winchell / February 20, 1972 / 74 / cardiac arrest DUE TO metastatic carcinoma of prostate

Marie Windsor / December 10, 2000 / 80 / Cardiopulmonary arrest DUE TO arteriosclerotic vascular disease

Natalie Wood / Found November 29, 1981 / 43 / Drowning

SOURCES

Death Certificates: There is no singular national source from which to obtain a death certificate. Each state records and files the original death certificate of resident citizens. In the United States only thirteen states are classified as "open states," meaning that the majority of death certificates in the country are no longer public records. Citing an interest to curb identity theft and protect national security, numerous state legislatures have prevented access to many historical documents. However, a researcher can request an "informational copy" or a non-certified copy without a raised seal as appears on an official document. Even within the closed states, many records are freed from restrictions of privacy after varying dates. For example, records in Florida filed before 1950 are open, while those recorded after that date require a special inquiry or request per document sought. Records used in this book were obtained from the following:

Alabama Vital Records: http://ph.state.al.us/chs/VitalRecords/
Alaska Bureau of Vital Statistics: http://www.hss.state.ak.us/dph/bvs/
Arizona Office of Vital Records: http://www.azdhs.gov/vitalrcd/death_index.htm
Arkansas Department of Health: http://www.healthyarkansas.com/
California Office of Vital Records: http://www.dhs.ca.gov/
Colorado Department of Public Health Environment: http://www.cdphe.state.co.us/
Connecticut Vital Records: http://www.dph.state.ct.us/PB/HISR/Vital_Records.htm
Delaware Office of Vital Statistics: http://www.dhss.delaware.gov/dhss/
District of Columbia Vital Records Division: http://www.dchealth.dc.gov/
Florida Department of Health: http://www.cdc.gov/nchs/howto/w2w/florida.htm
Georgia Department of Human Resources: http://health.state.ga.us/programs/
Hawaii State Department of Health: http://www.hawaii.gov/health/vital-records
Idaho Vital Statistics Unit: http://www.healthandwelfare.idaho.gov/Default.aspx
Illinois Department of Public Health: http://www.idph.state.il.us/
Indiana State Department of Health: http://www.in.gov/isdh/index.htm
Iowa Department of Public Health: http://www.idph.state.ia.us/
Kansas Office of Vital Statistics: http://www.kdheks.gov/vital/
Kentucky Office of Vital Statistics: http://chfs.ky.gov/dph/
Louisiana Office of Public Health: http://www.dhh.louisiana.gov/offices/

Maine Department of Human Services: http://www.maine.gov/

Maryland Department of Health and Mental Hygiene: http://www.vsa.state.md.us/

Massachusetts Registry of Vital Records and Statistics: http://www.mass.gov/

Michigan Vital Records: http://www.mdch.state.mi.us/

Minnesota Department of Health: http://www.health.state.mn.us/

Mississippi State Department of Health: http://www.msdh.state.ms.us/

Missouri Department of Health: http://www.dhss.mo.gov/BirthAndDeathRecords/

Montana Department of Public Health: http://www.dphhs.mt.gov/

Nebraska Vital Records: http://www.hhss.ne.gov/vitalrecords/

Nevada Office of Vital Records: http://health2k.state.nv.us/

New Hampshire Division of Vital Records: http://www.sos.nh.gov/vitalrecords/

New Jersey Vital Statistics: http://www.state.nj.us/health/vital/index.shtml

New Mexico Vital Records: http://www.health.state.nm.us/

New York State Vital Records: http://www.health.state.ny.us/

NYC Department of Health: http://www.nyc.gov/health

North Carolina Vital Records: http://www.schs.state.nc.us/SCHS/

North Dakota Department of Health: http://www.health.state.nd.us/vital/

Ohio Department of Health: http://www.vitalrec.com/oh.html

Oklahoma State Department of Health: http://www.health.state.ok.us/

Oregon Vital Records: http://arcweb.sos.state.or.us/reference.html

Pennsylvania Division of Vital Records: http://www.dsf.health.state.pa.us/health/

Rhode Island Department of Health: http://www.health.ri.gov/

South Carolina Office of Vital Records: http://www.scdhec.net/administration/vr/

South Dakota Department of Health: http://www.state.sd.us/doh/vitalrec/vital.htm

Tennessee Vital Records: http://www2.state.tn.us/health/vr/index.htm

Texas Department of Health: http://www.dshs.state.tx.us/vs/

Utah Office of Vital Records: http://health.utah.gov/vitalrecords/

Vermont Department of Health: http://healthvermont.gov/

Virginia State Health Department: http://www.vdh.state.va.us/

Washington Center for Health Statistics: http://www.doh.wa.gov/

West Virginia Vital Registration Office: http://www.wvdhhr.org/

State of Wisconsin Vital Records: http://www.dhfs.state.wi.us/vitalrecords/

Wyoming Vital Records Services: http://wdhfs.state.wy.us/vital_records/

Autopsy reports were obtained from Medical Examiner offices located in the county or municipality where the deaths occurred. Most accept requests from non-family members if the Coroner's report is not part of an ongoing criminal investigation, or specifically sealed by request of estate trustees, or Attorney General overseeing the jurisdiction of the particular ME office. The location of death cited on the death certificate will indicate the nearest Coroner office and from there determine if an autopsy was performed. The National Association of Medical Examiners (NAME) lists member pathologists and professionals in the field: http://www.thename.org/

Obituaries were obtained from Library of Congress: Newspaper Archives/Indexes/ Morgues: http://www.loc.gov/rr/news/oltitles.html; NewspaperArchive.com; NewsLibrary.com; Smalltownpapers.com; New York Times Archives: http://query .nytimes.com/; Chicago Tribune Archives: http://pqasb.pqarchiver.com/chica gotribune/advancedsearch.html; The Washington Post Archives: http://pqasb.pq

archiver.com/washingtonpost/search.html; Boston Globe Archives: http://www
.boston.com/tools/archives/; The San Francisco Chronicle Archives: www.sfgate
.com/; Philadelphia Inquirer: http://www.philly.com/mld/philly/archives/; Atlanta
Journal Constitution: http://pqasb.pqarchiver.com/ajc_historic/search.html.
Many of these online newspaper archives, some dating from the 1850s, have the best firsthand accounts of the deceased, as well as formal obituaries.

FURTHER READING AND SOURCES CITED

Introduction: Trilling, Lionel, *Matthew Arnold*, Norton (1939); McAndrew, Frank, et al.,
"Of Tabloids and Family Secrets: The Evolutionary Psychology of Gossip," *Journal
of Applied Social Psychology* 32 (2002): 1–20; Andrews, Robert, et al., *The Columbia
World of Quotations*, Columbia University Press (1996).

Obituary History: Hayles, D. J., "The Roman Census," *Buried History* 9 (1973): 113–32;
Graunt, John, "Natural and political observations on the Bills of Mortality," (1661)
Ed. Birch, T. 1759; Egerton, Frank N., III., "John Graunt," Gillispie, Charles (ed.),
Dictionary of Scientific Biography, Charles Scribner's, 1972, pp. 506–508; Coffin, Mar-
garet M., *Death in Early America*, Thomas Nelson Publishers, 1976; Zinnser, H., *Rats,
Lice and History*, Penguin, 1936; Moore, G. William, et al., "Determining cause of
death in 45,564 autopsy reports," *Theoretical Medicine and Bioethics* 9, no. 2 (1988);
Rosen, George, *History of Public Health*, Johns Hopkins University Press, 1993; Johnson, Marilyn, *The Dead Beat: Lost Souls, Lucky Stiffs, and the Perverse Pleasures of Obituaries*, HarperCollins Publishers, 2006; Hume, Janice, *Obituaries in American Culture*,
University Press of Mississippi, 2000; Sehdev A.E.S., Hutchins G.M. "Problems
with proper completion and accuracy of the cause-of-death statement," *Internal
Medicine* 161 (2001): 277–84.

Causes of Death: U.S. Department of Health and Human Services, Public Health Service,
National Center for Health Statistics. *Physicians' Handbook on Medical Certification
of Death*, Government Printing Office, 2003. Department of Health and Human
Services publication no. (phs)2003-1108; Baden, Michael, *Unnatural Death: Con-
fessions of a Medical Examiner*, Ballantine Books, 1990; Maples, Wm., *Dead Men Do
Tell Tales*, Main Street Books, 1995; Wecht, Cyril H., *Cause of Death,* Onyx, 1994;
Wilson, Keith, D., *Cause of Death*, Writers Digest Books, 1994; Knight, Bernard, *Fo-
rensic Pathology*, Hodder Arnold Publication, 1996; Elvis Presley Autopsy: Office of
the County Medical Examiner, Memphis, Tennessee, Case 77-1944; Middlebrook,
Diane Wood, *Anne Sexton: A Biography*, Houghton Mifflin, Co., 1991; Pellegrino Ed,
"From the couch to the grave: the Anne Sexton case," *Cambridge Q Healthclinical
Ethics* 5 (1996): 189–203; Sotos, John G., "Was President Taft cognitively impaired?"
Science News, October, 2003.

Television History: Burns, R.W., *Television: An International History of the Formative Years*,
London Institution of Electrical Engineers, 1998; Carey, G. R., "Seeing by Electric-
ity," *Scientific American* 42 (June 1880): 255; Brooks, Tim, *The Complete Directory to
Prime Time Network TV Shows*, Ballantine Books, 1981; Jackson, Ronald, *Classic TV
Westerns*, Carol Publishing Group, 1994; Meyers, Ric, *Murder on the Air: Television's
Great Mystery Series*, The Mysterious Press, 1989; Schwartz, David, et al. *The Ency-
clopedia of TV Game Shows*, Checkmark Books, 1999; Gwinn, Allison, ed., *The 100
Greatest Shows of All Time*, Entertainment Weekly Books, 1998; Jarvis, Everett, *Final*

Curtains, Carol Publishing Group, 1994; Braudy, Leo, *The Frenzy of Renown: Fame and Its History*, Oxford University Press, 1996; Lasswell, Mark, *TV Guide: Fifty Years of Television*, Crown, 2002; Lewis, Bradley, *My Father, Uncle Miltie*, Barricade Books, 1999; Graysmith, Robert, *The Murder of Bob Crane*, Crown Publishers, 1993; Cotter, Bill, *The Wonderful World of Disney Television: A Complete History*, Hyperion, 1997.

Music History: Armstrong, Louis, *Louis Armstrong in His Own Words*, Oxford University Press, 1999; Haney, Daniel Q., "Study: Marijuana Raises Heart Risks," *Medical Editorial*, (AP) March 3, 2000; Giddens, Gary, *Satchmo: The Genius of Louis Armstrong*, Da Capo Press, 2001; "Tommy Dorsey Chokes to Death on Food," *New York Times*, November 27, 1956, pp. 1, 2; "Duke Ellington, a Master of Music, Dies at 75," *New York Times*, May 25, 1974; Hayden, D., *Pox: Genius, Madness, and the Mysteries of Syphilis*, Basic Books, 2003; Fong-Torres, Ben, *The Hits Just Keep Coming*, Backbeat Books, 2001; Bronson, Fred, *Billboard's Hottest 100 Hits*, Billboard Books, 2003; Randel, Don Michael, *The Harvard Biographical Dictionary of Music*, Harvard University Press, 1996; Romanowski, Patricia, et al., *The Rolling Stone Encyclopedia of Rock & Roll*, Fireside, 1995; Tyler, Don, *Hit Parade*, William Morrow, 1985; "William Donaldson, 54, Song Writer Dies," *New York Times*, June 16, 1947; Crowther, Bruce, *The Jazz Singers*, Sterling Publishing Company, 1986.

Cinema and Culture: Bernstein, Jonathan, *Pretty in Pink: The Golden Age of Teenage Movies*, St. Martin's Griffin, 1997; Bodroghkozy, Aniko, "Reel Revolutionaries: An Examination of Hollywood's Cycle of 1960s Youth Rebellion Films," *Cinema Journal* 41, no.3 (2002): 38–58; Shipman, David, *The Great Movie Stars: The Golden Years*, Little, Brown & Co., 1995; MacQuarrie, Brian, "Slain Lottery Winner Leaves Mixed Legacy," *Boston Globe*, May 11, 1997; "Lottery winner dies of self neglect," Retrieved from BBC, Tuesday, 22 January, 2002; Brown, Adele Q., *What a Way to Go*, Chronicle Books, 2001; "Basil King Dead," *New York Times*, June 23, 1928; "Author of Pollyanna Dies," *New York Times*, May 23, 1920; "Booth Tarkington, Novelist Dead," *New York Times*, May 20, 1946; "Bruce Barton, Ad Man, Is Dead," *New York Times*, July 6, 1967; "M.E. Perkins, Scribner's Editor," *New York Times*, June 18, 1947; "Gerald Lee Dead," *New York Times*, April 4, 1944; "Walter B. Pitkin, Author," *New York Times*, January 26, 1953.

Ancient History: Apeles, Teena, *Women Warriors*, Seal Press, 2003; Pearson, Will, ed., *Mental Floss*, HarperCollins, 2005; Fines, John, *Who's Who in the Middle Ages*, Barnes & Noble Books, 1995; Boyle, David, et al., *History Makers*, Paragon Publishing, 2005; Matyszak, Philip, *Chronicle of the Roman Republic*, Thames & Hudson, 2003; Manley, Bill, *Penguin Historical Atlas of Ancient Egypt*, Penguin Books, 1996; Bagnall, Roger S., *Egypt in Late Antiquity*, Princeton University Press, 1993; Library of Congress Classical & Medieval History Links, http://www.loc.gov/rr/main/alcove9/classics.html

Inventions and Business: Pratt, Fletcher, *All About Famous Inventors*, Random House, 1955; Calhoun, Chris, ed., *52 McGs*, Citadel Press, 2001; Tomecek, Stephen, *What a Great Idea*, Scholastic, 2003; Brands, H.W., *Master of Enterprise*, Simon & Schuster, 1999; "Woolworth Died with Will Undisclosed," *New York Times*, April 15, 1919; "Mrs. Macy is Dead, Aided Miss Keller," *New York Times*, October 21, 1936; "Earle E. Dickson, Devised Band-Aid," *New York Times*, September 22, 1969; "Jesse W. Reno," *New York Times*, June 3, 1947; "Kool-Aid King Leaves Estate of $45 Million," *New York Times*, November 8, 1961; "Miss Mary Anderson," *New York Times*, June 30, 1953;

"Death List of a Day: Lewis Edson Waterman," *New York Times*, May 2, 1901; "Frank Waterman Dies Here," *New York Times*, May 7, 1938; "Dr. W. H. Carrier Dead Here at 73," *New York Times*, October 8, 1950; "Inventor Ferris Is Dead," *New York Times*, November 23, 1896; "Marconi Is Dead of Heart Attack," *New York Times*, July 20, 1937; Leo Gerstenzang, Head of Q-tip, 68," *New York Times*, February 2, 1961.

Heros and Pop Culture: Forbes, Malcolm, *They Went That-A-Way*, Barnes & Noble Books, 1989; McHenry, Robert, *Famous American Women*, G. & C. Merriam Company, 1980; Siegel, Marvin, ed., *The Last Word*, William Morrow, 1997; Adams, Rachel, *Sideshow U.S.A.*, University of Chicago Press, 2001; Bogdan, Robert, *Freak Show*, University of Chicago Press, 1988; Spignesi, Stephen J., *The U.S.A. Book of Lists*, New Page Books, 1990; Russo, Frank, et al., *Bury My Heart at Cooperstown*, Triumph Books, 2006; "City Forbids Human Flies to Climb Skyscraper Walls," *New York Times*, April 11, 1923; "Jockey Dies as He Wins His First Race," *New York Times*, June 5, 1923; "Parachute Leap off Statue of Liberty," *New York Times*, February 13, 1912; "Woman Goes Over Niagara in a Barrel," *New York Times*, October 25, 1901.

ACKNOWLEDGMENTS

Thankful to the members of HWA for the Bram Stoker Award, especially Peter Straub, Kathy Ptacek, Angeline Hawkins, Rob Reginald, Mike Arnzen, and many more than there is space to name. Appreciation for the support from Joanne Sinchuk and Bob Williamson of MWA. Gratitude to Lynn and Lewis Riggle, Steve and Patty Largo, Jared, Shafina, Colette, Erik, and Joey for their cheers. Recognition to Michael Largo, Jr., for his help in research, and my sweetheart wife, Susy, for living with me. Praise to my agent Frank Weimann of the Literary Group International, and to Joelle Yudin and Mauro DiPreta who embraced the project from the first. The book wouldn't be possible without the talented cast at HarperCollins, especially editor, Peter Hubbard, a gentleman and scholar; Carrie Kania, publisher; David Roth-Ey, editorial director; the sharp eyes of Dori Carlson, managing editor, and Kolt Beringer, assistant managing editor; Justin Dodd, designer; Nicole Reardon, marketing manager; ever-enthusiastic Courtney Morrow, publicist; and the many dedicated and fervent souls in the sales force. In closing, thank you to the family members of the many persons listed for their conversations and correspondence, knowing that I wish condolences for all.

PHOTOGRAPHIC
CREDITS

Where's the Proof: Sande, Joan van. National Library of Medicine; Bills of Mortality: National Library of Medicine; Counting the Dead: Collins, Marjory; Obituary vs. Reality: Illus. in: *Harper's Weekly* (1862); Adler: Library of Congress Prints and Photographs Division; Alexander the Great: Etched by Jacques Reich (1902); Musician Wrecks: Walcott, Marion. Office of War Information; Joan of Arc: United States Treasury Department; Inquisition: Brito, Jose. G. Barrie and Son (1901); Archimedes: Probert Encyclopaedia (1910); Armstrong: New York World-Telegram and the Sun Newspaper Photograph Collection; Astaire: George Grantham Bain Collection; Polka: Lee, Russell (1903); Astor: George Grantham Bain Collection; Attila: Library of Congress; Anonymous AX: Strohmeyer and Wyman (1899); Bach: State Historical Society of Colorado; Baer: New York World-Telegram and the Sun Newspaper Photograph Collection; Balboa: Cady, Annie C. Gebbie and Co. (1893); Ball: New York World-Telegram and the Sun Newspaper Photograph Collection; Baron: United States Department of Defense; Barry: New York World-Telegram and the Sun Newspaper Photograph Collection; Barrymore: French, Herbert E., National Photo Company; Beethoven: Library of Congress Prints and Photographs Division; Bergman: New York World-Telegram and the Sun Newspaper Photograph Collection; Berle: New York World-Telegram and the Sun Newspaper Photograph Collection; Berlin: Aumuller, Al. World Telegram; Blackwell: Illus. in: Blackwell Family Papers, Box 63, Library of Congress; Boone: Library of Congress Prints and Photographs Division; Borden: George Grantham Bain Collection; Tin Cans: Office of War Information, Overseas Picture Division; Bowser: Work Projects Administration Poster Collection; Brahms: Library of Congress Prints and Photographs Division; Brando: Special Media Archives Services Division, National Archives at College Park; Buck: Library of Congress Prints and Photographs Division; Burke and Wills: Courtesy of National Library of Australia; Burns: New York World-Telegram and the Sun Newspaper Photograph Collection; Burton: New York World-Telegram and the Sun Newspaper Photograph Collection; Camus: New York World-Telegram and the Sun Newspaper Photograph Collection; Cash: Jimmy Carter Library (NLJC) National Archives; Charles: Nixon Presidential Materials Staff (NLNS), National Archives; Carnegie: Library of Congress Prints and Photographs Division; Carrier: Horydczak, Theodor (1890); Carver: Rothstein, Arthur; Cary: Library of Congress Prints and Photographs Division; Cather: Carl Van Vechten Photographs; Chamberlain: Library of Congress Prints and Photographs Division; Chalibasvili: New York City W.P.A. Art Project; Cleopatra: Library of Congress Prints and Photographs Division; Death on Menu: H. A. Thomas and Wylie Lith. Co.; Cole: Courtesy Joe Romersa (www.shadowboxstudio.com); Colt: Library of Congress Prints and Photographs Division; Coltrane: New York World-Telegram and the Sun Collection; Columbus: Library of Congress Prints and Photographs Division; Confucius: Illus. by Johann G. Heck (1851); Conte: Library of Congress Prints and Photographs Division; Cortes: Library of Congress Prints and Photographs Division; Malintzin: W. H. Ferguson Company (1902); Crapper: The Meyer-Sniffen Co., Limited (1895); Crow: Frances Benjamin Johnston Collection; Curie: Press Illustrating Service, New York City; Curtis: Library of Congress Prints and Photographs Division; Dandridge: New York World-Telegram and the Sun Newspaper Photograph Collection; Darrow: NYC: Federal Art Project; Decatur: Illustration by H. R. Robinson; Dickson: Hine, Lewis W.; Dionysius: National Museum of Science and Technology; Disney: New York World-Telegram and the Sun Newspaper Photograph Collection; Doody: New York World-Telegram and the Sun Newspaper Photograph Collection; Drake: Library of Congress Prints and Photographs Division; Doss: U.S. National Archives and Records Administration; Eagels: Johnston, Alfred Cheney; Earhart: New York World-Telegram and the Sun Newspaper Photograph Collection; Eastman: George Grantham Bain Collection; Mr. Ed: Library of Congress Prints and Photographs Division; Edison: Library of Congress Prints and Photographs Division; Edwards: G. Eric and Edith Matson Photograph Collection; Einstein: Turner, Oren Jack; Ellington: Library of Congress Prints and Photographs Division; Epperson: Office of War Information, Overseas Picture Division; Fahrenheit: Library of Congress Prints and Photographs Division; Farnsworth: Gottscho-Schleisner Collection; Faulkner: Carl Van Vechten Photographs; Ferris: Photo by the Waterman Co.; Fitzgerald: Carl Van Vechten Photographs; Human Fly: National Photo Company Collection; Ford: National Photo Company Collection; Foster: Painting by A. B. Leisser; St. Francis: Laurent, J.; Fuller: Underhill, Irving; Gabor: National Child Labor Committee (U.S.); Gallo: Gottsch-Schleiner Collection; da Gama: Casanova, E. Ernesto; Garland: New York World-Telegram and the Sun Newspaper Photograph Collection; Garroway: New York Zoological Society (1906); Gautama: The Universal Photo Art Co.; Gehrig: U.S. National Archives and Records Administration; Geronimo: Wittick, Ben; Gershwin: George Grantham Bain Collection; Mr. Magoo: New York World-Telegram and the Sun Newspaper Photograph Collection; Gleason: New York World-Telegram and the Sun Newspaper Photograph Collection; Glidden: U.S. National Archives and Records Administration; Gorman: George Grantham Bain Collection; Malcomson: National Photo Company Collection; Grant: Office of War Information; Guthrie: New York World-Telegram and the Sun Newspaper Photograph

Collection; Guttenberg: Vermont Historical Society; Hale: Illus. in: *Harper's Weekly* (1860); Hannibal: D. Appleton and Company (1885); Harding: George Grantham Bain Collection; Hayes: Currier and Ives (1880); Hemingway: Library of Congress Prints and Photographs Division; Hendrix: Collier, John; Hepburn: New York World-Telegram and the Sun Newspaper Photograph Collection; Heron: Courtesy of www.mlahanas.com; Hitchcock: New York World-Telegram and the Sun Newspaper Photograph Collection; Hitler: Special Media Archives Services Division (NWCS-S), National Archives at College Park; Hoffmann: National Library of Medicine; Holiday: Carl Van Vechten Photograph Collection; Aeschylus: AP/Wide World Photos; Honnecout: Library of Congress Prints and Photographs Division; Jackson: Currier and Ives (1872); Jesus: Currier, N. (1848); Johnson: U.S. National Archives and Records Administration; Willie Johnson: Lomax Collection; Jones: New York World-Telegram and the Sun Newspaper Photograph Collection; Keller: Whitman, Chelsea; Kelly: New York World-Telegram and the Sun Newspaper Photograph Collection; Gilliard: Carl Van Vechten Photograph Collection; Key: Horydczak Collection; Keynes: New York World-Telegram and the Sun Newspaper Photograph Collection; Khan: Courtesy Collection of Roy Winkelman; Kubla Khan: Illus. in: Mongols and Romans, by John Ranking (1826); Killian: New York World-Telegram and the Sun Newspaper Photograph Collection; Mack the Knife: British Cartoon Prints Collection; Kovacs: Library of Congress Prints and Photographs Division; Kroc: Farm Security Administration. Office of War Information Photograph Collection; Landon: Department of the Interior; Lassie: State Historical Society of Colorado; Lee: Library of Congress Prints and Photographs Division; De Leon: from Denison, John Ledyard, ed. Illus. in: *"Die illustrierte neue welt"* (New York, H. Bill, 1858); Lewis: New York World-Telegram and the Sun Collection; Lincoln: Library of Congress Prints and Photographs Division; Richard the Lionhearted: Little, Th. G. (1859); Liston: New York World-Telegram and the Sun Newspaper Photograph Collection; Livingstone: Ferd. Mayer and Sons; French-Sheldon: Library of Congress Prints and Photographs Division; Lottery: Painting by Eward Hull, National Library of Medicine; Lottery Winner: Russell-Morgan Print; Lombardi: New York World-Telegram and the Sun Newspaper Photograph Collection; Magellan: Illus. in Narrative and Critical History of America, Winsor (1886); Vaughan: New York World-Telegram and the Sun Newspaper Photograph Collection; Harrison: New York World-Telegram and the Sun Newspaper Photograph Collection; Marciano: Herb Scharfman of International News Photos; Martians: DeMarsico, Dick; Marx: New York World-Telegram and the Sun Newspaper Photograph Collection; McDonald: Vachon, John. Office of War Information; McNamara: Endicott and Company; Mercer: New York World-Telegram and the Sun Newspaper Photograph Collection; Miller: Library of Congress Prints and Photographs Division; Mineo: Library of Congress Prints and Photographs Division; Mitchell: New York World-Telegram and the Sun Newspaper Photograph Collection; Montgomery: New York World-Telegram and the Sun Newspaper Photograph Collection; Monroe: U.S. National Archives and Records Administration; Montessori: George Grantham Bain Collection; Morrison: Largo, S.; Joplin: Kohn, Misch; Cocaine: Partnership for a

Drug-Free America, National Library of Medicine; The Who: Russell-Morgan Print; Morton: Library of Congress; Mozart: Drawing by Eugene A. Perry; Musician Murder: U.S. Printing Co. (1900); Nefertiti: E. B. Thompson Collection; Buddy Holly: New York World-Telegram and the Sun Newspaper Photograph Collection; Musicians Downed: Library of Congress Prints and Photographs Division; Nero: The National Ptg. and Eng. Co. (1913); Niagara Daredevils: Courtesy Rochester Public Library; Anna Edson Taylor: Library of Congress Prints and Photographs Division; Suttner: Library of Congress Prints and Photographs Division; Mother Teresa: U.S. National Archives and Records Administration; Pasternak: New York World-Telegram and the Sun Newspaper Photograph Collection; Patton: U.S. Army Signal Corps; Pericles: In album: Athens, Egypt, Rhine, Switzerland. Tyrol, Salzburg; Pizarro: D. M. Kelsey, National Publishing Company (1891); Plato: Library of Congress Prints and Photographs Division; Aristotle: Baldung Grien, Hans; Pocahontas: State Historical Society of Colorado; De Long: U.S. Naval Department; Peary: New York World-Telegram and the Sun Newspaper Photograph Collection; Minik Wallace: New York World-Telegram and the Sun Newspaper Photograph Collection; Cook: Library of Congress Prints and Photographs Division; Henry Robertson Bowers: National Library of Australia; Byrd: U.S. Department of Navy; Marco Polo: Illus. in: The Travels of Marco Polo ("Il milione"), 1298; Popes: Bouton, A. M. (1835); Pyle: U.S. Department of Navy; O'Neill: Carl Van Vechten Photograph Collection; Parker: New York World-Telegram and the Sun Newspaper Photograph Collection; Pemberton: Gottscho-Schleisner Collection; Perkins: Horydczak, Theodor; Pollack: Office of War Information Photograph Collection; Presley: Office of County Medical Examiner, Memphis, TN; Lone Ranger: New York World-Telegram and the Sun Newspaper Photograph Collection; Reality TV: U.S. Office of War Information; Remarque: New York World-Telegram and the Sun Newspaper Photograph Collection; Roddenberry: Wladyslaw, Theodore (1873); Roebling: Illus. in: Harper's Weekly (1883); Rosenthal: U.S. Department of Defense; Ruth: George Grantham Bain Collection; Sacagawea: U.S. Department of Treasury; Sartre: New York World-Telegram and the Sun Newspaper Photograph Collection; Savery: Royal Society of London; Socrates: Bijur, A. (1859); Solomon: Russell-Morgan Print (1899); Biblical longevity: Hariot, Thomas. (1590); De Soto: James Little and Co. (1866); Ramses II: G. Eric and Edith Matson Photograph Collection; Schubert: Detroit Publishing Co.; Sexton: Dorfman, Elsa; Shaw: Davart Company, NYC (1934); Sinatra: Franklin D. Roosevelt Library Public Domain Photographs; Shore: Detroit Publishing Co. (1905); Singer: New York World-Telegram and the Sun Newspaper Photograph Collection; Skelton: Library of Congress Prints and Photographs Division; Smith: Carl Van Vechten Photographs Collection; Spartacus: Ream, Vinnie; Steinbeck: Carl Van Vechten Photographs Collection; Serling: Library of Congress Prints and Photographs Division; Ed Sullivan: LaClaire, Maurice Carnes; John Sullivan: Fox, Richard K.; Joe Louis: Carl Van Vechten Photographs Collection; Superman: Office of War Information. Overseas Picture Division; Taft: Glackens, L. M. Louis; Tesla: George Grantham Bain Collection; Thorpe: U.S. National Archives and Records Administration; Pop Warner: Library of Con-